Cultural Heritage and Human Rights

D1355566

Editors

Helaine Silverman
University of Illinois at Urbana-Champaign
Urbana-Champaign, IL

and

D. Fairchild Ruggles
University of Illinois at Urbana-Champaign
Urbana-Champaign, IL

 Springer

Helaine Silverman
Department of Anthropology
University of Illinois at
    Urbana-Champaign
Urbana, IL 61801
USA
helaine@uiuc.edu

D. Fairchild Ruggles
Department of Landscape Architecture
University of Illinois at
    Urbana-Champaign
Champaign, IL 61820
USA
dfr1@uiuc.edu

ISBN: 978-0-387-76579-2   e-ISBN: 978-0-387-71313-7

Library of Congress Control Number: 2007926251

Cover illustration: Cover art courtesy Helaine Silverman and D. Fairchild Ruggles. The Bamiyan
Buddha photograph is a public domain image, courtesy of UNESCO: Buddha Statue 53 Meters Tall
in Bamiyan Valley, Afghanistan, taken in 1963.

Printed on acid-free paper.

9 8 7 6 5 4 3 2 1

springer.com

Preface

Laura Graham (2006) recently wrote that anthropologists are obligated to promote human rights and social justice. Her call to action, especially among vulnerable communities, is one felt in many disciplines. We take particular pleasure in the range of fields represented in this volume on cultural heritage and human rights: anthropology and archeology (Hugo Benavides, Jan French, Charles Orser, Anne Pyburn, Helaine Silverman, Laurajane Smith, Larry Zimmerman), architectural and landscape history (D. Fairchild Ruggles), landscape architecture and geography (James L. Wescoat, Jr.), cultural heritage conservation and urban geography (William Logan), urban planning (Chris Silver), and history, cultural studies, human rights, and international and public affairs (Elazar Barkan). The richness of perspectives herein reflects both the disciplines and the dialogues among the authors.

The volume is divided into two parts. Part I begins with an introduction, written by the editors, that provides an overview of the themes that emerged in the workshop that gave rise to this volume. It concludes with the text of the United Nations' Universal Declaration of Human Rights. Part II begins with William Logan's paper, which acts as a second introduction. There is a strong link between Logan's discussion of conflict and the specific South Asian case study presented in James L. Wescoat, Jr.'s essay. Like Wescoat, Chris Silver is concerned with conflicting claims to heritage sites in the context of tense local politics, local cultural antagonisms and tourism; his case study is Bali. The papers by Charles Orser, Jan French, Hugo Benavides, and Larry Zimmerman are united by their treatment of historically denigrated and disenfranchised populations. Orser deals with the Irish who, although a majority in their own country, faced centuries-long oppression from British colonialists that collided in the middle of the nineteenth century with the potato famine, thereby generating a mass migration and diaspora. The Africa-descended population of Brazil, discussed by French, is likewise a diaspora and one that faced terrible challenges due to the experience and legacy of slavery. Upon abolition this population still remained at the bottom of the social scale. Just as Irish-Americans have looked to their homeland in the construction of their cultural heritage, so, too, Afro-Brazilians are empowering their own trans-oceanic identity. The other great underprivileged group in Latin America is its own native peoples. Benavides is interested in the cognitive dissonances between an appropriated pre-Hispanic past in Ecuador and its Indian present as played-out at the country's largest archeological site. Attention to native people leads us to Zimmerman's paper on how Indians have participated in, or been excluded from, writing the narratives of national commemorative sites. Laurajane Smith also deals with native people in her discussion of one Australian Aboriginal group's struggle to manage its own cultural heritage. At the same time, Smith incisively explores the political aspects of heritage practice and heritage assertion. Those political perspectives resonate with Anne Pyburn's forthright goal of getting archeologists to aid grass roots political action by providing useful information to various groups of stakeholders who then can think about the past in ways that lead to actions other than violence and divisive politics. The volume concludes with Elazar Barkan's philosophical consideration of the problematic entanglements of human rights and cultural heritage understood as cultural property (in both tangible and intangible form), and the question of voice.

In recent years there has been a dramatic increase in scholarly attention to the topic of cultural heritage. Heritage is important because it provides symbolic and economic sustenance, meaning, and dignity to human lives. It legitimizes territorial and intellectual ownership, and it is a critical factor in the formation of social identity. Although heritage as a management practice has been the focus of numerous international conferences sponsored by UNESCO, ICOMOS, ICCROM, and other cultural organizations, the specific relationship between the free expression of cultural heritage and human rights has not been sufficiently explored. The relationship between cultural heritage and human rights is complex and cannot be adequately considered in a single volume such as this; however, it opens the door to further discussion. Cultural rights are a critical dimension of human rights and should be at the forefront of heritage studies. We hope the present volume draws attention to the vital intersections that must be engaged by scholars, practitioners, communities, and politicians in this area.

Our thanks go to the authors who have contributed such stimulating papers, and to our editor at Springer, Teresa Krauss, for providing us all with this important publication opportunity. The participants in this volume met in a workshop at the University of Illinois, Urbana-Champaign (UIUC) in 2006. That meeting, organized by the Collaborative for Cultural Heritage and Museum Practices (CHAMP), was made possible by generous support at UIUC from the Vice-Chancellor for Research, the Dean of Fine and Applied Arts, the Department of Landscape Architecture, the Department of Anthropology, Human Dimensions of Environmental Systems, and the Illinois Program for Research in the Humanities.

References

Graham, Laura R., 2006, Anthropologists Are Obligated to Promote Human Rights and Social Justice. *Anthropology News*, October: 4–5.

Contents

Contributors

Elazar Barkan, School of International and Public Affairs, Columbia University, New York, NY 10027

O. Hugo Benavides, Department of Sociology and Anthropology, Fordham University, Bronx, NY 10458

Jan Hoffman French, Department of Sociology and Anthropology, University of Richmond, Richmond, VA 23173

William S. Logan, Cultural Heritage Centre for Asia and the Pacific, Deakin University, Melbourne, Australia

K. Anne Pyburn, Department of Anthropology, Indiana University, Bloomington, IN 47405

Charles E. Orser, Jr., Department of Anthropology, Illinois State University, Normal, IL 61790

D. Fairchild Ruggles, Department of Landscape Architecture, University of Illinois at Urbana-Champaign, Champaign, IL 61820

Christopher Silver, College of Design, Construction and Building, University of Florida, Gainesville, FL 32611

Helaine Silverman, Department of Anthropology, University of Illinois at Urbana-Champaign, Urbana, IL 61801

Laurajane Smith, Department of Archaeology, The University of York, York Y01 7EP, UK

James L. Wescoat, Jr., Department of Landscape Architecture, University of Illinois at Urbana-Champaign, Champaign, IL 61820

Larry J. Zimmerman, Department of Anthropology, Indiana University-Purdue University at Indianapolis, Indianapolis, IN 46202

Part 1
Introduction

Chapter 1
Cultural Heritage and Human Rights

Helaine Silverman and D. Fairchild Ruggles

Introduction

Heritage is a concept to which most people would assign a positive value. The preservation of material culture – objects of art and of daily use, architecture, landscape form – and intangible culture – performances of dance, music, theater, and ritual, as well as language and human memory – are generally regarded as a shared common good by which everyone benefits. Both personal and community identities are formed through such tangible objects and intangible cultural perform-ances, and a formation of a strong identity would seem to be a fundamentally good thing. But heritage is also intertwined with identity and territory, where individu-als and communities are often in competition or outright conflict. Conflicts may occur over issues of indigenous land and cultural property rights, or between ethnic minorities and dominant majorities disputing the right to define and man-age the cultural heritage of the minority. At stake is the question of who defines cultural heritage and who should control stewardship and the benefits of cultural heritage. Thus, while heritage can unite, it can also divide. These contestations, when unresolved, can lead to resistance, violence, and war. The inherent conflict between world or national heritage and individual or local rights emerges at this critical point. Heritage is by no means a neutral category of self-definition nor an inherently positive thing: It is a concept that can promote self-knowledge, facilitate communication and learning, and guide the stewardship of the present culture and its historic past. But it can also be a tool for oppression. For this reason, heritage has an uneasy place in the United Nations' call for universal human rights and it merits examination as an urgent contemporary problem.

Current thinking about human rights traces its origins to 1948 when the United Nations (UN), motivated by the horrors of the Holocaust during World War II,[1]

---

[1] Goodale (2006) discusses anthropology's "Statement on Human Rights" that was written by Melville Herskovits and published in *American Anthropologist* one year earlier, in 1947. Goodale reconstructs that Herskovits was approached by the nascent UNESCO for advice on the UN's Universal Declaration on Human Rights, then in progress in the Commission on Human Rights chaired by Eleanor Roosevelt.

H. Silverman and D. F. Ruggles (eds.), *Cultural Heritage and Human Rights*.
© Springer 2007

promulgated the Universal Declaration of Human Rights. This document affirms basic liberties such as life, liberty, security, recourse to legal tribunals; freedom of movement both within and between nations; and freedom from torture and slavery. It affirms a person's "right to freedom of thought, conscience and religion; this right includes freedom to change his religion or belief, and freedom, either alone or in community with others and in public or private, to manifest his religion or belief in teaching, practice, worship and observance." Article 27 specifically states "Everyone has the right freely to participate in the cultural life of the community, to enjoy the arts and to share in scientific advancement and its benefits." This article, in particular, introduced the idea that culture was an aspect of human rights, although it did not elucidate the specific relationship between individuals, communities, and nations, and did not clarify how conflicts among these three entities could or should be resolved.

In 1966, to resolve the potential tension between constituents with differing allegiances (provoked by the Universal Declaration of Human Rights), the UN's International Covenant on Civil and Political Rights (ICCPR) and International Covenant on Economic, Social, and Cultural Rights (ICESCR) were passed. The ICCPR proposed that the universal inalienable rights of individuals are superior to claims of national sovereignty (Hakki 2002: 85). However, because individuals belong to cultural groups, there is the potential for a collision between the desire for cultural self-determination by one group and the claim of universal human rights principles on the part of different and competing groups or the overarching nation-state. Elazar Barkan considers this topic in this volume, arguing that although a universal minimum of human rights exists, "many 'universal' rights have meaning mostly as they are applied within local variation."

As argued by Nagengast and Turner, "Universal human rights was one of the earliest global discourses" (1997: 269). An excellent critique of the universalist notion of "one world: a global ethic" is found in Trigg (2005). He considers how local loyalties may be reconciled with so-called global responsibilities, acknowledging the specificity of the moral foundations of the West's political way of life and concluding that morality is not "natural" and human nature is inherently ambiguous; morality is historically contingent and the product of social arrangements.

Universality is still a subject of heated and complex debate in the UN and among anthropologists (American Anthropological Association 1947; Goodale 2006). It was particularly resisted in non-Western countries that objected to the very idea of universal standards externally imposed because they regarded these standards as reflecting not so much universal as Western values and codes of behavior (e.g., Messer 1997; Nagengast and Turner 1997). One response to this was the Nara Convention, drafted in Japan in 1994 as a response to the 1964 Venice Charter's assumption that architectural "authenticity" could be universally defined. Specifically, the Nara Convention stated that authenticity could be culturally determined, which opened the door to different preservationist values. For example, instead of the Western priority given to fixity of physical material, other cultures might place value on the significance of a site, the ritual associated with it, or the periodic renewal or replenishment of its architectural fabric.

In addition to the criticisms that have been levied against UNESCO's claims to universality,[2] the agency has been faulted for paying insufficient attention to the realm of culture and the arts. Ghanea and Rahmani (2005: 134) observed that "The Commission on Human Rights and the UN human rights system has been historically criticised for the emphasis it has placed on civil and political rights rather than economic, social and cultural rights." Worldwide, cultural heritage does not figure prominently in the extensive literature on human rights, but this does not mean that it is an issue of minor importance or without significant social impact. Freedom of religion, political expression, movement, and freedom from violence, torture, and hunger are human rights of paramount importance and correctly deserving of protection, vigilance, and continued analytical study. But heritage ought to rank with these as an essential component of human rights because the very concept of heritage demands that individual and group identities be respected and protected. Heritage insists on the recognition of a person or community's essential worth. The notion of "world cultural heritage" may, in fact, promote tolerance (see Begag 1998), whereas the lack of tolerance for the identity of others often leads to the repression of minority cultural expressions. This can take the form of suppression of intangible manifestations of culture, such as language, dress, and ritual, or the outright physical destruction of material objects and buildings. There are fundamental conflicts between universal and individual heritage and rights, which are not entirely resolvable.

UNESCO's Declaration Concerning the Intentional Destruction of Cultural Heritage (2003) states that, with reference to monuments, "cultural heritage is an important component of the cultural identity of communities, groups and individuals, and or social cohesion, so that its intentional destruction may have adverse consequences on human dignity and human rights." UNESCO declarations and recommendations, which are collective policy statements used as instruments for preservation worldwide, are often written in nonspecific terms so as to facilitate majority approval in the General Assembly and to satisfy the greatest number of national "clients." However, scholars are not as adverse to conflict; their works are intended not to set policy but to critique it. Thus, Meskell (2002: 564) writes more forcefully: "The loss of heritage can easily be decried as a crime that [a]ffects multiple generations, erasing cultural memory and severing links with the past that are integral to forging and maintaining modern identities. Yet it is dangerous to place commensurate value on people and things and to couch these acts in a language reserved for genocide, since they do not inhabit the same order of existence." In this, Meskell points to the difference between human lives and material culture. An equally important distinction is that which exists between different human communities. The differences between the values of one group and another − whether defined in terms of religion, tribal identity, or caste − are expressed in cultural manifestations, and likewise, the conflicts between groups will be enacted both in the human and material realm. It is precisely

---

[2] Here we do not consider the issue of *world* cultural heritage as a manifestation of UNESCO's concept of universality, which is also debated (see e.g., Bianchi and Boniface 2002; Cleere 2000, 2001; Meskell 2002: 568–570).

because cultural heritage is a significant aspect of identity that it is the arena where conflict occurs.

We have seen that the Declaration of Human Rights included a statement on culture. Since then, other transnational legislation also has been concerned with culture, if not cultural heritage directly. The Protocol of San Salvador, which was added in 1988 to the American Convention on Human Rights of the Inter-American Commission on Human Rights (an autonomous organ of the Organization of American States [OAS]), addresses the "Right to the Benefits of Culture" in its Article 14. This article states that people benefit from culture, art, science, and technology, which should be conserved and developed. Although "cultural heritage" per se is not mentioned, it can be understood to be encompassed by the protocol. Similarly, the Indian National Trust for Art and Cultural Heritage (INTACH) has drafted a memorandum whose purpose is to stimulate awareness, documentation, and preservation of the Indian cultural and natural heritage.

At the 19th meeting of its General Assembly in 1998, the International Council of Museums (ICOM) passed Resolution No. 1 concerning museums and cultural diversity. Among other observations, the resolution recognizes the continuing significance of the Universal Declaration of Human Rights, expresses concern with continuing tensions in different parts of the world derived from inadequate cultural understanding, commits to the promotion of cultural rights of all peoples through a reaffirmation of the values embedded in the 1948 document, supports the 1994 UN Draft Declaration on the Rights of the World's Indigenous Peoples, and advocates the development of museums as sites for the promotion of heritage values of significance to all peoples through cross-cultural dialog.

It is clear that since 1948 there has been a gradually growing interest in the UN and in organizations at the national level in the area of the cultural dimension of human rights. Regarding the UN, Ghanea and Rhamani write that "at the recent session of the Commission [on Human Rights] . . . 15 resolutions were passed under the agenda item of economic, social and cultural rights and 16 under civil and political rights" (2005: 134). This shift is most graphically demonstrated by a recent advertisement of the United Nations published in *Foreign Policy* (November/December 2005: 7). It touts six major UN accomplishments in 2005, including "Preserve World Heritage Sites in 137 countries".[3] Other international entities, such as the OAS and ICOM, have expressed concern with cultural heritage and human rights in several of their decrees.

It is evident from the above that human rights and cultural heritage are not self-contained; they may overlap and in doing so may conflict with each other. The essays in this volume consider those kinds of conflicts in terms of indigenous rights (which are often articulated in resistance to national identity), war and other violence

---

[3] The other accomplishments listed before it are "Help 8.4 million Iraqis get to the polls. Provide food aid to 2 million tsunami-affected people. Maintain peacekeeping operations in 16 countries. Vaccinate millions of children around the world. Inspect nuclear and related facilities in over 140 countries."

(political, ethnic, religious), access to and exclusion from shared sacred sites, the impact of economic development on cultural heritage of local populations, memory/forgetting, and intellectual property rights. We also include, in this essay, a brief consideration of the human rights aspects of site looters and squatters as they impact the tangible cultural heritage.

Indigenous Rights and Traditional Lands

In her review of anthropological engagement with human rights, Messer (1993) emphasizes indigenous land rights. The literature on the topic of indigenous rights is vast but relatively little of it is phrased in terms of cultural heritage. However, the linkage of land, cultural heritage, and human rights is quite well known, the case of Australia's Aboriginal population being a good example. Morphy (1995) writes about landscape and the reproduction of the Aboriginal ancestral past and generation of the Aboriginal present. Layton (1995) emphasizes the links between everyday knowledge of the land as a source of subsistence, ritual knowledge of the landscape, the landscape as a source of personal identity and people as the embodiment of the ancestral heroes of the Creation Period, and how these have been mobilized in Aboriginal land claims. Moreover, he explicates the natural as well as cultural heritage aspect of Aboriginal claims, for the Aboriginals regard themselves as emplaced custodians of the land (Layton 1995: 223–224). Taçon deals especially with the "dreaming tracks" of the Aboriginals, emphasizing that Aboriginal connections with the landscape are reaffirmed through art and ritual "as a vital part of both their physical and spiritual survival" (1999: 51). Rhona Smith (2001), a British lawyer, explores the relationship between Aboriginal people and the land, arguing that re-establishment of "traditional ties to the land would be a major step to preserving the culture of one of the world's oldest civilizations." Problems in her formulation, however, include the location of agency, reference to the Aboriginals as a "civilization," and lumping of Aboriginals as a single cohesive people, making them into the equivalent of a nation, and all the values thus implied. It is not the Australian state that would be preserving Aboriginal culture through devolution of land title, nor is that culture enclosed in a jar of formaldehyde. Rather, decades of agitation by Australian Aboriginal peoples and their Anglo supporters resulted in the Native Title Act of 1993 (Glaskin 2003), which has permitted them (to the degree permitted by this still inequitable legal agreement) to reclaim ancestral lands, thereby enabling them to live their cultural lives to a greater degree than before. Moreover, Australia's 1979 Burra Charter (revised 1981, 1988, and 1999) for the conservation of places of cultural significance recognizes the social value that a *place* (not just an architectural monument or site) may have as a "focus of spiritual, political, national, or other cultural sentiment to a majority or minority group," thereby justifying its conservation. Although the term "human rights" is not used, it is implicit in the Burra Charter for it deals specifically with living culture as embodied in actual people, not simply the physical remains of societies that belong to the past.

The land rights–human rights dimension of cultural heritage is by no means restricted to Australia, an excellent case study of which is provided by Laurajane Smith in this volume. It is also central to the research of Hugo Benavides and Jan French whose essays in this volume deal with historically disenfranchised peoples in South America and the formation of identity with respect to land, race, indigeneity, nationalism, and global capitalism. Land also figures in Larry Zimmerman's essay, which considers the importance of place for the identity of Native American tribes. Charles Orser, in his contribution to the volume, develops a different aspect of the attachment of heritage to land. He considers the case of the Irish who voluntarily or necessarily left their land, and he explores the various ways that those communities participate as stakeholders in decisions about how that heritage is represented and managed. His study provokes the question: Is possession of heritage a matter of physical residency, blood genealogy, memory, or perhaps simple desire?

War

In 1954, UNESCO passed The Hague Convention for the Protection of Cultural Property in the Event of Armed Conflict. Like the Universal Declaration of Human Rights, this convention was written in response to the terrible destruction of World War II. That war saw the bombing of the baroque-style city of Dresden (Germany), the destruction of the medieval monastery of Monte Cassino (Italy), and the loss, disappearance, or theft of huge numbers of artworks. The Hague Convention states that cultural property must be safeguarded as the common heritage of humankind. These sentiments were reiterated in the 1972 World Heritage Convention, which states that "damage to cultural property belonging to any people whatsoever means damage to the cultural heritage of mankind, since each people makes its own contribution to the culture of the world." But, as the recent Balkan War, Gulf War, conflicts in Afghanistan, and Iraq War have shown, The Hague Convention has been little respected. In the case of the Balkan War – a civil conflagration between cohabiting communities – cultural monuments were specifically targeted for annihilation. Thus, the toppling of a minaret or dome was a powerful sign intended as an assault on not just the architecture but the religious identity of the entire Muslim community. The sixteenth-century Mostar Bridge (Bosnia), which historically linked largely Muslim and Christian neighborhoods, was pounded over and over by Croats until it finally fell in 1993, as if to sever the historic relationship by removing the bridge.

The Director-General of UNESCO (1987–1999), Federico Mayor, explained the deliberate destruction of cultural heritage in the context of war as an assault calculated to produce trauma "because of the much greater difficulty of people's rehabilitation when everything dear and known to them has been swept away" (quoted in Gamboni 2001). The connection between cultural heritage and human rights is clear; it is less clear how any national or international agency, including the UN, can prevent devastation in times of war. The UN's current course is mostly that of advocacy and censure.

Access and Exclusion

The right of access to sacred sites and the pain of exclusion from them fall within the realm of human rights and cultural heritage and constitute a prime venue for armed struggle. For instance, from establishment of the State of Israel in 1948 until the 1967 War when Israel (re)claimed the eastern half of the city from Jordan, Jews had been excluded by force from the Western Wall, sometimes called the Wailing Wall (the remaining wall of the Second Temple in Jerusalem), the holiest and, indeed, only shrine for this religious community. Perhaps of all the factors contributing to strife in this part of the Middle East, nothing is more fraught with tension than Jerusalem, for this city contains sites of critical importance to three religions: in addition to the Western Wall of the Second Temple, it includes the Holy Sepulchre (the tomb of Jesus) and the Dome of the Rock (site of Muhammad's Night Journey).

An equally difficult example would be the tensions between Hindus and Muslims in India over religious sites claimed by both. The case of Ayodhya stands out. The historically important Babri Mosque in Ayodhya (Uttar Pradesh), built in 1528 by Babur, was razed by militant Hindus in 1992 who charged that it occupied the site of the birthplace of the Lord Rama (Lal 2001; Rao and Reddy 2001). The violence was the catalyst for sectarian rioting on a national scale, leaving 2,000 people dead, and prompting anxiety about the stability of India's secular government. While the fight was ostensibly about the legitimacy of the Islamic monument versus the endurance of a prior claim (also a pertinent factor in Israel's stewardship of Jerusalem), it became a powerful rallying point for Hindu nationalist extremism. Thus, the monument and its fate stood in for a larger political agenda, and architectural preservation was intimately entangled with the human rights question of the freedom of expression of religious identity.

Exclusion may also be perpetrated on ethnic grounds. For instance, Clifford (1997) and Mortensen (2006) discuss the exclusion of the Maya descendant communities from the great archeological sites of their ancestors at Palenque and Copán, respectively. The exclusion is driven in part by tourism, but it is framed by the vicious internal wars of terror that were waged by various Central American government militaries and nongovernmental militias against their own indigenous enclaves.

A paradigmatic case of exclusion on the basis of race occurred in Zimbabwe where both physical and interpretive factors colluded. At Great Zimbabwe, a huge complex built in the thirteenth–fourteenth century, early excavators literally mined the site of its stone and destroyed almost all evidence of its African origin. Its rich imported goods were incorrectly interpreted as evidence of a "long lost centre of the Phoenician empire, a comforting reminder of an ancient white civilization in a remote and strange land" for its colonizers (Fagan 1981: 45). Zimbabwe raises the

issue of the relationship of scientific knowledge to particular historically disenfranchised groups. Throughout the lifespan of colonial Rhodesia, the majority black
population was denied its cultural heritage by the government's racist ideology,
which excluded the African from regional prehistory (MacKenzie and Stone 1990;
Hall 1984; Schmidt 1995: 126–127). Unlike Bosnia, where the bridge itself was
demolished in order to insist on the exclusive rights of the Christian Croat community, in Zimbabwe the narrative attached to the monument was written so as to insist
on the colonizers' own claims to heritage. Material forms are powerful signs, and
today Great Zimbabwe constitutes the premier emblem for the building of the
imagined community known as the nation. But in contradistinction to the recent
past, it is a postcolonial nation that now asserts its African identity there.

Just as indigenous Africans were excluded from prehistory and contemporary
civic life in colonial sub-Saharan Africa, Native American history was wholly
ignored in the United States. The "myth of the Moundbuilders" excluded Native
Americans from a role in the rise of pre-Columbian civilization in the national territory
(Feder 2006: 147–174). Archeology corrected this factual error, but relations
between the field of archeology and Native Americans are frequently chilly as
archeological data collide with native North American oral tradition and cosmology
(Mason 2000). Zimmerman discusses indigenous resistance to archeological examination in his contribution to this volume: his use of the terminology of colonialism
helps to highlight the pain and alienation that indigenous communities may feel yet
archeologists fail to recognize. Indigenous communities rarely thank the archeologist:
according to Benavides, in this volume, if the archeologist expects such gratitude,
that presumption reflects the patriarchal, colonial role of archeologists as articulators
of heritage for the mute, bestowers to the bereft.

A cognate situation occurred among the indigenous peoples of Bolivia. Until the
Agrarian Reform of 1953, the Indians were not even considered persons and lacked
the most basic civil rights (Mamani 1989: 46). (This was similarly seen in North
America where recognition of native Americans and African Americans as human
beings meriting the full rights of citizenship was [and is] a hard fought battle.)
Nineteenth-century scholars believed that the Aymara, the native people of the alti-
plano on which is located the great site of Tiwanaku (flourished 500–900 CE), were
inferior and lacked the sophistication to have ever produced a civilization such as
Tiwanaku (Stanish 2002: 171). In the early twentieth century, the leading Bolivian
scholar Arthur Posnansky (1912) confirmed this racist perspective, arguing that the
ancestors of the Aymara could not possibly have created the site and culture.
Archeology has since proven unequivocally the local origin of Tiwanaku, and, in
an important vindication, the surrounding Aymara have appropriated the site. They
now legally control it and interpret it according to their own ideology and ideals.
This point is developed by Mamani who writes that the past and its remains are, for
the Aymara (of which he is one), "sources of moral strength and a reaffirmation of
our cultural autonomy." The Indians are not, he emphasizes, "only prehistory, a
dead and silent past" (Mamani 1989: 49–58). In 2006, Evo Morales, an Aymara
Indian, was elected president of Bolivia and held a ritual inauguration at the site
(see *American Indian* Summer 2006: 12).

Just as archeologists have sometimes refused to acknowledge evidence that does not accord with their own political and ideological beliefs, in other cases evidence has been deliberately emphasized in order to reinforce a particular notion of the past. The former Shah of Iran bestowed his attention on Persepolis, in 1971 staging there celebrations of the 2500th anniversary of Cyrus the Great's founding of the Persian Empire. He did this to legitimate the idea of an Iranian nation and place it again on the world stage. In addition, by emphasizing Persian antiquity and using it as the inspiration for Iranian modernization, he tried to create a counternarrative calculated to marginalize the growing Islamist movement in Iran.

The most egregious example of the misuse of scholarship in the realm of cultural heritage and human rights occurred under the Nazis in mid-twentieth century Germany. The Nazis appropriated the pasts of other people as a means of justifying ethnic cleansing and racial slaughter (Arnold 1992). In history, archeology, and, to a lesser degree, philology, the Nazis used popularized "scientific" work on India's ancient languages and peoples to assert their theory of a Nordic (and essentially white) Aryan race (Hock 2003: 2–3). Hans Hock has shown that even among modern scholars nationalism and racial attributions still permeate the interpretations of historical evidence for contact between Aryan and non-Aryan language groups in South Asia (Hock 1999). Although in archeology, the deliberate use of archeology to underscore political and racial ideology culminated with the Nazi rise to power, it had its origins in the work of late nineteenth-century scholars such as Friedrich Delitzsch who looked to the ancient past for the origins of what they regarded as fixed racial types.

Michel-Rolph Trouillot's (1995) classic interrogation of power and the production of history is everywhere present in the field of cultural heritage. Because the denial or distortion of history/prehistory has proven to be a contributing factor in genocide, ethnic cleansing, and oppression to an extreme degree in recent centuries, history often becomes a human rights issue. Among the lessons learned is that the freedom or ability to articulate one's own cultural heritage and express one's own identity is vitally important.

Cultural heritage is threatened when it is neglected and allowed – sometimes intentionally – to deteriorate. It is also damaged when the natural integrity of a site or people is deluged by external influences. In the summer of 2006, the international news media gave glowing reports about China's new train service between Beijing and Lhasa, Tibet. A CNN travelogue showed the beauty of the route and the care taken by the Chinese authorities to protect the wildlife along the way. A *Newsweek* article, however, was more sanguine (Liu 2006). It raised the issue of China's problematic policy toward Tibet, which is aimed at the commodification of traditional Tibetan culture for Chinese tourism, subordinating it to larger nationalist claims and ultimately diminishing it. The influx of millions of Han Chinese to the Tibet Autonomous Region is an ethnic inundation that extends the breadth of Han culture while destroying the integrity of Tibetan culture (Margolis 2006). One traveler observed, "Tibetans seem fated to become extras in a tourist theme park while millions of Chinese move up the new railroad to the top of the world" (Margolis 2006).

In Tibet, heritage preservation is bound up with questions of legitimate ownership. China's stewardship of Tibet was won by force: after the British invaded Lhasa in 1904, they gave nominal suzerainty of the country to China; China invaded Tibet soon after the 1949 revolution and, although the autonomy of Tibetan religious, cultural, and political institutions were guaranteed in a document known as the Seventeen Point Agreement, China failed to keep its promises. The Tibetans rebelled in the famous 1959 uprising, at which point the Dalai Lama and the Tibetan government fled to exile in India. As recently as 1989, martial law was imposed by China. Thus, when the worldwide press trumpets the expansion of tourism to Tibet by means of a luxury train, one has to wonder exactly who is extending the invitation to visit Tibet, and at the same time who is invited or excluded from that invitation.

The question of national versus local development of cultural heritage is developed in Christopher Silver's essay in this volume. In Indonesia, tourism – the country's third major source of income – began in the Dutch colonial era. Under the authoritarian presidencies of Sukarno and Suharto (1945–1998), the development of natural and cultural heritage for tourism continued to figure prominently on the national agenda, always privileging national unity over cultural pluralism. With radical shifts in Indonesia's economic structure and the liberalization of its political system since 1998, however, the tourism industry shows signs of devolving into a more locally based system in which not only the economic benefits may accrue to individual regions but also the expression of cultural localism. In both China and Indonesia, militant force and resistance has played a role in how heritage is expressed and by whom, but Indonesia's relationship to its minority communities and distinct locales seems to be heading in a direction opposite to that of China and its relation to Tibet.

What to Remember, What to Forget

Cultural heritage requires memory. It is not enough for things and monuments to exist on a landscape: in order to be cultural heritage they must be remembered and claimed as patrimony, even if their original meaning is lost or poorly understood. In this sense cultural heritage is always, to some degree, intangible. For tangible and intangible cultural heritage to have meaning and potency, the heritage must be active, dynamic, used, and performed, rather than existing inert and static. Johnson observes that "landscapes, sites and monuments are always emergent and processual, whose meaning(s) and significance are continually being remade through various material and discursive practices" (2001: 75).

Moreover, cultural heritage may be positive and pleasant, or negative and painful, or it can be both, even for the same group of stakeholders. Such a complex range of potential behavior suggests why cultural heritage is readily contested and even rejected. "Selecting particular pasts to conserve is necessarily a matter of continuous negotiations among all interested parties" (Mondale 1994: 15). The connection we see with human rights concerns that which may be commemorated and how the commemoration plays out in the present. A few examples will suffice.

In March 2001, the world looked on in horror as the Taliban blew up the Bamiyan Buddhas in an act of cultural iconoclasm, political assertion, and religious fervor. Although the Buddhist heritage belonged to history, not the lives of the present inhabitants, the de facto rulers rejected all pasts and presents save their own radical version of Islam and consequently this famous site was not accepted as Afghanistan's cultural heritage. While many observers understood this as an extreme form of Islamic iconoclasm, the obliteration was "not a timeless response to figuration but a calculated engagement with a culturally specific discourse of images at a particular historical moment" (Flood 2002). The destruction was politically designed to focus Afghan history on Islam and marginalize its Buddhist past, not unlike the way that the Shah of Iran had marginalized Iran's Islamic history in order to insist upon an older (and theologically inert) identity. The Taliban argued that destruction as a concept was culturally constructed and that the right to make the decision about the statues' survival belonged locally to them. In this sense, their narrow definition of heritage mirrored their narrow view of human rights. But ironically, the Taliban's justification for this publicly reviled act of erasure was predicated on some of the same principles that elsewhere have been used to guide preservation while admitting cultural difference (Meskell 2002: 565).

"Never forget" became the impassioned plea of the remaining world Jewry after the Holocaust, an exhortation directed not just at the Jewish community, but to the entire world in the hope that such a horror would never be repeated to any group anywhere. After almost 2000 years of widespread, often violently manifested anti-Semitism, it is painful for Jews to claim discrimination and genocide as a component of an extraordinarily rich, temporally deep cultural heritage. Yet as a people whose human rights have been abrogated in the most shocking manner, general consensus among Jews clearly favors remembrance over oblivion. Where the issue becomes more complicated is in its tangible form in the countries whose citizens were the Holocaust's perpetrators (Germany) and willing supporters (Austria, Poland, and others). Should they facilitate the cultural heritage of their tiny surviving Jewish populations (and the Romani) as part of their own national identities by building museums of remembrance? Would doing so embrace the concept of human rights? (see Klein 2001; Bunzl 2003). And should they preserve the built environments of their shame such as concentration camps (Koonz 1994) and buildings occupied by Nazi offices? These are active heritage issues, and – as the generation of Holocaust survivors passes away – the issue of how memorials can preserve human experience becomes an urgent one.

The United States has attempted to atone for the cruel treatment of its Native American population through the funding of the new National Museum of the American Indian in Washington, DC, the design and content of which were left to the communities represented, perhaps even exceeding the scenario of participation described by Zimmerman at Sand Creek National Historic Site. In the new museum, the script is celebratory. Cultural heritage is not so much predicated upon the pre-Columbian past as the present. And hemispheric Indianism complements, perhaps overrides, tribal identities. However, while the museum may give prominence to Native American culture, it may distract attention from another injustice that is more painful and difficult to resolve. There is a deep irony in the fact that many lawsuits in which indigenous communities are seeking to reclaim land or reparations for its illegal seizure remain unsettled. At stake is the question of legitimate ownership in which native claims counter those of residents (and, of course, these are not opposite categories). The National Museum of the American Indian allows a diverse American public to celebrate indigenous culture in a way that does not demand confrontation with issues of contested territory. Perhaps honoring and contestation each have their time and place, but it is important to recall, as Laurajane Smith urges in her contribution to this volume, that heritage is not ultimately just about the struggle to possess objects and sites, nor simply to hold them "in trust for future generations." It is a performed negotiation: "what is both done at, and with, heritage sites, objects and places."

The remembrance and commemoration of communism in countries formerly behind the Iron Curtain – an era not known for its human rights behavior or advocacy – poses other issues. Light (2000), for instance, has referred to the heritage of communism in Romania as an "unwanted past." In contrast to Romania's hesitation, the oppressive communist past of the former East Germany is undergoing a selective revival through a phenomenon known locally as *ostalgie*, nostalgia for the East, specifically in terms of ordinary items of daily life (Berdahl 2005).

The terrorist attacks of 11 September 2001 lamentably offer new opportunities for consideration of cultural heritage and human rights. The planned murder of thousands of civilians that day at the World Trade Center (now called Ground Zero), the Pentagon, and Johnstown, Pennsylvania, is an atrocity that has caused lasting trauma. What makes the events of September 11 unique is the instantaneity with which they became scripted as cultural heritage of the country and with virtually no contestation. As noted by Meskell (2002: 557), "World Monuments Watch moved quickly to feature Ground Zero in its October 2001 issue as a place of heritage, requiring both salvage and commemoration. The site was suprapositioned, listed as site 101 in their register of 100 endangered sites around the globe." Meskell describes Ground Zero as "'negative heritage,' a conflictual site that becomes the repository of negative memory in the collective imaginary." The future of the site has been debated for 5 years, albeit with little change in the general public perception of the terrorist attack itself. At issue is how the site is to be scripted for civic and ritual commemoration and, inexorably, rehabilitation for commerce and profit.

Intellectual Property Rights

Human rights and cultural heritage intersect in the area of property rights, defined both as real territory and as other forms of ownership such as memory, traditional knowledge, and even genes. Nicholas and Hollowell (2004: 6) state that "descendent communities have legitimate concerns about the procurement, dissemination and exploitation of 'traditional knowledge' as intellectual property. As commodifications of cultural pasts and claims over uses of the past continue to expand, questions about sharing the benefits of research and concerns about unauthorized or commercial uses of knowledge, images, stories, and designs will persist and fuel debate, or even lawsuits." It is not farfetched for a group to claim its sacred knowledge – a part of its culture heritage – as an inviolable intellectual property right and to contend that they have the right to protect themselves from prying, whether by governments, missionaries, or anthropologists.

Similarly, Elazar Barkan, in his essay in this volume, describes resistance on the part of indigenous peoples to the collection and cataloging of their genes. There is a clear conflict between the desire of the scientific community to study genetic material and make the knowledge obtained from it available worldwide, and non-Western peoples who claim to own their genes and whose cultures have radically divergent views on the meaning of their bodies and the activities to which those bodies should be subjected.

Looters and Squatters

As we saw above, destruction of heritage can occur deliberately, but it can also occur as a result of neglect, impoverishment, and looting. A recent, well-reported example of all three factors is the looting and illegal export of antiquities and works of art that took place in Afghanistan and Iraq under the noses of the occupying forces.

Vandalism directed against tangible cultural heritage, such as architectural monuments and archeological sites, occurs as a result of mischief, greed, political protest, religious intolerance, poverty, and a multitude of other reasons. In the case of the looting of historically important sites such as tombs, the culprits are often local people seeking to supplement their meager income – what we would call subsistence looting. Sometimes they sell objects of art for profit, ripping the work from the contexts that allow archeologists and historians to determine date and meaning. In other instances, they simply quarry a site for its stone and brick, and in doing so, damage the structural integrity of the building. A related issue is "invasion" or "squatting" on archeological sites where the appeal is not the historical value of the site but the availability of the land on which it is built. Landless people will move into what appear to be unclaimed sites in order to take advantage of the well-built floors, walls, and roofing. Their choice of location is typically what drew ancient people to the same place, such as accessible land and water. What are the human rights ethics of these cases? Should the concept of cultural heritage meriting protection be privileged over the immediate needs of the local dwellers? Is possession of heritage determined by place of current residence? Past residence? By claims made on the basis of ethnic or religious ties to a place? These questions are complicated. One has sympathy for the subsistence looter, especially because of the miniscule returns that he/she receives in an antiquities market organized by middlemen and dealers (e.g., Nagin 1990).

Whether enacted by local or external agents, looting destroys a community's heritage, thereby contributing to the destruction of its culture, traditions, and very survival (e.g., Udvardy et al. 2003). The valuable objects ripped out of context for sale need not be ancient and buried to cause cultural loss in their communities of origin. Lobo (1991, 1993; also Bubba 1996) writes about the robbery of sacred weavings from a small Aymara community in highland Bolivia in the 1970s and 1980s. The textiles were esteemed in Coroma "not only as garments of beauty and warmth but also as objects of veneration and status. Many of the weavings have social meanings that are integral to the continuity of community life" (Lobo 1993: 30). Although some were hundreds of years old, they played an active role in ritual life in Coroma.

It is very clear that looting destroys the contexts that give objects their meaning; it is to be condemned. But the moral implication of historic (and archeological, artistic, etc.) objects bought by wealthy collectors from impoverished sellers is more complex. While the original context may be well documented and the commercial exchange entirely legal, the question of meaning is still deeply problematic. If an artifact – especially a sacred object – is taken from its cultural setting and placed in another, its meaning changes. Reception theory teaches us that meaning occurs in the space between an object and its audience (Holub 2002). It is unclear what the role of the heritage preservationist should be in that case.

In Peru, where basically all unfarmed land without private title is state property, there is a widespread phenomenon called *invasión* by which squatters occupy land held by the state and establish shantytowns. Eventually through hard work and perseverance with the intractable bureaucracy, some of these become legally recognized communities. While from the perspective of fair housing and social justice these are successes, the results for heritage preservation are less salutary because often archeological sites are present on these reclaimed grounds. Whether of minor or major significance, the state ought to commission archeologists from its National Institute of Culture to do a salvage project to recover the necessary data before allowing contemporary human occupation on a site. However, this process can take years or even decades and to hold in reserve for potential future excavation a remote site that no one seems eager to study could be regarded as excessive "retentionism." But, some sites of *invasión* are World Heritage Sites, such as Chan Chan, a huge city dating to the eleventh through fifteenth centuries, where for decades Peru's National Institute of Culture has been battling squatters. And at Sacsayhuaman, the magnificent stone-walled complex above the Inca capital of Cuzco, squatters have attempted to entrench themselves in the more distant parts of the site. In these latter cases, it might well be argued that ethically the sites do more good for the public welfare in terms of tourist revenue and archeological significance than is to be derived from permitting squatter settlements.

Yet sometimes squatters and local residents can be the best stewards of a site. At Champaner–Pavagadh in Gujarat (India), a small unsophisticated village spatially divided between the foot and midpoint of a sacred mountain, various temple trusts and citizen organizations assume this role. The mountain's summit has a shrine to the goddess Kali, a sacred Hindu temple that is visited annually by two million pilgrims who make the arduous ascent by bus, jeep, and foot. At its base is an Islamic city of magnificent mosques, tombs, and palaces that flourished in the fifteenth century before the city's abrupt decline. The Heritage Trust of Baroda has spent more than a decade working on plans to preserve the huge, historically complex site. The Trust has found that, while the undeeded plots with shops and humble dwellings along the pilgrimage trail sometimes occlude the dramatic views and crowd too near to the monuments under the protection of the Archaeological Service of India, these same shopkeepers and hawkers may be the most promising guardians of the site. For example, with only modest means and minimal urging, they formed an association to clean litter and debris from one of the plateaus, the busiest rest point. This is a case (like that analyzed by Anne Pyburn herein) where the benefits to the stakeholders were visible. In contradistinction to Luxor (Egypt) where local inhabitants have profited from tomb robbing for centuries, the key in Champaner seems to be that the residents recognize the spiritual (if not the historical) significance of their site, closely identify with it as their own, and are aware that they are positioned to reap the benefits of whatever improvements they can make (Sinha et al. 2003). As Wescoat's essay in this volume shows, during the 2002 riots in Gujarat, sites in Champaner–Pavagadh remained safe even while monuments elsewhere were the target of hostility, suggesting that cultural heritage can provide a kind of common ground in times of strife.

Conclusion

The issue of power is pervasive throughout the case studies examined in this volume. We see that cultural heritage and human rights are entangled with relations of power, and power relations necessarily impact the ideology of universalism underwriting current cultural heritage discourse (Woodiwiss 2005). Western countries have had the power for many years – certainly since the time of high imperialism in the nineteenth century – to determine and dictate policy concerning cultural heritage, both tangible and intangible. That power has been exercised in actions ranging from innocuous to the use of military force.

Falk (2000: 2) has written, "Realizing human rights is tantamount to achieving global justice." While global justice is a huge and fraught goal, various authors in this volume see a direct linkage between human rights and cultural heritage at the local scale, which, in turn, ultimately contributes, in the aggregate, to fulfillment of the global goal. The present volume directs attention to this objective in all of its complexity.

William Logan explains in his essay the relationship between human rights and cultural heritage and the challenges faced by UNESCO in trying to establish priorities between them. Because cultural rights can sometimes be invoked to justify, or at least excuse, violations of human rights, human rights must necessarily supersede cultural rights, and yet the right to the free articulation of heritage is an important aspect of human rights. He points out that cultural rights have both collective and individual assertions, and these may conflict with each other. Human and cultural rights are not always separable, and yet sometimes they must be separated in order to insist on the overarching claims of human rights. He also points to the ways that these discourses have played out internationally, one nation exposing another nation's suppression of cultural expression to shame them and also to gain the political high ground.

Ultimately UNESCO, as the most powerful international heritage organization, will play the largest part in setting worldwide policy regarding the definition and protocols for heritage management, expression, and preservation. However, because UNESCO is a government entity itself, it valorizes national governments. Minority communities within nation states, whether in repressive regimes or democratic republics, are left in a paradoxical situation: when they are at odds with the agenda of the nation, they are forced to seek mediation and redress from the very entity, that is, their adversary. In his Kadaku versus Australia example, Logan shows the important role of UNESCO in adjudicating in such a conflict, but he cautions that it was a rare case of bypassing the national level to negotiate directly with the minority community. This volume contains other examples of minority communities in India, Ecuador, Brazil, Australia, Indonesia, the United States, and elsewhere whose interests are not the same as those of the nation-state that imposes its majority values upon them, and one can think of countless others.

Local contestations of power against the backdrop of heritage assertions are particularly evident in Hugo Benavides' work in Ecuador. He discusses differing notions of power and how the CONAIE (Confederation of Indian Nationalities of Ecuador) recently was able to paralyze the nation several times during week-long strikes, oust two democratically elected presidents, and face off the International Monetary Fund. The irony he recognizes is that the CONAIE's national success has secured its own form of political/gender domination, reconfiguring power in a truly unpredictable way in the context of a population proudly proclaiming its indigenous heritage and future aspirations. As UNESCO grapples with its newly adopted *Convention for the Safeguarding of Intangible Heritage* (approved 2003, operational in 2006), the issue of how to resolve minority/majority conflict may emerge yet more forcefully. In the arena of human rights and cultural heritage, this may be the next frontier.

References

Cultural Heritage Instruments

Burra Charter (http://www.icomos.org/australia/burra.html).
Declaration Concerning the Intentional Destruction of Cultural Heritage, UNESCO, 2003 (http://portal.unesco.org/en/ev.php-URL_ID=17718&URL_DO=DO_TOPIC&URL_SECTION=201.html).
Draft Declaration on the Rights of Indigenous Peoples, UN, 1994 (http://www1.umn.edu/humanrts/instree/declra.htm).

Hague Convention for the Protection of Cultural Property in the Event of Armed Conflict, UNESCO adopted 1954, ratified 1956 (http://www.icomos.org/ hague/hague.convention.html).

Indian National Trust for Art and Cultural Heritage (INTACH) (www.intach.org/pdf/list).

International Covenant on Civil and Political Rights, UN adopted 1966, ratified 1976 (http://www.ohchr.org/english/law/ccpr.htm).

International Covenant on Economic, Social and Cultural Rights, UN adopted 1966, ratified 1976 (http://www.unhchr.ch/html/menu3/b/a_cescr.htm).

Protocol of San Salvador, added to the American Convention on Human Rights in the Area of Economic, Social and Cultural Rights, Inter-American Commission on Human Rights, 1988 (http://www.cidh.oas.org/Basicos/basic5.htm).

Resolution No. 1, 19th meeting of the General Assembly of ICOM (International Council of Museums), 1998 (http://icom.museum/resolutions/eres98.html).

The Nara Document on Authenticity, 1994 (http://www.international.icomos.org/ naradoc_eng.htm).

Universal Declaration of Human Rights, UN, 1948 (http://www.un.org/Overview/ rights.html).

World Heritage Convention, UNESCO, 1972 (http://whc.unesco.org/en/conventiontext/).

Published Works

American Anthropological Association, 1947, Statement on Human Rights. *American Anthropologist* 49(4): 539–543.

Arnold, Bettina, 1992, The Past as Propaganda: How Hitler's Archaeologists Distorted European Prehistory to Justify Racist and Territorial Goals. *Archaeology* July–August: 30–37.

Barakat, Sultan, Craig Wilson, Vjekoslava Sankovic Simcic, and Marija Kojakovic, 2001, Challenges and Dilemmas Facing the Reconstruction of War-Damaged Cultural Heritage: The Case Study of Pocitelj, Bosnia-Herzegovina. In *Destruction and Conservation of Cultural Property*, edited by Robert Layton, Peter G. Stone, and Julian Thomas, pp. 168–181. Routledge, London.

Begag, Azouz, 1998, Culture as an Antidote to Intolerance. In *Cultural Heritage and Its Educational Implications: A Factor for Tolerance, Good Citizenship and Social Integration*, pp. 27–31. Proceedings, Seminar, Brussels (Belgium), 28–30 August 1995. Cultural Heritage No. 36. Council of Europe.

Berdahl, Daphne, 2005, Expressions of Experience and Experiences of Expression: Museum Re-presentations of GDR History. *Anthropology and Humanism* 30(2): 156–170.

Bianchi, Raoul, and Priscilla Boniface, 2002, Editorial: The Politics of World Heritage. *International Journal of Heritage Studies* 8(2): 79–80.

Branka, Sulc, 2001, The Protection of Croatia's Cultural Heritage During War 1991–2005. In *Destruction and Conservation of Cultural Property*, edited by Robert Layton, Peter G. Stone, and Julian Thomas, pp. 157–167. Routledge, London.

Brown, K. S., 1998, Contests of Heritage and the Politics of Preservation in the Former Yugoslav Republic of Macedonia. In *Archaeology Under Fire*, edited by Lynn Meskell, pp. 68–86. Routledge, London.

Bubba Zamora, Cristina, 1996, Collectors Versus Native Peoples: The Repatriation of the Sacred Weavings of Coroma, Bolivia. *Museum Anthropology* 20(3): 39–44.

Bunzl, Matti, 2003, Of Holograms and Storage Areas: Modernity and Postmodernity at Vienna's Jewish Museum. *Cultural Anthropology* 18(4): 435–468.

Cleere, Henry, 2000, The World Heritage Convention in the Third World. In *Cultural Resource Management in Contemporary Society: Perspectives on Managing and Presenting the Past*, edited by Francis P. McManamon, pp. 99–106. Routledge, London.

—, 2001, The Uneasy Bedfellows: Universality and Cultural Heritage. In *Destruction and Conservation of Cultural Property*, edited by Robert Layton, Peter G. Stone, and Julian Thomas, pp. 22–29. Routledge, London.

Clifford, James, 1997, Palenque Log. In *Routes*, edited by James Clifford, pp. 220–237. Harvard University Press, Cambridge.

Colwell-Chanthaphonh, Chip, 2002, Dismembering/Disremembering the Buddhas. *Journal of Social Archaeology* 3(1): 75–98.

Cowan, Jane K., 2006, Culture and Rights after Culture and Rights. *American Anthropologist* 108(1): 9–24.

Fagan, Brian, 1981, Two Hundred and Four Years of African Archaeology. In *Antiquity and Man. Essays in Honor of Glyn Daniel*, edited by John D. Evans, Barry Cunliffe, and Colin Renfrew, pp. 42–51. Thames and Hudson, London.

Falk, Richard, 2000, *Human Rights Horizons*. Routledge, New York.

Feder, Kenneth L., 2006, *Frauds, Myths and Mysteries*, 5th edition. McGraw-Hill, New York.

Flood, Finbarr Barry, 2002, Between Cult and Culture: Bamiyan, Islamic Iconoclasm, and the Museum. *The Art Bulletin* 84(4): 641–659.

Gamboni, Dario, 2001, World Heritage: Shield or Target? *Conservation* 16(2), Summer. http://www.getty.edu/conservation/resources/newletter/16_2 (accessed 31 May 2006).

Ghanea, Nazila, and Ladan Rahmani, 2005, A Review of the 60th Session of the Commission on Human Rights. *International Journal of Human Rights* 9(1): 125–144.

Glaskin, Katie, 2003, Native Title and the Recognition of Indigenous Land Rights in Australia. *Anthropology News*, December: 8.

Goodale, Mark, 2006, Introduction to 'Anthropology and Human Rights in a New Key.' *American Anthropologist* 108(1): 1–8.

Hakki, Murat Metin, 2002, The Silver Anniversary of the UN Human Rights Committee: Anything to Celebrate? *International Journal of Human Rights* 6(3): 85–102.

Hall, Martin, 1984, The Burden of Tribalism: The Social Context of Southern African Iron Age Studies. *American Antiquity* 49(3): 455–467.

Hock, Hans, 1999, Through a Glass Darkly: Modern "Racial" Interpretations vs. Textual and General Prehistoric Evidence on āya and dāa/dasyu in Vedic Society. In *Aryan and Non-Aryan in South Asia: Evidence, Interpretation, and Ideology*, Proceedings of the International Seminar on Aryan and Non-Aryan in South Asia, University of Michigan, Ann Arbor, 25–27 October, 1996, edited by Johannes Bronkhorst and Madhav Deshpande, pp. 145–74. Harvard Oriental Series, Opera Minora, 3.

—, 2003, Did Indo-European Linguistics Prepare the Ground for Nazism? Lessons from the Past for the Present and the Future. In *Language in Time and Space: A Festschrift for Werner Winter on the Occasion of his 80th Birthday*, edited by B. L. M. Bauer and G. -J. Pinault. Mouton de Gruyter, Berlin.

Holub, Robert C., 2002, *Reception Theory*. Routledge, London.

Johnson, Mark, 2001, Renovating Hue (Vietnam): Authenticating Destruction, Reconstructing Authenticity. In *Destruction and Conservation of Cultural Property*, edited by Robert Layton, Peter G. Stone, and Julian Thomas, pp. 75–92. Routledge, London.

Klein, Julia M., 2001, The Jewish Museum Berlin: Amid Clutter, At Odds with Itself. *The Chronicle of Higher Education*, November 9: B15–B17.

Koonz, Claudia, 2004, Between Memory and Oblivion: Concentration Camps in German Memory. In *Commemorations. The Politics of National Identity*, edited by John R. Gillis, pp. 258–280. Princeton University Press, Princeton.

Lal, B. B., 2001, A Note on the Excavations at Ayodhya with Reference to the Mandir-Masjid Issue. In *Destruction and Conservation of Cultural Property*, edited by Robert Layton, Peter G. Stone, and Julian Thomas, pp. 117–126. Routledge, London.

Layton, Robert, 1995, Relating to the Country in the Western Desert. In *The Anthropology of Landscape. Perspectives on Place and Space*, edited by Eric Hirsch and Michael O'Hanlon, pp. 210–231. Clarendon, Oxford.

Light, Duncan, 2000, An Unwanted Past: Contemporary Tourism and the Heritage of Communism in Romania. *International Journal of Heritage Studies* 6(2): 145–160.

Liu, Melinda, 2006, Bound to the Tracks. On the Maiden run of the Train to Lhasa, Where Environmentalism Travels First Class – But Human Rights to Do Not. *Newsweek*, July 17.

Lobo, Susan, 1991, The Fabric of Life, Repatriating the Sacred Coroma Textiles. *Cultural Survival* 15(3): 40–46.

—, 1993, Sacred weavings returned. *Cultural Survival Quarterly*, Spring: 3–4.

MacKenzie, Robert, and Peter Stone, 1990, Introduction: The Concept of Excluded Past. In *The Excluded Past. Archaeology in Education*, edited by P. Stone and R. MacKenzie, pp. 1–14. Unwin Hyman, London.

Mamani Condori, Carlos, 1989, History and Prehistory in Bolivia: What About the Indians? In *Conflict in the Archaeology of Living Traditions*, edited by R. Layton. Routledge, London.

Margolis, Eric, 2006, *Tibet: The Lost Kingdom* (July 10). http://www.ericmargolis.com/archives/2006/07/tibet_the_lost.php.

Mason, Ronald J., 2000, Archeology and Native North American Oral Traditions. *American Antiquity* 65(2): 239–266.

McGowan, Keith, 2002, *Human Rights*. Lucent Books, Farmington Hills, MI.

Meskell, Lynn, 2002, Negative Heritage and Past Mastering in Archaeology. *Anthropological Quarterly* 75(3): 557–574.

Messer, Ellen, 1993, Anthropology and Human Rights. *Annual Review of Anthropology* 22: 221–249.

—, 1997, Pluralist Approaches to Human Rights. *Journal of Anthropological Research* 53(3): 293–317.

Mondale, Clarence, 1994, Conserving a Problematic Past. In *Conserving Culture. A New Discourse on Heritage*, edited by Mary Hufford, pp. 15–23. University of Illinois Press, Urbana.

Morphy, Howard, 1995, Landscape and the Reproduction of the Ancestral Past. In *The Anthropology of Landscape. Perspectives on Place and Space*, edited by Eric Hirsch and Michael O'Hanlon, pp. 184–209. Clarendon, Oxford.

Mortensen, Lena, 2006, Copán: The Authenticity of Stone. In *Archaeological Site Museums in Latin America*, edited by Helaine Silverman, pp. 47–63. University Press of Florida, Gainesville.

Nagengast, Carole, and Terence Turner, 1997, Introduction: Universal Human Rights Versus Cultural Relativity. *Journal of Anthropological Research* 53(3): 269–272.

Nagin, Carl, 1990, The Peruvian Gold Rush. *Art & Antiques* 7(5): 99–146.

Nicholas, George, and Julie Hollowell, 2004, Intellectual Property Issues in Archaeology? *Anthropology News*, April: 6, 8.

O'Sullivan, Declan, 2000, Is the Declaration of Human Rights Universal? *International Journal of Human Rights* 4(1): 25–53.

Posnansky, Arthur, 1912, *Guía General Ilustrada para la Investigación de los Monumentos Prehistóricos de Tihuanacu e Islas del Sol y la Luna (Titicaca y Koati)*. Hugo Heitmann, La Paz.

Rao, Nandini, and C. Rammanohar Reddy, 2001, Aydohya, the Print Media and Communalism. *Destruction and Conservation of Cultural Property*, edited by Robert Layton, Peter G. Stone, and Julian Thomas, pp. 139–155. Routledge, London.

Schipper, Friedrich T., 2005, The Protection and Preservation of Iraq's Archaeological Heritage, Spring 1991–2003. *American Journal of Archaeology* 109: 251–272.

Schmidt, Peter R., 1995, Using Archaeology to Remake History in Africa. In *Making Alternative Histories. The Practice of Archaeology and History in Non-Western Settings*, edited by Peter R. Schmidt and Thomas C. Patterson, pp. 119–147. School of American Research Press, Santa Fe.

Sinha, Amita, D. Fairchild Ruggles, and James L. Wescoat Jr., 2003, *Champaner–Pavagadh Cultural Sanctuary, Gujarat, India*. Department of Landscape Architecture, University of Illinois, Champaign.

Smith, Rhona K. M., 2001, Traditional Lands and Cultural Rights: The Australian Experience. *International Journal of Human Rights* 5(3): 1–18.

Stanish, Charles, 2002, Tiwanaku Political Economy. In *Andean Archaeology I: Variations in Sociopolitical Organization*, edited by William H. Isbell and Helaine Silverman, pp. 169–198. Kluwer/Plenum, New York.

Taçon, Paul S. C., 1999, Identifying Ancient Sacred Landscapes in Australia: From Physical to Social. In *Archaeologies of Landscape*, edited by Wendy Ashmore and A. Bernard Knapp, pp. 33–57. Blackwell, Oxford.

Trigg, Roger, 2005, *Morality Matters*. Blackwell, Malden, MA.
Trouillot, Michel-Rolph, 1995, *Silencing the Past. Power and the Production of History*. Beacon, Boston.
Udvardy, Monica, Linda L. Giles, and John B. Mitsanze, 2003, The Transatlantic Trade in African Ancestors: Mijikenda Memorial Statues (Vigango) and the Ethics of Collecting and Curating Non-western Cultural Property. *American Anthropologist* 105(3): 566–580.
Woodiwiss, Anthony, 2005, *Human Rights*. Routledge, New York.

Appendix
Universal Declaration of Human Rights*

http://www.un.org/Overview/rights.html

Preamble

Whereas recognition of the inherent dignity and of the equal and inalienable rights of all members of the human family is the foundation of freedom, justice, and peace in the world,

Whereas disregard and contempt for human rights have resulted in barbarous acts which have outraged the conscience of mankind, and the advent of a world in which human beings shall enjoy freedom of speech and belief and freedom from fear and want has been proclaimed as the highest aspiration of the common people,

Whereas it is essential, if man is not to be compelled to have recourse, as a last resort, to rebellion against tyranny and oppression, that human rights should be protected by the rule of law,

Whereas it is essential to promote the development of friendly relations between nations,

Whereas the peoples of the United Nations have in the Charter reaffirmed their faith in fundamental human rights, in the dignity and worth of the human person, and in the equal rights of men and women and have determined to promote social progress and better standards of life in larger freedom,

Whereas Member States have pledged themselves to achieve, in co-operation with the United Nations, the promotion of universal respect for and observance of human rights and fundamental freedoms,

Whereas a common understanding of these rights and freedoms is of the greatest importance for the full realization of this pledge.

Now, therefore, The General Assembly proclaims This Universal Declaration of Human Rights as a common standard of achievement for all peoples and all nations, to the end that every individual and every organ of society, keeping this Declaration constantly in mind, shall strive by teaching and education to promote respect for

---

* Adopted and proclaimed by the United Nations General Assembly resolution 217 A (III) of 10 December 1948.

these rights and freedoms and by progressive measures, national and international, to secure their universal and effective recognition and observance, both among the peoples of Member States themselves and among the peoples of territories under their jurisdiction.

Article 1

All human beings are born free and equal in dignity and rights. They are endowed with reason and conscience and should act towards one another in a spirit of brotherhood.

Article 2

Everyone is entitled to all the rights and freedoms set forth in this Declaration, without distinction of any kind, such as race, colour, sex, language, religion, political or other opinion, national or social origin, property, birth or other status. Furthermore, no distinction shall be made on the basis of the political, jurisdictional or international status of the country or territory to which a person belongs, whether it be independent, trust, non-self-governing or under any other limitation of sovereignty.

Article 3

Everyone has the right to life, liberty and security of person.

Article 4

No one shall be held in slavery or servitude; slavery and the slave trade shall be prohibited in all their forms.

Article 5

No one shall be subjected to torture or to cruel, inhuman or degrading treatment or punishment.

Article 6

Everyone has the right to recognition everywhere as a person before the law.

Article 7

All are equal before the law and are entitled without any discrimination to equal protection of the law. All are entitled to equal protection against any discrimination in violation of this Declaration and against any incitement to such discrimination.

Article 8

Everyone has the right to an effective remedy by the competent national tribunals for acts violating the fundamental rights granted him by the constitution or by law.

Article 9

No one shall be subjected to arbitrary arrest, detention or exile.

Article 10

Everyone is entitled in full equality to a fair and public hearing by an independent and impartial tribunal, in the determination of his rights and obligations and of any criminal charge against him.

Article 11

(1) Everyone charged with a penal offence has the right to be presumed innocent until proved guilty according to law in a public trial at which he has had all the guarantees necessary for his defence.
(2) No one shall be held guilty of any penal offence on account of any act or omission which did not constitute a penal offence, under national or international law, at the time when it was committed. Nor shall a heavier penalty be imposed than the one that was applicable at the time the penal offence was committed.

Article 12

No one shall be subjected to arbitrary interference with his privacy, family, home, or correspondence, nor to attacks upon his honour and reputation. Everyone has the right to the protection of the law against such interference or attacks.

Article 13

(1) Everyone has the right to freedom of movement and residence within the borders of each state.
(2) Everyone has the right to leave any country, including his own, and to return to his country.

Article 14

(1) Everyone has the right to seek and to enjoy in other countries asylum from persecution.
(2) This right may not be invoked in the case of prosecutions genuinely arising from non-political crimes or from acts contrary to the purposes and principles of the United Nations.

Article 15

(1) Everyone has the right to a nationality.
(2) No one shall be arbitrarily deprived of his nationality nor denied the right to change his nationality.

Article 16

(1) Men and women of full age, without any limitation due to race, nationality, or religion, have the right to marry and to found a family. They are entitled to equal rights as to marriage, during marriage and at its dissolution.
(2) Marriage shall be entered into only with the free and full consent of the intending spouses.
(3) The family is the natural and fundamental group unit of society and is entitled to protection by society and the State.

Article 17

(1) Everyone has the right to own property alone as well as in association with others.
(2) No one shall be arbitrarily deprived of his property.

Article 18

Everyone has the right to freedom of thought, conscience and religion; this right includes freedom to change his religion or belief, and freedom, either alone or in community with others and in public or private, to manifest his religion or belief in teaching, practice, worship, and observance.

Article 19

Everyone has the right to freedom of opinion and expression; this right includes freedom to hold opinions without interference and to seek, receive and impart information and ideas through any media and regardless of frontiers.

Article 20

(1) Everyone has the right to freedom of peaceful assembly and association.
(2) No one may be compelled to belong to an association.

Article 21

(1) Everyone has the right to take part in the government of his country, directly, or through freely chosen representatives.
(2) Everyone has the right of equal access to public service in his country.
(3) The will of the people shall be the basis of the authority of government; this will shall be expressed in periodic and genuine elections which shall be by universal and equal suffrage and shall be held by secret vote or by equivalent free voting procedures.

Article 22

Everyone, as a member of society, has the right to social security and is entitled to realization, through national effort and international co-operation and in accordance with the organization and resources of each State, of the economic, social and cultural rights indispensable for his dignity and the free development of his personality.

Article 23

(1) Everyone has the right to work, to free choice of employment, to just and favourable conditions of work and to protection against unemployment.
(2) Everyone, without any discrimination, has the right to equal pay for equal work.
(3) Everyone who works has the right to just and favourable remuneration ensuring for himself and his family an existence worthy of human dignity, and supplemented, if necessary, by other means of social protection.
(4) Everyone has the right to form and to join trade unions for the protection of his interests.

Article 24

Everyone has the right to rest and leisure, including reasonable limitation of working hours and periodic holidays with pay.

Article 25

(1) Everyone has the right to a standard of living adequate for the health and well-being of himself and of his family, including food, clothing, housing and medical care and necessary social services, and the right to security in the event of unemployment, sickness, disability, widowhood, old age or other lack of livelihood in circumstances beyond his control.
(2) Motherhood and childhood are entitled to special care and assistance. All children, whether born in or out of wedlock, shall enjoy the same social protection.

Article 26

(1) Everyone has the right to education. Education shall be free, at least in the elementary and fundamental stages. Elementary education shall be compulsory. Technical and professional education shall be made generally available and higher education shall be equally accessible to all on the basis of merit.
(2) Education shall be directed to the full development of the human personality and to the strengthening of respect for human rights and fundamental freedoms. It shall promote understanding, tolerance and friendship among all nations, racial or religious groups, and shall further the activities of the United Nations for the maintenance of peace.
(3) Parents have a prior right to choose the kind of education that shall be given to their children.

Article 27

(1) Everyone has the right freely to participate in the cultural life of the community, to enjoy the arts and to share in scientific advancement and its benefits.
(2) Everyone has the right to the protection of the moral and material interests resulting from any scientific, literary or artistic production of which he is the author.

Article 28

Everyone is entitled to a social and international order in which the rights and freedoms set forth in this Declaration can be fully realized.

Article 29

(1) Everyone has duties to the community in which alone the free and full development of his personality is possible.
(2) In the exercise of his rights and freedoms, everyone shall be subject only to such limitations as are determined by law solely for the purpose of securing due recognition and respect for the rights and freedoms of others and of meeting the just requirements of morality, public order and the general welfare in a democratic society.
(3) These rights and freedoms may in no case be exercised contrary to the purposes and principles of the United Nations.

Article 30

Nothing in this Declaration may be interpreted as implying for any State, group or person any right to engage in any activity or to perform any act aimed at the destruction of any of the rights and freedoms set forth herein.

Part 2
Connotations, Conflicts, Conundrums, Communities

Chapter 2
Closing Pandora's Box: Human Rights Conundrums in Cultural Heritage Protection

William S. Logan

Introduction

On 20 January 2006, Romania became the 30th State Party to sign UNESCO's *Convention for the Safeguarding of Intangible Heritage*. This meant that the Convention, which had been approved by UNESCO's General Conference in 2003, entered into force on 20 April 2006 (as it required 30 signatories to become operational). The Convention signaled the expansion of the global system of heritage protection from the *tangible* (that is, heritage places and artifacts) to the *intangible*. Article 2 of the Convention describes intangible cultural heritage as "practices, representations, expressions, knowledge, skills" – in other words, heritage that is embodied in people rather than in inanimate objects. It is an expansion that many heritage professionals, including some in UNESCO itself, see as opening up a Pandora's box of difficulties, confusions, and complexities.

Concern has been voiced that the Convention was prepared too rapidly, with many key issues, such as the criteria for the new *Representative List of Intangible Heritage*, still needing to be clarified. Without such criteria – or the hurdle of "authenticity" used in dealing with heritage places under the 1972 World Heritage Convention – how will the list be drawn up? How will it be possible to limit the size of the list? The conservation of inanimate objects – places and artifacts – is difficult enough; but the protection of heritage embodied in people raises a whole new set of ethical and practical issues.

This chapter canvasses these concerns, focusing on the "newer," intangible form of heritage. The concerns are clearly important and we need to find ways to deal with them – as practitioners, policy-makers, researchers, and educators – and for the public whose cultural heritage we are talking about. In particular, the chapter focuses on the issue of how we might – indeed must – use the notion of human rights as a way of limiting the proposed Intangible List. The chapter will outline the ways in which the protection and preservation of cultural heritage is especially linked to "cultural rights" as a form of human rights. This linkage is too often ignored or inadequately understood by scholars working in the cultural heritage field. Indeed, it could be said that this deficiency is part of the larger problem facing

H. Silverman and D. F. Ruggles (eds.), *Cultural Heritage and Human Rights.*
© Springer 2007

the field, which the Smithsonian (2005) recently pointed out – that is, the "vastly under-theorized" condition of the very concept of "cultural heritage."

This linkage is also not clearly understood by cultural heritage practitioners in many countries who too frequently view their work merely as technical. And it seems, too, to be poorly understood by human rights workers, despite the abundance of opportunities around the world to witness people struggling to assert their cultural rights in order to protect their cultural heritage and their cultural identity. Perhaps UN Chief of the Permanent Forum on Indigenous Issues Secretariat, Elsa Stamatopoulou, is correct in suggesting that human rights experts and international law specialists tend to avoid discussion of cultural rights "lest the lurking issue of cultural relativism appear, implicitly, or explicitly, to undermine the delicate and fragile universality concept that has been painstakingly woven over the last five decades" (Stamatopoulou 2004).

The chapter deals mostly with global efforts to protect cultural heritage, although much also applies at the national and local levels. It aims to set a broad agenda for the specific, detailed case studies that must follow as well as for educational curricula in heritage studies. The chapter reflects my personal involvement in the cultural heritage field over three decades, including extensive work with UNESCO and other global agencies, notably ICOMOS and ICCROM, although I hasten to add that the opinions expressed are my own and are not intended to represent the official views of any of these organizations.

Cultural Diversity and Heritage

Heritage usually comprises those things in the natural and cultural environment around us that we have inherited from previous generations – or were sometimes created by the current generation – and that we, as communities and societies, think are so important we want to pass them on to the generations to come. As previously noted, these things can be tangible (places, artifacts) and intangible (practices and skills embodied in people). This chapter started with reference to the Intangible Heritage Convention, though, in fact, the cultural heritage field concentrated, historically, first on the tangible and only in the last 15 years has it turned its attention to the intangible. The World Heritage Convention (to give it its full name, *Convention Concerning the Protection of the World Cultural and Natural Heritage*) deals with heritage places and dates from 1972; the Intangible Heritage Convention came three decades later.

Heritage is the result of a selection process. It is not everything from our history – heritage and history are not one and the same. The aim of heritage protection is to pass on this selection of things with their values intact and in authentic condition. Or at least this is how we think about tangible heritage. There are serious doubts about whether these concepts are relevant to intangible cultural heritage and can be used in identifying the significant things that should be inscribed under the 2003 Convention.

Heritage has acquired enormous economic value, notably as one of the mainstays of the vast tourism industry. But it is also fundamental to cultural identity; it is those things that underpin our identity as communities – national, regional, local, even family. These are things about which we are usually proud; but sometimes they may be important and worthy of conservation because they are reminders of how societies can go wrong; they provide salutary lessons for present and future generations.

Heritage, tangible and intangible, provides the basis of humanity's rich cultural diversity. The flyer for the conference that led to this book asked whether cultural heritage matters enough to go to war for. Clearly large parts of the world think so. Conflicts over cultural heritage and cultural identity abound the world over and are the subject of media scrutiny and academic scholarship, from local disputes through to ethnic cleansing over larger regions and to Samuel P. Huntington's grand clash of civilizations.

UNESCO and Cultural Diversity

At the global level, UNESCO is the peak organization engaged in shaping attitudes to, forming statements of principle about, and engaging with its Member States in projects to protect cultural heritage and cultural diversity. These interests were present in UNESCO's program from the outset: its Constitution refers to the preservation of the "integrity and fruitful diversity of the cultures" of the Member States. But the organization's emphasis has made a number of significant shifts since its establishment in 1946 (Yusuf 2005). In the immediate post-World War II years (late 1940s and 1950s), UNESCO emphasized "intercultural dialogue" as a key strategy for peace building. During the period of rapid postwar decolonization, UNESCO's General Conference adopted in 1966 a *Declaration on the Principles of International Cultural Cooperation*, Article 1 of which states that: "Each culture has a dignity and value which must be respected and preserved," that "every people has the right and duty to develop its culture," and that "In their rich variety and diversity, and in the reciprocal influences they exert on one another, all cultures form part of the common heritage belonging to all mankind."

"Establishing the link between human rights, human dignity and culture," according to Abdulqawi Yusuf, Director of UNESCO's Office of International Standard and Legal Affairs, in a presentation to the third Forum on Human Development in January 2005, "was an important step in bringing culture into the political mainstream of international cooperation, making it constitutive and not only expressive of individual and group identity and independence. This was particularly important for the newly independent countries" (Yusuf 2005: 2).

In the 1970s and 1980s, the emphasis of UNESCO's work on cultural relations shifted to the "culture and development" relationship and to the protection of cultural heritage. The objective was, Yusuf (2005: 2) says, "to ensure the promotion of cultural identity within the context of a global development strategy, which was at the time being fostered by the international community." Following the 1982 World Conference on Cultural Policies in Mexico, an important conceptual shift occurred in the manner in which UNESCO considered culture in its work. The earlier definition focusing on traditional "arts and literature" was replaced by a new definition that saw culture "in its widest sense, [as] the whole complex of distinctive spiritual, material, intellectual, and emotional features that characterize a society and social group. It includes not only the arts and letters, but also modes of life, the fundamental rights of the human being, value systems, traditions and beliefs" (Mexico Declaration on Cultural Policies 1982).

It was during the 1990s that the diversity theme, and especially the protection of diversity, began to emerge as a major focus of UNESCO activities, in large part due to fears that globalization is antithetical to the survival of cultural diversity. The UN had declared the years 1988–1997 as a "Decade for Cultural Development," with "cultural diversity" as a key theme (Lacoste 1994). The Decade ended with the 1998 Stockholm Intergovernmental Conference on "Cultural Policies for Development," which recommended that Member States should "promote the idea that cultural goods and services should be fully recognized and treated as being not like any other form of merchandise." The World Commission on Culture and Development, meanwhile, presented its final report under the title *Our Creative Diversity* in 1995.

During 2000, the then recently appointed UNESCO Director General, Koïchiro Matsuura, established a scheme called *Proclamation of Master Pieces of the Oral and Intangible Heritage of Humanity*, which became the advance guard of the 2003 Intangible Heritage Convention. Then, in October 2000, UNESCO's Executive Board invited the Director General to identify the basic elements of a UNESCO declaration on cultural diversity. In doing so the Executive Board referred explicitly to the need to strengthen UNESCO's role in "promoting cultural diversity in the context of globalization."

The resulting instrument, the *UNESCO Universal Declaration on Cultural Diversity*, was adopted unanimously by the 185 Member States represented at the 31st session of the General Conference in 2001. The UNESCO Web site (2006) refers to it as the founding act of a new ethic being promoted by the organization at the dawn of the twenty-first century, particularly because it provides the international community, for the first time, with a "wide-ranging standard-setting instrument to underpin its conviction that respect for cultural diversity and intercultural dialogue is one of the surest guarantees of development and peace."

Limiting the Scope of Cultural Heritage Deemed Worthy of Protection

The *Universal Declaration on Cultural Diversity* maintains that cultural diversity is the "common heritage of humanity," "a source of exchange, innovation and creativity," and "as necessary for humankind as biodiversity is for nature." Most of us would agree that the protection of cultural diversity alongside biological diversity is a worthwhile enterprise. There is a richness in the world worth keeping.

There is a claim, often implicit, in the UNESCO documents, however, that conservation should be directed at *all* cultural heritages equally. As an intergovernmental organization, UNESCO has to work diplomatically to achieve consensus, and consequently the emphasis on equal treatment is generally necessary. But there are patently some dimensions of our own culture that we might not want to keep at all – and some elements of other people's cultures that we might hope they would abandon. With tangible forms of heritage, we might just let them disintegrate over time; with intangible forms – living heritage, embodied in people – the issue is not as simple. It is not ethically possible to "own" people in the way that we can own, buy and sell, destroy, rebuild, or preserve physical property – places and artifacts.

Nevertheless, some cultural practices have been eradicated in the past, including social forms such as Chinese foot-binding, and economic forms such as "New World" slavery. The Indian practice of suttee has largely died out. It was banned by the British in the 1820s, but continued to be practiced. The last Indian legislation was as recent as 1987, following the death of a 17-year-old girl, Roop Kanwar, on her husband's funeral pyre in Rajasthan.

Other forms continue today but are actively discouraged by some sections of the world community. These include the burning of female children in northern India (reported on the BBC during April 2006) or female and male genital mutilation practiced by some religious groups. These practices are justified on religious (i.e., cultural) grounds. In the case of the child burning, the perpetrators (village men) believe that these sacrifices to the Hindu goddess of destruction, Kali, bring them a better life in this world. Apparently some 200 cases are known to India's police.

The difficulty with the anthropological definition of culture lies in its breadth, making it possible to claim almost all aspects of human behavior as part of one's "culture." Thus even political behavior like Ku Klux Klan rituals can be seen as a cultural manifestation – one example of many cultural forms held to be important by communities and groups within various countries. Unlike the World Heritage system for heritage places, where the Operational Guidelines (last revised in early 2005) contain a list of ten criteria to be used in the listing process, the Intangible Heritage Convention contains, at present, no criteria – no prescription about which elements within cultures might be regarded as significant and worthy of protection. This may be relatively unproblematic while dealing with exotic art forms, such as traditional music or dance; but it is clearly unsatisfactory when a broader view of culture is taken.

The Convention requires the establishment of two lists: the *Representative List of the Intangible Cultural Heritage of Humanity* and the *List of Intangible Cultural Heritage in Need of Urgent Safeguarding*. As the title of the first, main list indicates, the intangible heritage system is opting for heritage elements that are "representative" rather than the best or the unique. This, too, is problematic: representative of what? How will it be possible to limit the number of representatives on the list? The Convention refers to a future intergovernmental Committee that will have the responsibility of drawing up a set of criteria for the establishment, updating, and publication of the lists and submitting to the General Assembly for approval the criteria (Articles 16.2 and 17.2). UNESCO advice at the present time times is that "the raw material for these criteria can be found in the Convention's definition of Intangible Cultural Heritage and elsewhere in the text of the Convention".

How then are we to choose which elements of cultures to protect and which to let perish? As I have said, increasingly the issue of preserving cultural heritage is linked to cultural rights as a form of human rights. But where is the universal right to the preservation of cultural heritage articulated? Does recourse to the notion of human rights and to the human right instruments solve our problems completely? My conclusion is that we can, of course, take recourse to the range of international statements (or instruments) concerning human rights and cultural heritage to support our endeavors – but this does not eliminate all our problems as the cases I will raise shortly demonstrate.

Indeed, even within the human rights statements and in the interpretative discourse surrounding them, a deficiency is noted with regard to how the key concepts are seen to interrelate with each other. One human rights scholar, Rodolfo Stavenhagen, writing in 1998, made the point that "Cultural rights [a term we may take to include the right to maintain and enjoy one's own cultural heritage] have not been given much importance in theoretical texts on human rights and . . . are treated rather as a residual category" (1998: 1). This was certainly true in the earlier statements. Asbjørn Eide and Allan Rosas (2001: 289) note that, in both the *Universal Declaration of Human Rights* (1948) and the *International Covenanton Economic, Social and Cultural Rights* (1966), "cultural rights" seem like a left-over category coming at the end of the rights listed in both documents.

Another major difficulty in many of the human rights instruments, such as these two, as well as in much of the discourse, is that they are concerned more with individual than group, community, or societal rights. The *International Covenant on Civil and Political Rights* (1966), moves more clearly beyond individual human rights, particularly in Article 27:

> In those States in which ethnic, religious or linguistic minorities exist persons belonging to such minorities shall not be denied the right, in community with other members of their group, to enjoy their own culture, to profess their own religion, or to use their own language.

This approach, underlining the protection of minority group human rights, is strengthened by the 1992 UN *Declaration on the Rights of Persons Belonging to National or Ethnic, Religious, and Linguistic Minorities.*

The 2001 *Declaration on Cultural Diversity* and the 2003 *Convention for the Safeguarding of Intangible Heritage* bring human rights to the foreground. Article 4 of the 2001 Declaration deals specifically with human rights as the guarantor of cultural diversity and limits the application of the instrument to those aspects of cultural heritage that do not infringe human rights. This is extended in Article 5 dealing with cultural rights as an enabling environment for cultural diversity. The preamble of the Intangible Heritage Convention also starts by referring to existing international human rights instruments, and Article 2 includes the statement that:

> For the purposes of this Convention, consideration will be given solely to such intangible cultural heritage as is compatible with existing human rights instruments, as well as with the requirements of mutual respect among communities, groups and individuals, and of sustainable development.

In summary, one of the complexities flying out of Pandora's box seems to be dealt with adequately. As Ayton-Shenker said in a 2003 background paper for a Commonwealth Parliamentary Association conference in Bangladesh:

> Every human has the right to culture, including the right to enjoy and develop cultural life and identity. Cultural rights, however, are not unlimited. The right to culture is limited at the point at which it infringes on another human right. No right can be used at the expense or destruction of another, in accordance with international law.

However, in practice the issue is not settled: this resolution, while having the appeal of apparent simplicity, is insufficient in theory and practice. Moreover, it is being ignored by many regimes around the world.

The Clash Between Universalism and Cultural Relativism

This chapter does not dwell on the theoretical issues, other than to highlight two difficulties that impact seriously on human rights practice. The Academy of European Law (2005) puts its finger on the first difficulty when it notes that:

> Cultural rights are torn between two different but linked meanings: first, as a sub-category of human rights, cultural rights are endowed with universal character, which is a major characteristic and postulate of human rights as a whole; second, cultural rights are clearly related to cultural diversity and cultural diversity is an obvious challenge to the very idea of universal human rights.

That is, there is an apparent disjuncture between human rights, as universal and all-encompassing, and cultural diversity and cultural heritages, which are by definition culturally and temporally specific.

This leads inevitably to the thorny conflict between universalism and cultural relativism. I have written elsewhere about the ways in which the former – universalism – is linked to the modernist way of conceiving the world, which prevailed at the time UNESCO was established, while the latter – cultural relativism – is closely tied with the postmodernist view of the world (Logan 2002). It is a tension that is seen in the makeup of UNESCO itself, an inherent contradiction between UNESCO as a modernist organization with globalizing impacts, and UNESCO as a supporter, from the outset, of cultural diversity. This contradiction permeates the various UNESCO legal instruments.

The postmodern outlook should lead, one would hope, to a greater awareness of the need for intercultural sensitivity. In the cultural heritage field, this would mean taking greater note of local opinions and involving local professionals and communities in genuine rather than token ways. It would reinforce efforts to protect traditional popular arts and crafts and vernacular buildings alongside the "high" forms that once tended to dominate official conservation efforts. It would mean fully engaging indigenous minorities in the conservation of their own cultural heritage.

Unfortunately these hopes are not always translated into practice. The insistence of the right of all voices to be heard does not necessarily imply end goals of conciliation or reconciliation. Indeed, while the argument that "local communities know best" has often been associated with the term cultural relativism, another term – cultural exceptionalism (Franck 2001) – is sometimes also invoked by local communities that want to reject negotiated outcomes.

The second key difficulty has already been mentioned – the residual nature of cultural considerations in the various human rights instruments. This seems to be largely by accident rather than design, the result of the relatively late recognition of cultural rights. But this in turn probably reflects a perception in the general community (and particularly the legal community drawing up the human rights instruments) that cultural matters are less critical than the economic, political, and social. At times, however, it might be useful in practice if a hierarchy of human rights forms was generally accepted. I will try to show, using some case studies drawn from around the world, how this would help settle many of the cases where conflicting human rights arguments are being made on the basis of cultural heritage claims.

Cultural Heritage, Cultural Rights, and Cultural Politics

The implications of the various cultural heritage instruments are, of course, deeply political, with potentially major impacts, especially for suppressed minority cultural groups in many countries but also for governments and for dominant ethnic groups which feel their power is being undercut by efforts to raise the status of minority groups and their cultures. It is clear that in some countries the 2001 *UNESCO Universal Declaration on Cultural Diversity* and the 2003 *Intangible Cultural Heritage Convention* reinforce the political anxieties held by the national governments.

At least three broad types of conflict can be defined in which the interrelationships between cultural heritage and human rights issues are implicated. These might form a useful starting point for the development of new university research and teaching agendas in the cultural heritage field.

1. *Cultural right of minority groups to maintain their intangible cultural heritage is threatened.*

Albro and Bauer, editors of a recent (2005: 31) issue of *Human Rights Dialogue* focused on "cultural rights," note that cultural rights claims are being recognized as an "important means for the recuperation of identity and as an essential basis for advancing social justice." They comment that this process has been slow, despite the fact that cultural rights have long been enshrined in international law. The weak political commitment to cultural rights is explained, they argue, by a series of political considerations made by national governments. Governments of states where there is a cultural majority population see a threatening linkage between cultural rights, arguments for self-determination, and threats to the state-based model of sovereignty.

Thus Myanmar and Laos, both countries with significant tensions between dominant and minority ethnic cultural groups, are not among the 30 countries that have ratified the Convention at this stage, although, perhaps surprisingly, China, Vietnam, and India have.

In the case of Myanmar, it is clear that the Myanmar junta is using Buddhist heritage conservation projects, especially religious monuments, as a way of legitimizing its own position, strengthening the dominance of the majority ethnic group, and marginalizing the cultures of the Karen and Mon minorities so as to force these groups to assimilate (Philp 2004). Here the definition of democracy is important: democracy is not simply the rule of the dominant electoral group, but a respect for minority rights. While it might be argued that the government is serving the interests of the numerically stronger Burmese group, there is no democracy in that country and the winner of the last democratic elections, Aung San Suu Kyi, is, as we know, still under house arrest. UNESCO's World Heritage Center officers have had to be exceedingly wary about engaging with Myanmar under these circumstances.

It is much more difficult for us to find a theoretical solution – much less a practical one – about the conflict between democratic principles and maintenance of cultural diversity and cultural heritage that has been taking place in Fiji. Here we can argue that the protection of the country's cultural diversity requires support for both the indigenous Fijian culture and the culture of the Indian immigrant population. However, the Indian population has grown numerically to the point where it was able to win a democratic national election. The indigenous population perceived this as losing control of its very homeland.

Clearly many nation states experiencing conflicts over language, religion, and ethnicity fear "balkanization." The Declaration and the 2003 Convention raise the concern that cultural heritage may be used as emblems around which resistance by minority groups to government policies can be mobilized. Indonesia seems to fall into this category, its national *Pancasila* principles being challenged by the post-Suharto devolution of powers to the provinces, the independence of Timor Leste and the secessionist movements in Aceh and West Irian.

As far as I know, the United States shows no sign of ratifying the Convention, nor has the Australian Government. I do not know the reasons for the US decision, but its stance in UNESCO, having rejoined in 2003 after a 17-year absence, seems to be that culture looks after itself and needs no government intervention. This is easy to say when American culture is promoted globally by Hollywood, the music recording industry and dominance of print and television media.

I am on safer ground hypothesizing that the Australian Government sees the Convention as strengthening multiculturalism, a policy approach it has been winding back. Perhaps it fears that cultural divisions will be reinforced by any renewed emphasis on minority cultures. This is not to say that the Australian Government has no interest in promoting cultural heritage. In fact the opposite is true. It does have some low-level commitment to indigenous heritage through the Maintenance of Indigenous Languages and Cultures and media access programs administered by the national Department of Communication, Information Technology and the Arts (DCITA). And it argues that it also shows commitment to intangible cultural heritage protection generally through its funding of agencies such as the National Sound and Screen Archives.

It is using a carefully selected set of cultural heritage items as the core around which they are seeking to reshape the nation. Thus we have great government interest (and expenditure) on places like Anzac Cove in Gallipoli, Turkey, and negotiations with the Turkish Government have taken place to find a way to inscribe Anzac Cove on the Australian National Heritage List. Gallipoli was the site of a disastrous encounter with the Turkish army in World War I, but it has acquired iconic status as a place where Australians finally realized that their future had to be one of independence from Britain.

On the other hand, the Australian Government has occasionally put the cultural heritage of minority groups on the line, as in the case of World Heritage-listed Kakadu in the Northern Territory. Here the conflict was between the Government, acting for the transnational company mining uranium, and the Mirrar people who, while numerically small, are the traditional landowners of the area. Transnational business corporations have frequently ignored cultural rights, as can be seen in the many disputes between corporations and traditional peoples. The case caused a major headache for the World Heritage Committee and all concerned. It seems far from over, with the current push toward the development of Australia's uranium industry.

2. Selective interpretations of cultural heritage are used to influence mainstream cultural identity and opinion to the detriment of human rights.

Cultural heritage can, of course, be used to manipulate people. Governments commonly use cultural heritage to try to weld disparate ethnic groups into a more cohesive and harmonious national entity. They use cultural heritage to shape public opinion. All of these manipulative activities may be benign if they promote tolerant states and societies based on human rights. Interpretations of the past can be opened out so as to recognize the roles played by minority groups in the national story, to engage them more fully in celebration of the nation's achievements, and to recognize injustices done to them in the past. Efforts to rediscover "unpleasant" episodes in our national histories can result in the empowering of indigenous minorities.

But the use of heritage can be malign as well as benign. In too many cases governments have used selective versions of the "national cultural heritage" to force minority groups to adopt the dominant culture, effectively wiping out their own cultural identity. The Myanmar case has been mentioned. The "Troubles" in Northern Ireland are seen as being a clash of religion-based cultures. Protestant and

Catholic areas are demarcated with kerbsides painted in orange or green, flags, and wall painting. But we have to be careful to ensure that cultural heritage is not taking the rap for social problems which, in fact, have deeper economic and political causes. Indeed, "cultural heritage" is in danger of getting a bad name when often it is not warranted.

Worse, selective appropriations of the past are too often used by state leaders to boost jingoism and facilitate aggression toward others outside national borders. Despite the UNESCO *Convention for the Protection of Cultural Property in the Event of Armed Conflict* (The Hague Convention of 1954) and all the best efforts of the International Blue Shield Committee, it is still a deliberate strategy in wars to attack the physical manifestations of the enemy's cultural identity and to lower the enemy's morale by so doing.

This applies to civil wars as well as international wars, as evidenced in February 2006 by the bombing of the Al-Askari Mosque in Samarra, a major holy place of Iraqi Shiites, and the counterattack on Sunni mosques. In Africa, where the chief forms of heritage are intangible, the deliberate slaughter of opponent tribes has been atrocious. I recall the speech of a Rwandan at the 2001 Forum UNESCO international seminar making the point that his people's heritage died with every victim of the genocide that occurred there in the 1990s. The catastrophe in Cambodia under Pol Pot very nearly wiped out the country's rich cultural heritage of dance and music. Fortunately a few ageing women in the Cambodian diaspora have been able to return to train a new generation of young dancers and musicians in traditional techniques.

It is therefore important to have the declarations by UN, UNESCO, and other global bodies, including recently even the WTO under former President James Wolfensohn (1999), reaffirming the ethical position that the right to protect cultural diversity and cultural heritage is a cultural right, part of the panoply of human rights.

3. *Cultural practice claimed as a human right, even though the practice contravenes local laws and/or fundamental human rights instruments.*

The third type of conflict is in many ways the most difficult to deal with in that the problems lie in the inherent contradictions in the human rights framework of concepts and instruments themselves. "Cultural rights arguments have their detractors across the political spectrum," according to Albro and Bauer (2005), and even when defended, as by human rights workers themselves, cultural rights are "perceived to be a challenging arena for advocacy." This is because cultural rights can be in direct conflict with other human rights, particularly the rights of individuals and children and women as groups.

What really is the cultural heritage value of the fine west Asian rugs and carpets in cases where they are made using child labor? In Australia there continues to be arranged marriages of girls in certain ethnic communities and the restriction of female student participation in certain school subjects, such as sport or music. Attempts to outlaw particular cultural manifestations within a society often reflect the prejudices of the majority and such biases are often fiercely resisted. Prohibiting the wearing of the Muslim veil in French schools has caused bitter controversy in that country and beyond. Such resistance, at its most extreme, can feed into separatist movements as witnessed in the last decade from Aceh to Chechnya.

Ambiguities and Contradictions Within the Human Rights Instruments

Three problems within the cultural rights and human rights instruments themselves are worth commenting on here. First, there are, as we have seen, problems in defining the very concept of "culture" and it is used in different ways at the international and national levels, so that the standards of cultural rights and cultural diversity and heritage protection are inconsistent. The concept of "cultural heritage," being subsidiary, shares the same problem.

The most fundamental conceptual contradiction is that, while human rights constitute a universal category, the concept of cultural heritage is culturally, temporally, and geographically specific. This disjuncture does not merely occur when one term or the other is inappropriately used or misunderstood, but rather is written into the structure of human rights instruments at a fundamental level. Articles 22, 27, and 29 of the *Universal Declaration of Human Rights* (1948) acknowledge cultural heritage matters *as* human rights. This creates problems of interpretation when specific cultural practices are claimed as intangible heritage in cases that contravene the universal human rights instruments in other ways.

Second, there is also the problem that cultural rights, as human rights, have both a collective and individual dimension. As rights with a collective dimension, they may come into conflict with individual human rights or individual perceptions of human rights (Academy of European Law 2005). Tensions arise relating to the role of the state in seeking to adjudicate between the collective and individual dimensions: To what extent should the state remain tolerant in respect of cultural practices that appear to restrict the enjoyment of some human rights by members of a community? To what extent should it enforce individual rights even in relation to religious, ethnic, and cultural communities?

Take an example. The Indian Ocean island of North Sentinel has a population of about 250 people living in traditional manner – loin-clothed hunter-gatherers, with their Sentinelese language intact. The island is off-limits to the outside world, with Indian laws prohibiting visitors from landing. On 12 February 2006 the *Observer* reported that two poachers from another Andaman Island had drifted ashore and had been slaughtered by Sentinelese tribesmen. According to the *Observer*, "The local authorities, under pressure from international preservation groups and a largely sympathetic local [Andaman] population, are reluctant to pursue the matter." Here, it seems to me, the heritage (cultural rights) argument has to take back seat. Maintenance of human life must be seen as the highest "human right" – our highest priority.

Take another example from Myanmar. Nwe and Philp (2002: 153) describe the way that the Myanmar junta, the State Peace and Development Council (SPDC), has consistently denied allegations of human rights abuses as they relate to forced labor on state projects, including restoration of heritage monuments. One would think that such practices would be irreconcilable with Article 4 of the *Universal Declaration of Human Rights*, which prohibits slavery in any form, and Article 5, which stipulates that "No one shall be subjected to torture or to cruel, inhuman or degrading treatment or punishment." Yet the junta argues that their labor practices are part of the Burmese heritage and linked to traditional Buddhist concepts of merit-making. In other words, Myanmar makes the case that cultural heritage overrides these other notions of human rights.

This is where an accepted hierarchy of human rights would be helpful. But this is not to be found in the UDHR or other instruments. The most help we get is the view referred to above, that "no right can be used at the expense or destruction of another, in accordance with international law." In any case, many governments, agencies, and members of threatened cultural minorities ignore instruments such as the UDHR when making decisions over contested cultural heritage.

An Indonesian case that blew up in 2006 comes to mind here – a case in which one form of universal human rights (freedom of religion) is pitted against another form (women's rights). But the case is made more complicated because the cultural heritage protection program involved (protection of Islamic culture) is a form of identity manipulation that has nationalistic ideological and political motivation. Additionally, the various protagonists are making selective use of human rights principles, highlighting the ambiguities, and contradictions within them. No one seems to be talking in terms of the agreed but vague position in international law that no right can be invoked at the expense of another.

The case centers around the attempt by the Indonesian government to crack down on pornography in Indonesia (Forbes 2006a: 19). The Indonesian Parliament is considering an "antipornography" law that would impose a 5-year imprisonment term on couples who kiss in public, or persons (presumably women only) who flaunt a "sensual body part," including the navel. Tight clothing would also be outlawed. Into this controversy has stepped an Indonesian feminist, Gadis Arriva, making media headlines around the world. "This law is something very alien to us," she argues. Indonesians have a sensuality, she maintains, that is part of their culture: women wear tight dresses and there are bare-breasted women in Bali and Papua. She claims the law is "part of an agenda to reshape Indonesia, with pornography a symbol of Western culture to the many Muslims who believe globalization aims to destroy their culture" (Forbes 2006b: 19).

The director of Balinese Provincial Government's tourism authority, Gede Nurjaya, is also concerned about the impact of the proposed law on the struggling tourism-based economy in Bali. Traditional Balinese art and dance could become illegal, he fears, and certainly tourists who want to bathe in mixed company would be deterred. The conflict continues at the time of writing (May 2006), with tens of thousands of demonstrators marching in Jakarta in favor of the proposed legislative crackdown.

Last year Vietnam celebrated the addition of its "Tay gong-playing skills" to the 90-strong list of intangible heritage items proclaimed by UNESCO as "Masterpieces of the Oral and Intangible Heritage of Humanity." This focused the world's attention, if briefly, on the plateaus of the mid-Tay Nguyen (Vietnam's Central Highlands) where gong-playing is an essential part of the birth, wedding, harvest, and funeral rituals practiced by the Ba Na, Xo Dang, Gia Rai, and others of the 54 ethnic minorities officially recognized by the Vietnamese Government in Hanoi. In this case study the key issue is the claims to cultural autonomy made by the Central Highland minorities and the claims to religious freedom made by those seeking to intervene in the lives of the ethnic groups.

Some background is necessary. There has been a long history of political instability and resistance to mainstream Kinh Vietnamese governments, whether of the capitalist south or communist north. This goes back to French colonial days when the French authorities attempted to buy off the ethnic minorities, especially the White Thai in Tonkin and the Hmong in Laos, by turning a blind eye to their opium smuggling. This had political impacts as well as public health and social problems associated with opium production, smuggling, and consumption that still persist among these groups today.

During the early 1960s the Central Highlands fought President Ngo Dinh Diem's transplantation of northern Catholics onto their lands; in the 1970s and 1980s they resisted the government of Ho Chi Minh and formed a minor insurgency group known as FULRO (from the French *Front Uni pour la Libération des Races Opprimées*); and in the last 10 years there have been a number of land rights-based clashes with the authorities. Complicating the picture in recent times is the fact that American Protestant missionaries have been working in the area, fanning Hanoi suspicions of CIA involvement and leading to some crack down on missionary activities.

How does one judge this scenario in terms of cultural rights? Should the missionaries be stopped because they are undermining the traditional culture of the ethnic minority group? Or would that infringe the minority group's right to choose whatever religion they want? Should they be stopped because they represent interference in the running of Vietnam by its duly elected government? Is this a case where national sovereignty rights are threatened by external forces? Without more facts it is difficult to know for certain.

What is clear, though, is the relevance of concepts of "power" to the case. On the one hand, the US does not acknowledge involvement in the missionary activities in Vietnam, in the same way that it does not officially back the Fa Lun Gong in China. On the other hand, to use Joseph Nye's (2004) concept of "soft power," the US seeks to exert influence by setting the discourse, using human rights arguments to undercut Vietnamese and Chinese status in the world's eyes. Such tactics fit the US state interest. One conclusion that might be drawn is that this is primarily about power in the global setting, and only secondarily about human rights.

On their side, the dominant Kinh Viet group has never held the ethnic minority groups, or their human rights, in high regard. For long their term for the minorities was "moi" – primitives – and they have exerted their political and economic power over the past 50 years to force the minorities to toe the line. Patricia Pelley (1998) provides an excellent analysis of the efforts made by the Vietnamese government from the 1950s to "sedentarize the nomads." So what does the listing of the Tay gongs have to do with this? Does the newly found interest in the ethnic minority's culture mark the abandonment by the Hanoi government of its assimilationist approach? The answer is probably no, although perhaps there is a softening of that approach. It is more likely to be part of an attempt to use cultural heritage as a focus of national pride and to win the closer cooperation of the ethnic minority groups in Vietnam's increasingly lucrative cultural tourism industry.

Cultural Heritage, Human Rights, and Democratic Rights

A number of the preceding cases revolve around conflicts between desires to protect cultural diversity and cultural heritage and arguments about the rights of individuals and groups to have some say in determining their life circumstances through democratic institutions of government and the rights of democratically elected governments to govern. In the case of Fiji, the democratically elected Indian-dominated government was seen in 2000 to represent a threat to Fijian cultural identity. In the cases of Vietnam and China, there are fears of external interference deriving from the US. Let me return to the Kakadu case in Australia's Northern Territory, to demonstrate another form of international interference – the conflict between conceptions of national sovereignty and perceptions of inter-ference from the global heritage bodies themselves. I was involved in this conflict as member of the Australia ICOMOS national executive and then as president and then, a few years later, as an intermediary called in by the Mirrar people to assist in sorting out their options for future action.

Kakadu National Park was inscribed on the World Heritage List in 1981 as a natural site. The boundaries were extended in 1987 and it was reinscribed in 1992 for its cultural values (Aplin 2004). These cultural values are essentially intangible, being the sacred meaning given to the landscape by the local indigenous people. A small central area of these exceptionally beautiful wetlands had been excluded from the site on the basis of an agreement negotiated in 1982 between the Mirrar traditional land-owners (through the Northern Lands Council) and the national government. The government issued a uranium mining permit to the Pan-Continental mining company for that excluded area. By 1998, the situation had changed considerably. The Jabiluka mining rights had been acquired by Environmental Resources of Australia and the leadership of the Mirrar people had passed to Yvonne Margarula who disputed whether her father had clearly understood the agreement he was making back in 1982. Furthermore, leakages of contaminated water from the mine had occurred and the Mirrar perceived these as threatening the natural and cultural values of their land and the World Heritage site.

Frustrated by the stonewalling of the national government, which was seen as siding with the mining company, the traditional owners, acting through the

Gundjehmi Aboriginal Corporation, broke the normal UNESCO protocols, by-passed Canberra, and went directly to the World Heritage Committee asking it to place Kakadu National Park on the "World Heritage in Danger" list. The government was both fearful and furious – fearful that it would face a gigantic compensation claim from the mining company if the mining contract was cut short and furious – and embarrassed – that the case had been taken to Paris and out of its jurisdiction. UNESCO was forced to adjudicate on the merits of the Mirrar's case and sent in a delegation of experts. This was taken as an infringement of national sovereignty by the government and a restriction on its powers as a democratically elected government. Australia ICOMOS was in a difficult position because it sided with the Mirrar. The government considered this disloyal, overlooking the fact that Australia ICOMOS is the national committee of ICOMOS international, an organization of professionals that is supposed to be independent of governments.

Thus, despite the predictions of scholars who saw globalization reducing the power of nation states, national interests continue to loom large in human rights, cultural rights, and cultural heritage issues. At the global level of cultural heritage protection this is especially true since UNESCO is an international governmental organization. National governments place enormous importance on UNESCO listing, whether this relates to places on the World Heritage List or intangible elements under the 2003 Convention (or indeed Memory of the World, or other UNESCO programs). Their interest is multifaceted and includes the economic benefits of tourism but particularly the international status that comes from having part of the national heritage recognized as of world significance and the electoral status from having made a successful submission to the World Heritage Committee. There is very often a loss of face in having something put on the World Heritage in Danger list or the list of Intangible elements "in need of urgent safeguarding."

The difficulty is that, being an IGO like the UN, UNESCO, the World Heritage Committee and its secretariat, the World Heritage Center, cannot be openly critical of a Member State. Diplomatic maneuvers are usually used to achieve difficult ends. In the case of Kakadu, however, and for the overall good of the global heritage conservation system, the World Heritage Committee was forced to take a legalistic approach and to resolve the previously ambiguous issue of whether it could place an inscribed site that was in trouble onto the World Heritage in Danger List *without the prior consent* of the government concerned. After taking legal advice and after numerous bitter committee meetings, it was finally decided that the 1972 Convention should be interpreted to allow this possibility. In the event this was not necessary in the Australian case, although Nepal's Katmandu Valley was immediately placed on the In Danger list despite the opposition of the Nepalese government.

Kakadu was a clash between neoliberal politics, on the one hand, and intangible cultural heritage and cultural rights on the other. While the sacred nature of the area threatened by mining expansion was relevant, in the end the case before UNESCO turned on the scientific evidence about the damage to natural heritage values. In other cases, religious values play a much more definitive role and are often more complex because of it.

The Power to Decide: Challenges for the Conservation Profession

Conservation policy-makers, practitioners, researchers, and educators face many key challenges, especially arising out of the extension of practice into the intangible cultural heritage field. To what extent should and do we take these considerations into account in their practice?

Of course, issues bearing on human rights exist in relation to *tangible* heritage. But the World Heritage system has found ways to use conservation as a positive force supporting the maintenance and extension of human rights. In particular, it uses the conservation of cultural heritage places to remind us of our responsibilities to protect the human rights of people. The island of Gorée in Senegal is listed because of its infamous role as a slave camp, a rounding up point from which Africans were shipped to the New World. Auschwitz is another listed place – a memorial to those who perished there and a warning to people today and in the future about the depths of depravity to which we can sink if we abandon human rights principles.

This is not limited to World Heritage. The torture chamber at Tuol Sleng in Cambodia, for instance, is not listed. But there are national places in Australia that we should perhaps be conserving for similar reasons. The Woomera Detention Center and other places in Australia's deserts and tropical islands where refugees, including children, have been detained for inordinate lengths of time might some day become national heritage sites reflecting the theme of "pain and shame" and acting to remind future generations of the lapse that is currently taking place in Australia in relation to the protection of basic human rights.

Another World Heritage example – the Rice Terraces of the Philippines Cordillera – demonstrates some of the negative issues. The terraces were listed in 1995 under the new Cultural Landscape category as an "Organically evolved landscape" of the subtype: "Continuing landscape which retains an active social role in contemporary society associated with a traditional way of life and in which the evolutionary process is still in progress and where it exhibits significant material evidence of its evolution over time." Unfortunately for the listing, the local population has grown weary of the rigors of this traditional way of life and see better prospects in jobs elsewhere in the Philippines.

In short, the problem here was that the decision to inscribe was made not by the local population whose heritage it is, but by professionals and policy-makers in Manila and Paris. Here again we see the underlying issue of power – who has the power to decide that a place has heritage significance and to impose heritage controls. The inscription was imposed to protect an exotic landscape, but it overlooked the fact that the landscape depends on the intangible heritage bound up in the local community's life style and skills in irrigation and terrace construction practices. In fact the inscription could only succeed if it denied the human rights of the local population – their right to determine their own life circumstances.

Situations like this can often be avoided where the local community is engaged in the decision-making process from the outset. The response of the professions globally has been to argue for greater involvement of the local communities in the processes of identification, inscription, and management of World Heritage sites. Let the community choose, as best it can, given that community dynamics are far from perfect.

Such involvement is part of "cultural rights" as defined in the instruments I have talked about, part of "human rights." But how absolute is this "right"? In practice it varies from country to country, regime to regime, totalitarian through to democratic. However, in all countries, local ambitions need to be negotiated against broader community, regional and national interests and, indeed, between various interests within the same local community.

With intangible cultural heritage, the newcomer in the heritage conservation field, these problems are still to be broached. Although, as "living heritage embodied in people" it is the form of heritage most directly connected to human right principles and their abuse, we have yet to see a professional response emerge to take up the challenge. It is clear that both the destruction of monuments and the restriction of living cultural practices demoralizes indeed de-legitimizes people, inhibits intercultural understanding, and impedes economic development based on heritage tourism. Much research is needed to explore the apparent disjuncture between human rights, as universal and all-encompassing, and cultural heritages, which are by definition culturally and temporally specific. And there are an infinite number of cases where various forms of human rights are themselves in conflict – a rich subject for university scholarship.

Our work as researchers is committed; the goal is to win greater social justice. We need to see cultural heritage within the wider human rights framework. The less well-known part of the Pandora legend is that, along with pestilence, crimes, and suffering, she released from the box a final creature – hope. One can hope that UNESCO will move quickly to sort out the issues that at present seem to militate against the successful implementation of the *Convention on Intangible Cultural Heritage*. The General Assembly of States Parties to the Convention met for the first time in June 2006. One of their tasks was to incorporate those of the items proclaimed as Masterpieces of the Oral and Intangible Heritage of Humanity that lie on the territory of a State Party (that is, the 45 signatories at that time – the other UNESCO members will have to wait). To do this, a list of selection criteria will have to be settled. This task is delegated to an elected subset of the General Assembly, the Intergovernmental Committee for the Safeguarding of the Intangible Cultural Heritage, and should be completed during 2007.

One would also hope that the international human rights and aid communities will incorporate cultural diversity and cultural heritage protection more fully into their work. This will mean clarifying the ambiguities and contradictions within and between the various instruments and finding ways to ensure that conservation goals are effectively implemented. In the end, however, the UNESCO systems and the human rights and aid communities cannot alone achieve a reduction in the number of culture-based conflicts. This ultimately depends on the world's governments and an increased sense of global responsibility.

Acknowledgments This chapter was produced as part of a larger project on cultural heritage and human rights being conducted by the Cultural Center for Asia and the Pacific at Deakin University, Melbourne, Australia. I would like to thank my two research assistants on the project – Dr. Brad Warren and Fiona Erskine – for marshalling relevant documents and illustrations.

References

Academy of European Law, 2005, *Cultural Rights as Human Rights*. http://www.iue.it/AEL/Projects/CulturalRights.shtml (13 December 2005).

Albro, Robert, 2005, Making Cultural Policy and Confounding Cultural Diversity. *Cultural Comment*. http://www.culturalcommons.org/comment-print.cfm (13 December 2005).

Albro, Robert, and Joanne Bauer, 2005, Introduction. *Human Rights Dialogue: An International Forum for Debating Human Rights*, series 2(12): 2–3.

Aplin, Graeme, 2004, Kakadu National Park World Heritage Site: Deconstructing the Debate, 1997–2003. *Australian Geographical Studies* 42: 152–174.

Ayton-Shenker, Diana, 2003, *The Challenge of Human Rights and Cultural Diversity*. United Nations Background Note, 49th Commonwealth Parliamentary Association Conference, 4–12 October 2003, Bangladesh. www.cpahq.org/uploadstore/docs/16.pdf (8 January 2007).

Eide, Asbjørn, 1995, Cultural Rights as Individual Human Rights. In *Economic, Social and Cultural Rights: A Textbook*, edited by Asbjørn Eide, Catarina Krause, and Allan Rosas, pp. 289–301. Martinus Nijhoff, Dordrecht.

Eide, Asbjørn, and Allan Rosas, 2001, Economic, Social and Cultural Rights: A Universal Challenge. In *Economic, Social and Cultural Rights: A Textbook*, edited by Asbjørn Eide, Catarina Krause, and Allan Rosas, pp. 3–7. Martinus Nijhoff, Dordrecht.

Forbes, Mark, 2006a, Flesh Gets the Flick in Indonesian Porn War. *The Age* (newspaper), 25 February, p. 19.

—, 2006b, Nudity Part of Culture, says Feminist. *The Age* (newspaper), 25 February, p. 19.

Franck, Thomas M., 2001, Are Human Rights Universal? *Foreign Affairs* 80(1): 191–204.

Lacoste, Michel Conil, 1994, *The Story of a Grand Design: UNESCO 1946–1993*. UNESCO, Paris.

Logan, William S., 2002, Globalizing Heritage: World Heritage as a Manifestation of Modernism and Challenges from the Periphery. In *20th Century Heritage – Our Recent Cultural Legacy. Proceedings of the Australia ICOMOS National Conference 2001*, edited by David Jones, pp. 51–57. University of Adelaide and Australia ICOMOS, Adelaide and Melbourne.

Nwe, Than Than, and Janette Philp, 2002, Yangon, Myanmar: The Re-Invention of Heritage. In *The Disappearing "Asian" City. Protecting Asia's Urban Heritage in a Globalizing World*, edited by William S. Logan, pp. 147–165. Oxford University Press, Hong Kong.

Nye, Joseph S., 2004, *Soft Power: The Means to Success in World Politics*. Public Affairs, New York.

Pelley, Patricia, 1998, "Barbarians" and "Younger Brothers": The Remaking of Race in Postcolonial Vietnam. *Journal of Southeast Asian Studies* 29: 374–391.

Philp, Janette, 2004, *Cultural Politics and the Appropriation of Theravada Buddhism in Contemporary Burma (Myanmar)*. Unpublished Ph.D. dissertation. Deakin University, Geelong, Australia.

Shelton, Dinah, 2005, The U.N. Human Rights Committee's Decisions. *Human Rights Dialogue: An International Forum for Debating Human Rights*, series 2(12): 31–33.

Smithsonian Center for Folklife and Cultural Heritage, 2005, *Theorizing Cultural Heritage*. http://www.folklife.si.edu/opportunities/fellowships_RF.html (20 December 2005).

Stamatopoulou, Elsa, 2004, Why Cultural Rights Now? Edited transcript of remarks made at The Case for Cultural Rights Workshop, New York City, 23 September. http://www.cceia.org/printerfriendlymedia.php/prmID/5006 (13 December 2005).

Stavenhagen, Rodolfo, 1998, Cultural Rights: A Social Science Perspective. In *Cultural Rights and Wrongs*, edited by H. Niec, pp. 1–20. UNESCO, UK.

UNESCO, 1954, *Convention for the Protection of Cultural Property in the Event of Armed Conflict* (The Hague Convention).

—, 1972, *Convention Concerning the Protection of the World Cultural and Natural Heritage* (The World Heritage Convention).

—, 2001, *Universal Declaration on Cultural Diversity*.

—, 2003, *Convention for the Safeguarding of the Intangible Cultural Heritage* (The Intangible Heritage Convention).

United Nations, 1948, *Universal Declaration of Human Rights*.

—, 1995, *Our Creative Diversity. Report of World Commission on Culture & Development*. EGOPRIM, Paris.

Wolfensohn, James D., 1999, Global City Regions: Reaching the Poor. *Paper Presented to the Global City-Regions in the 21st Century Conference*. Getty Museum, Los Angeles.

Yusuf, Abdulqawi A., 2005, *Toward a Convention on Cultural Diversity: Background and Evolution*. Presentation to the Third Forum on Human Development, Paris, 17 January.

Chapter 3
The Indo-Islamic Garden: Conflict, Conservation, and Conciliation in Gujarat, India

James L. Wescoat, Jr.

Introduction

I begin with the passage from Rajmohan Gandhi's *Revenge and Reconciliation: Understanding South Asian History* that inspires this chapter: "A word, finally, on Delhi, for we started this study by noting Delhi's *djinns*, its great load of unrepented cruelty and unshared sorrow. ... Can Delhi's accumulated offences be washed away? Can some atonement or penance – or some God-sent blessing or grace – expiate the guilt of centuries, and generate a breeze of forgiveness that blows away the smells of torture and revenge?" (Gandhi 1999: 410). A paragraph later, Gandhi suggests an answer, "Every tree planted, or cubic foot of water conserved, is a celebration of life, a proclamation of the worth of the future, and a garden or a river may calm sad or angry hearts. Every caring act – of fellowship, considerateness, nursing, apology, forgiveness, greening, or flowering – perhaps heals something of Delhi's torment, maybe calms one of its djinns, and a healing process in Delhi might speak to all of South Asia" (Gandhi 1999: 410) – and the world beyond.

This chapter on planting trees and conserving water at the newly designated World Heritage Site of Champaner–Pavagadh in the state of Gujarat, which was shaken by violent cultural conflict in 2002, strives to envision new linkages between cultural landscape conservation and conciliation (Fig. 1).

It employs a logic of *design inquiry* that aims to generate landscape solutions to an ill-defined suite of jointly social and environmental problems (cf. Schon 1990). As one who has interpreted Mughal paradise gardens as places of social conquest and control, I have a strong interest in landscape criticism (Wescoat 1991, 1997, 1999). However, I am increasingly concerned that the sophisticated power of critique in landscape scholarship is beginning to surpass skills in generative inquiry that broaden the range of choice among alternatives worthy of critique (Wescoat 1992, 1997). I know that this landscape design approach to cultural heritage conflict faces pitfalls, including naïve interventions that may do more harm than good. Conservation designers have a mixed record of working with factious stakeholder groups; we argue among ourselves; how can we begin to think about

H. Silverman and D. F. Ruggles (eds.), *Cultural Heritage and Human Rights.*
© Springer 2007

Provinces and Capitals of the Mughal Empire

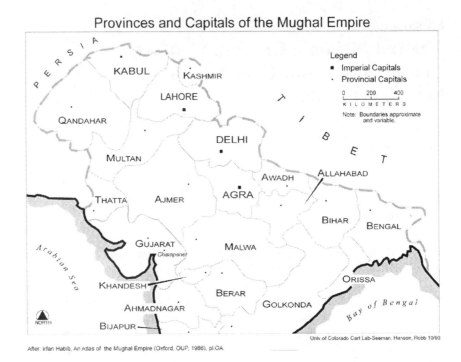

After: Irfan Habib, An Atlas of the Mughal Empire (Oxford, OUP, 1986), pl.OA.

Fig. 1 Map of Gujarat during the Mughal period (base map created by the University of Colorado Cartography Lab for the author)

addressing issues of violent cultural conflict through design? That is the question I want to address.

I will first introduce the Champaner–Pavagadh Project led by the Baroda Heritage Trust in collaboration with People for Heritage Concern and the Department of Landscape Architecture at the University of Illinois at Urbana-Champaign, and briefly describe the landscape approach to cultural heritage conservation. I then turn to a topic neglected in that project, which involves cultural violence of the sort that occurred in Gujarat in 2002, noting its historical roots and theoretical explanations for it. It is important to note that while hundreds of religious structures – mainly mosques and shrines – were destroyed in 2002, cultural sites at Champaner–Pavagadh experienced less physical destruction. It seems important to understand why, and to ask how conservation can address the spectrum of heritage conflicts, including those that involve human rights abuses. The main section of this chapter situates violent cultural conflicts within this broader spectrum of heritage conflicts, and presents landscape design alternatives that attempt to address those conflicts at Champaner–Pavagadh.

The Advent of Landscape Heritage Conservation at Champaner–Pavagadh

The cultural heritage project at Champaner–Pavagadh was conceived and organized by Architect Karan Grover of the Baroda Heritage Trust (Vadodara). In 2001, he invited Professor Amita Sinha of the University of Illinois, Department of Landscape Architecture to organize the first design studio in May 2001 at this magnificent site, which is briefly introduced below.

Pavagadh Hill is a dramatic volcanic cone, an outlier of the southern Aravalli range that rises 700 m above the surrounding cultivated plains. It has long served as a regional pilgrimage center in western India (Fig. 2).

A pilgrim's path ascends the hill through medieval Rajput and Sultanate fortifications and gateways, past Jain and Hindu temples, shops, and rest areas, culminating at the goddess temple complex of *Kalika Mata* on the summit. Strong breezes, which by one account gave Pavagadh Hill its name, drive monsoon winds up the steep hillslopes, feeding a chain of reservoirs (*talaos*) perched on each plateau (Fig. 3).

The names of these reservoirs reflect the water's descent from pure milk (*Dudhiya talao*) to yoghurt and oil (*Chassiya* and *Teliya talaos*). The water system feeds the residential settlements of Champaner before discharging into a large irrigation tank and channel.

The fifteenth century Sultanate ruler Mahmud Begada established Champaner as his capital, symbolically constructing its dramatic Jami Masjid (Friday Mosque) when besieging a local Rajput ruler encamped on Pavagadh Hill in 1484 CE.

Fig. 2 Pavagadh Hill with Kalika Mata temple on the summit. (Photo by author, January 2005)

Fig. 3 Water collection reservoir at Naulakha Kothar. (Photo by author, January 2005)

Situated on a strategic route between the rival provinces of Gujarat and Malwa, Champaner grew in size and architectural patronage until its sack by the Mughal ruler Humayun in 1534 CE, after which the capital of Gujarat shifted back to Ahmedabad, and the medieval complex of Champaner–Pavagadh returned to its frontier situation for roughly four centuries (Goetz 1949). As regional pilgrimage expanded during the twentieth century to hundreds of thousands of pilgrims annually, archeological excavations led by Mehta (1977, 1986) revealed the extensive urban settlement pattern that had been covered by scrub vegetation centuries ago. Tourism has grown at a slow rate that will accelerate as the Champaner–Pavagadh becomes known as a World Heritage Site.

The Baroda Heritage Trust sponsored three cultural landscape heritage workshops between 2001 and 2005. These design workshops developed a landscape approach that embraces the complex pressures of pilgrimage, tourism, economic development, forest management, and archeological protection. The landscape approach has five guiding principles:

1. It extends beyond monuments and sites to the rich topographic sense of place.
2. It focuses on relationships between environmental and social processes.
3. It encompasses multiple historical layers from the medieval to the postmodern.
4. It operates on multiple geographic scales from the site to the region.
5. It uses these lines of landscape analysis to generate design alternatives that harmoniously reconnect people and places.

Using this approach the conservation design teams mapped relationships among historical features, contemporary landscape experiences, and complex cultural meanings. They developed master plans for an archeological park that focused on Champaner City (People for Heritage Concern 2001; Thakur 2000, 2002, 2004), a cultural sanctuary focused on Pavagadh hill (Sinha et al. 2003), and a system of five trails that link Champaner and Pavagadh (Sinha et al. 2004). During the course of these studies, the Archeological Survey of India (ASI) and Baroda Heritage Trust nominated Champaner–Pavagadh for the World Heritage List. In July 2004, UNESCO added Champaner–Pavagadh to the World Heritage List for its joint significance as a living Hindu pilgrimage center, its cluster of Jain temples, its remarkably preserved medieval urban fabric, its exquisite sandstone-carved mosques and tombs, and its intangible heritage values (Fig. 4).

While this chapter could focus entirely on local heritage management challenges at Champaner–Pavagadh, the Gujarat riots of 2002 raise broader and deeper heritage problems that have not been directly addressed to date.

Fig. 4 Outstanding sandstone architectural heritage at the Friday Mosque. (Photo by author, January 2005)

Social Conflict and Cultural Heritage in Gujarat

Widespread violence broke out in Gujarat on 27 February 2002 after a train car of 57 passengers was set ablaze allegedly by Muslims on the railway station platform at Godhra, the capital of Panchmahals District. Some passengers were Hindu nationalist volunteers (*kar sevaks*) returning from the contested historic site known as the Babri Masjid–Ramjanmabhoomi (Babur's Mosque – Rama's Birthplace) in the city of Ayodhya, Uttar Pradesh state (some 1,000 km northeast of Godhra) where preparations were underway to build a new temple on the site of the sixteenth-century mosque demolished by Hindu nationalists in 1992 – torn down by the mob because that mosque was purportedly built on the ruins of an earlier temple marking Rama's birthplace.

Retaliation to the carnage at Godhra began almost immediately in nearby towns in Panchmahals district. Attacks against Muslim neighborhoods were carried out in the urban centers of Ahmedabad and Vadodara, as well as smaller cities. An estimated 1,000–2,000 Muslims were killed and hundreds of thousands were rendered homeless in 17 of the 24 districts of Gujarat. Mobs destroyed some 270 dargahs, shrines, and mosques in 3 days – heritage sites as well as people and livelihoods were objects of violence (Communalism Combat 2003). Backlash occurred against a number of Hindu neighborhoods and religious sites, notably the Akshardham temple in Gandhinagar where 30 people were killed and 100 wounded. Subsequent reports estimated that as many as 650 mosques, shrines, and tombs were destroyed (Sreenivas 2004a,b).

Champaner and Pavagadh were affected, though not as violently as the nearby towns of Halol and Lunawada or the *mohallas* of larger cities, where murders and human rights violations hearkening back to the horrors of partition were reported. Newspapers reported that Muslims in Champaner were threatened, driven out of town, and their shops damaged and looted (Waldman 2002; Bunsha 2006). Most local Muslim families (reportedly 49 in number) fled for their safety, and when several tried to return in December 2002 they were reportedly again driven off (Kotwal 2002). Threats at polling places occurred in December 2002 (Bunsha 2002, 2003). Two years later, only eight Muslim families had returned to Champaner–Pavagadh. They remained fearful of attacks and avoided public visibility by wearing non-Muslim types of clothing; some reported being forced to utter the Hindu pilgrim's cry of "Jai, Mataji!" (Vora 2004). Others reported economic boycotts and forcible exclusion from their work as van drivers, telephone booth operators, and shopkeepers, especially on Pavagadh Hill (Bunsha 2006; Taneja 2004; *Times of India* 2004). Some towns in Gujarat avoided even these types of conflicts through intercommunal peace tactics (Bhatt 2002). One report from Champaner suggested that Muslims would be permitted back if they retracted police charges against 52 men accused of looting (Waldman 2002; charges were ultimately dismissed in 2006 for lack of sufficient evidence). The boycott of Muslim residents' economic and social rights in Champaner–Pavagadh continues (Bunsha 2006).

Politicians of various parties have manipulated these events. An opposition Congress Party leader took out a political procession beginning on Pavagadh hill to appeal across communal lines (Midday 2004). The Government of Gujarat staged Navratri festivals in October 2004 that made ambivalent symbolic gestures to Muslim heritage sites in Gujarat (Sreenivas 2004a,b). A year later, the Government of Gujarat launched a Year of Tourism at Champaner–Pavagadh, in part to draw tourists back to the state. But violent episodes continued especially in the major urban centers of Vadodara and Ahmedabad where temples as well as mosques have been targeted, with more extensive yet less widely reported incidents in the countryside. Most recently, Vadodara municipal authorities destroyed structures encroaching on public land, including the *dargah* of one of the city's most prominent medieval Sufi saints, Syed Rashiduddin Chishti, failing to consider thoughtfully how a medieval grave can encroach on a modern roadway right-of-way or the social consequences of demolishing it.

A host of journalistic accounts, academic panels, public inquiries, and criminal charges followed the 2002 riots (e.g., Social Science Research Council 2002). A Concerned Citizens' Tribunal (2003) chaired by former Supreme Court justice Krishna Iyer compiled detailed accounts of incidents. Early reports by nongovernmental organizations such as Communalism Combat (2003), Forum Against Oppression of Women (2002), and People's Union for Democratic Rights (2002) asserted state and police collusion during the initial days of killing. International organizations such as Human Rights Watch (2002, 2003a,b, 2004) protested government's subsequent failures to halt the violence, arrest those reported, prosecute those arrested, or protect witnesses.

The Gujarat–Ayodhya connection in 2002 was anything but new. Twelve years earlier, in 1990, L.K. Advani, then president of the BJP party, led a *rath yatra* (chariot procession) from Somnath in western Gujarat toward Ayodhya. Why Somnath? In 1024 CE, the Muslim general Mahmud of Ghazni destroyed the temple at Somnath during his ninth expedition into India – an event invoked by Hindu nationalist parties to mobilize political support almost a millennium later. While one source reports that Mahmud destroyed the idol for treasure it contained and while others state that he destroyed it for ideological reasons, historical research is eclipsed by historicist renderings of the heritage destruction at Somnath (Amin 2002; Elliott 1976 reprint, pp. 434–478).

After the abortive rath yatra of 1990, a conclusive assault on the Babri mosque occurred in 1992. Immediately following its destruction, riots broke out in Bombay, Delhi, and many other towns in northern India. I was in Lahore, Pakistan, known today as the Mughal "city of gardens." Mobs came out in the streets and, not having lived with Hindus since 1947, tore down structures like Sikh gurudwaras and a school that had a temple-like ornament that had been attended by only Muslim children for decades. The Mughal gardens of Lahore like Shalamar, by contrast, were quietly beautiful in those days with a few picnickers, tourists, and no rioters. Fourteen years later, inquiry into the destruction at Ayodhya continues (Rediff 2006). And then in 2002, *kar sevaks* returning from a temple reconstruction rally in

Ayodhya were killed at Godhra, transforming the context, history, and challenges of landscape heritage conservation at places like Champaner–Pavagadh.

How are we to understand this unfolding situation in which multicultural heritage has acquired world heritage status, while the Muslim cultural group has fled, and the wider region has suffered gross human rights abuses? Most scholarly writing on the 2002 Gujarat pogrom employs explanations drawn from comparable communal and ethnic violence in northern India. Table 1 lists some of the major lines of interpretation, building upon Paul Brass' (2003) review of the literature in *The Production of Hindu–Muslim Violence in Contemporary India*, and adding several additional lines of inquiry that set the stage for a landscape approach.

Although the shorthand list in Table 1 does not do justice to the subtleties of the works cited, it does indicate the wide range of frameworks used to interpret communal violence in India (cf. also Asher 2004; Ruggles 2000). These general approaches are useful but not sufficient for understanding heritage sites that become the focus of violence, such as Ayodhya and Somnath, which have their own case-specific literatures.

Champaner–Pavagadh lies somewhere in between these situations where heritage becomes an object and context of conflict, and it thus requires a contemporary as well as historical perspective. In contemporary terms, it has been affected by recent regional violence and continuing local economic violence, but not direct physical human rights violations. At the same time, in historical terms, it has a record of armed violence that is part of its "heritage."

Table 1 Interpretations of communal conflict in India

Contemporary approaches

1. Descriptive analyses of political, economic, and nationalist determinants of postindependence riots (Engineer 1984)
2. Comparative analysis of effective and ineffective civil society institutions (Varshney 2002 on Ahmedabad vis-à-vis Surat)
3. Ethnographic accounts of violence and recovery (Das 1990)
4. Breakdown of justice institutions (Baxi 2002)
5. Psychoanalytic diagnoses of narcissistic anxiety and rage (Kakar 1996)
6. Detailed political analyses of an "institutionalized riot machine" that operates from the mohalla to state scale (Brass 2003)

Historical perspectives

7. Origins in an agonistic culture suppressed by millennia of ritual tradition, released by stresses of modernization (Heesterman 1985)
8. Colonial imputations of irreconcilable cultural differences and historical injustices that erupt in irrational spontaneous ways and that cannot be contained without the intervention of a third (colonial) party
9. Postcolonial critique of British and early nationalist constructions of communalism (Freitag 1989; Gossman 1999; Pandey 1990)
10. Postcolonial perspectives on precolonial conflict and coexistence (e.g., Bayly 1985; Gaborieau 1985)

All heritage conservation is a historicist project, i.e., a selective interpretation of the evidence that addresses modern concerns, especially when it involves environmental design that features some artifacts while transforming, sacrificing, or ignoring others (Lowenthal 1998). Delineating the heritage to be preserved, restored, or changed; designing facilities and spaces for accomplishing those aims; emphasizing some events and sites over others; inferring and inscribing selected landscape meanings and anticipating a wide range of inferences and inscriptions by others – all of these activities recast the landscape heritage of a place. They require an approach that is both contemporary and historical, in this case dating back to the medieval era, and an approach that in modern terminology spans from human rights violations to other spheres of cultural heritage conflict (cf. Gaborieau 1985).

The Spectrum of Cultural Heritage Conflict

Violent cultural conflict, even the hint of it, can put a halt to cultural heritage conservation. It is such a sensitive subject that it is rarely explicitly discussed during conservation projects. At the same time, we know that some heritage conservation actions purposely or unwittingly aggravate cultural conflict while others ameliorate it.

One approach to this dilemma is to widen the scope of discussion to encompass six broad relationships between cultural conflict and heritage conservation (see Table 2).

Relationship 1. Cultural Heritage in the Context of Armed Conflict
Concern about cultural heritage sites has arisen in many wars, including recent examples in Bosnia and Iraq, as archeologists alert the state and defense departments to impacts of war on cultural resources. The UN *Convention for the Protection of Cultural Property in the Event of Armed Conflict*, in force since 1956 does not apply to internal civil strife of the sort that occurred in Gujarat (United Nations 1954a,b, 1956, 1999; Toman 1996). Indeed, no international or national protocols address this situation, even when it involves strategic use of cultural sites in armed conflict, such as the siege of the Church of the Holy Sepulchre (Jerusalem) in 2003, the stand-off between US and Iraqi militia at the tomb of Ali in Najaf in 2004, and numerous instances where mosques, temples, churches, etc. are strategically used

Table 2 Varieties of heritage conflict

1. Cultural heritage in the context of armed conflict
2. Places of violence as cultural heritage
3. Heritage as the object of conflict, destruction, and desecration
4. Conflict between proposals for economic development and heritage conservation
5. Conflict among heritage stakeholders over material control and symbolic interpretation of a site
6. Conflict among heritage professionals over different concepts and methods of conservation

in warfare. The price of strategic miscalculation can be huge as evidenced by the assassination of Prime Minister Indira Gandhi and subsequent anti-Sikh pogrom in Delhi in 1984 following Operation Bluestar at the Sikh Golden Temple in Amritsar (Das 1990). In the larger context of warfare, historic sites are casualties of larger territorial struggles in which the land itself is the primary heritage at stake.

Partition of India and Pakistan in 1947 is the great regional design conflict in South Asia. It may sound odd to refer to it as design, but that is what it was, complete with cartographers, civil engineers, and constitutional lawyers as a first wave, followed by redesign of the Indus River system, the largest river basin project ever financed by the World Bank. Partition cost over one million lives and unfathomable suffering for tens of millions. The connection with Gujarat is tenuous but real: some actors in 2002 blamed the attack on Hindu travelers at Godhra on Pakistani agents, while others blamed the subsequent pogrom on Hindu nationalists striving to drive Muslims out of India (and they succeeded as some Gujarati Muslims fled not to Pakistan but to the Gulf, Europe, the US, and safer parts of India).

Relationship 2. Places of Violence as Cultural Heritage
Some sites of collective violence, such as battlefields and places of tragedy, become cultural heritage. Geographer Kenneth Foote (2003) distinguishes four processes of cultural response to places of tragedy that he terms sanctification, designation or listing, rectification through rebuilding, and obliteration. At Champaner–Pavagadh, pilgrimage and World Heritage listing contribute to sanctification and designation but the full story remains somewhat veiled. For example, many of the protected archeological remnants were built as military fortifications or in the course of military campaigns. The *Mirat-i Sikandari* reports that Sultan Mahmud Begara built the great Friday Mosque of Champaner town while besieging Rajput rivals in hillslope forts, with the aim of communicating his resolve (Sikander bin Muhammad [1611] 1886). The "pilgrim's path" winds its way up Pavagadh hill through a series of Rajput and Sultanate fortifications. In addition to stone ramparts, these structures include sophisticated gateways designed to enable defenders to survey, regulate access, and drop stones on attackers; catapults; and fortified passages to waterworks designed to withstand long periods of siege. Vegetation has overtaken these fortifications, which now seem powerless to the ascending pilgrim, tourist, and vendor.

Relationship 3. Heritage as an Object of Conflict, Destruction, and Desecration
A Draft UN Convention addresses intentional destruction of heritage (UNESCO 2003). Destruction ranges from vandalism of the sort that every designer now anticipates and strives to minimize through materials and surveillance, to massive damage such as the Taliban destruction of Buddhist statues; heritage "cleansing" of the sort documented in Bosnia; and complete leveling as occurred at the Babri mosque at Ayodhya in 1992. The important point here is that while hundreds of religious sites were desecrated in Gujarat during the 2002 riots, the destruction of religious sites at Champaner–Pavagadh was limited. A modern village mosque was damaged but historic mosques were not: was this because they were deemed "monuments," economically valuable as a source of tourism, or culturally valuable to the

wider community? Pilgrimage routes also can become paths of conflict when they pass through rival territories and heritage sites, but the pilgrimage routes and religious places related to Champaner–Pavagadh had no reported violence.

Relationship 4. Conflict, Economic Development and Heritage Conservation
Far more widespread are conflicts between infrastructure development, economic competition, and tourism development that contribute to site destruction. Fragmentation of bureaucratic authority aggravates the inherent tensions between past and future landscapes. Examples in South Asia are legion: colonial mining of Harappan sites in the Indus Valley for railway ballast; clearance of settlements for roads, parks, and other infrastructure; more recent construction of religious and cultural theme parks; and unauthorized development near historic sites. At Champaner–Pavagadh, there are intense development pressures to construct Dharamsalas for pilgrims, a new ropeway up the mountain for tourists and pilgrims, highway construction through the site, along with roadside vending and hawking (Sinha et al. 2002; Thakur 1987). Competition across economic sectors involves diverse socioeconomic and elite constituencies, which makes these struggles political and economic as well as cultural, as the next section elaborates.

*Relationship 5. Conflict among Heritage Stakeholders over Material
and Symbolic Control*
Throughout the world, there are conflicts over the uses and meanings of World Heritage Sites, whether the Grand Canyon in the US where tribes and agencies disagree over appropriate behaviors, or the Taj Mahal which is overseen by several disparate offices of the ASI. Struggles over the control, succession, rituals, and funds at shrines and temples are common.

Champaner–Pavagadh faces institutional fragmentation among national, state, local, and private organizations whose efforts are not well coordinated. At the national level there are ASI protected sites but little ASI presence compared with state archeology, forest, and irrigation districts. The Panchmahals district headquarters in Godhra has jurisdiction over local roads, schools, and public finance. Champaner town is a separate entity from settlements on the hill. The Ropeway coalition and Champaner Hotel have concessions to operate and make a profit on the site. And temple trusts and various NGOs on Pavagadh hill organize to maximize their interests while protecting against some forms of site impacts, e.g., NGO programs of tree planting and reservoir desilting. The 2002 riots exposed the links between economic interests and cultural conflict at Champaner–Pavagadh.

Relationship 6. Conflict Among Heritage Conservationists
Conflicts arise among heritage conservationists about the appropriate concepts, methods, and techniques for conservation. Historic landscapes are inherently dynamic, and they change over time in ways that invite debates, e.g., at Humayun's tomb in Delhi where debates have focused on what historical levels should be restored with what plants, materials, and meanings. Similarly, at Champaner–Pavagadh there are intense debates about conserving different strata of archeological, historical, and

living cultural resources. Some argue that policies must be established first, while others argue for master plans and/or prototype designs, and for greater or lesser emphasis on pilgrimage heritage relative to architectural and archeological heritage; natural heritage has received less attention to date.

These six types of heritage conflict may occur in any situation, but they come together dynamically and sometimes tragically at Indo-Islamic sites in India as exemplified by the riots in Gujarat in 2002. The next section describes how we have approached some of those conflicts at Champaner–Pavagadh.

Landscape Heritage Conflict, Conservation, and Design

As noted earlier, the Baroda Heritage Trust advocates a landscape approach to heritage conservation that strives to reconnect people and places. This means reconnecting Champaner City and Pavagadh Hill through its historical paths, waterworks, vegetation, and settlements. The guiding hypothesis for these conservation design proposals is that they can help harmonize contemporary tourist and pilgrim interests; illuminate the manifold historical contributions of Sultanate, Rajput, Jain, and tribal groups; and thereby deepen contemporary appreciation of the pluralistic cultural legacy at Champaner–Pavagadh. The following four design proposals develop this hypothesis.

Proposal 1. Redesign the Transportation System to Reconnect Champaner and Pavagadh
At present, travelers approach the site on an east–west highway that bisects the site with "Champaner" to the north and "Pavagadh" to the south (Fig. 5).

Increasing truck traffic, roadway paving, fencing, widening, and commercial development have accentuated this spatial and cultural divide – degrading the core of the site and the entry to both the Pilgrim's Path to the south along which the historic Hindu temples are located, and the Champaner Royal Enclosure to the north where most of the Muslim architecture is located. Before the highway, travelers approached the city from the west, north, and northeast through a more varied network of primary and secondary roads than that of the present East–West highway. Indeed, in a modern folk painting depicting the historical continuity of Champaner and Pavagadh, the current highway is absent and a series of gates leads through the city and up the hill. The proposed transportation redesign has three main components that strive to reestablish those historical relationships:

1. *A highway bypass around the site to the north.* The proposed bypass would divert thru-traffic around Champaner–Pavagadh. It would begin between Halol and the buffer zone on the west, swing north of the site around the outer walls of the old city, following existing smaller roads, and rejoin the highway east of the buffer zone.

Fig. 5 East–west highway entry to Champaner city. (Photo by author, January 2005)

2. *Off-site multimodal transportation centers.* Major transportation centers would be located where the new bypass road takes off from the existing highway on the east and west sides of the site. Smaller transportation nodes would be built near the old gateways and entry roads on the north and northeastern sides of Champaner. Private vehicles would be parked at these transportation nodes, and visitors would be conveyed to the site by battery-powered vehicles, bicycles, or on foot as now occurs at the Taj Mahal and other World Heritage Sites. These off-site facilities would offer new economic opportunities that, in a postconflict situation, could aim to provide restitution for lost opportunities in town and on the hill. At the same time, restricting vehicular access to the site would shift some automobile-based businesses from Pavagadh Hill to the lower slopes and outlying areas, which may generate new social and economic conflict. Those lost opportunities would have to be matched by new opportunities on the hill and off.
3. *A low-traffic "medieval thoroughfare."* The road through the site could then be converted to a thoroughfare akin to that of the medieval era in width, surfacing, and planted edges. At each of the gates, an original stone road surfacing based on remnants found on Pavagadh Hill would be reestablished for a distance of 10 m or more to transform the initial experience of the walled city.

Proposal 2. Improve Interpretive Trails that Reconnect Champaner with Pavagadh

The main trails presently take off from the state highway up Pavagadh Hill or through the historic city of Champaner. No modern trails connect the two areas as they did

Fig. 6 Improved trail along the Old Pilgrim's Path. (Photo by author, January 2005)

during the medieval era. The one exception from the Royal Enclosure gate to the pilgrim's path is unsafe and environmentally degraded by a busy intersection.

Design of a new interpretive trail system would link Champaner and Pavagadh at historical north–south connections. These connections include paths that approach and ascend the hill via passages used by hill defenders, the old pilgrim's path, and an old path from the Friday Mosque (Jami Masjid) along the northeast hillslope (Fig. 6).

These trails would clarify the spatial structure of the city's gates, walls, and forts. Historically, urban streets proceeded through a series of internal gates of Rajput and Sultanate fortifications on the lower slopes of Pavagadh hill. Identifying these thresholds would communicate the spatial logic of the site during the medieval era.

It could also provide guided and open-ended walking narratives. On the one hand, trails would guide tourists through historical routes and places within the overall complex, i.e., sequences of gates, baths, markets, mosques, residences, forts, tanks, temples, etc. Community members would be recruited for these new economic opportunities as guides. Even when destinations are crystal clear, such as the pilgrim's path to the Kalika Mata temple, pilgrims would be invited to consider features constructed for travelers by other patrons, gates that controlled access, and topographic progressions that have shaped the pilgrimage experience. These experiences are currently short-circuited by buses, jeeps, and ropeways that accelerate pilgrims' journey up the hill.

Some connective trails could also provide what Mehta and Chatterjee (2001) call "walking narratives" of former conflicts, suffering, and hopefully rehabilitation.

Some experiences can only be uttered or recalled silently in transit, passing by sites of historical conflict and conciliation and through disputed public spaces that are renegotiated in postconflict community life, in part through acts of therapeutic walking that range from individual safe passage, to friends walking together, to consciously peaceful processions.

Proposal 3. Conserve Culturally Hybrid Sites

Sites at Champaner and Pavagadh have acquired a cultural complexity that should neither be reduced to a single historical layer nor represented as intrinsically syncretic features. Two examples illustrate this design concept. The first is the great Friday Mosque. The second is the pilgrimage summit composition.

The Friday mosque at Champaner is one of the finest examples of medieval Gujarati architecture, a tradition distinguished by its exquisite sandstone-carved screens, panels, ceilings, and *mihrab* – stone carving that grew in part out of temple architecture in Gujarat. It has a large octagonal ablution pool reached by flights of steps similar to those in Gujarati stepwells built by Hindu as well as Muslim patrons. The pool has also served as a site for evening festivals with oil lamps. Gottschalk (2000: 173) describes an analogous situation at a large village well known to Hindu villagers as the *hathi kua* (elephant well) and to Muslim villagers as the *hath kua* (hand well, implying its use for ablution before prayers). The mosque courtyard includes a small grave (*qabr*) of an unknown saint, a common yet doctrinally ambiguous feature found in mosque architecture across South Asia. Today, the mosque courtyard (*sahn*) is also graced with grass lawns and plants laid out in what originally was an area for rest and overflow from the prayer hall. It exhibits horticultural tastes dating to the early twentieth century. These conjunctions of mosque, shrine, pool, and garden give the site an intriguing, well-tended hybrid character. Conserving these diverse cultural facets of the Friday Mosque area today could cultivate an appreciation for the hybrid heritage of Champaner–Pavagadh.

The best example of joint heritage occurs at the pilgrimage summit itself (Fig. 7). The courtyard has a Champa tree, reminding one of the city of Champaner below. After taking *darshan* from the mother goddess, one can ascend to the roof where a small grave exists for a Sufi saint known as *Pir Baba*. The goddess' power (*sakti*), experienced visually, is augmented by the saint's power (*barakat*), experienced by physical proximity and prayers. The reverence shown on both levels of the building underscores communal continuities rather than oppositions.

Proposal 4. Conserve Historical Water Systems from the Summit to the Plains

Standing on Pavagadh summit, one keenly senses the passage of clouds and action of monsoon rains cascading through steep ravines in all directions. Returning from the summit, one appreciates the sophisticated systems of water catchment carved into each plateau, wells that filter drinking water from those catchments, small ghats for bathing and washing, and channels that convey runoff to the tanks and excess water to overflow drains. These fascinating water systems suffer from increasing

Fig. 7 Kalika Mata temple complex. (Photo by author, January 2005)

pollutant loading, solid waste disposal, accelerated erosion and sedimentation, and poorly constructed public-works-style concrete repairs (Fig. 8).

Community groups have organized to address some of these problems, e.g., slope revegetation and tank desilting projects on the Mauliya plateau. Sumesh Modi (2002) has documented historical water systems, but there has as yet been no systematic effort to examine water conservation measures from the summit to the plains that may improve human well-being. Just as trails lead from the plains up the hill, connecting Champaner and Pavagadh, the water system progresses downslope from a rock-cut water tank near the Pavagadh summit to an earthen irrigation reservoir on the plains beyond Champaner.

Conserving traditional waterworks requires both systems and site-specific approaches (Agarwal and Narain 1999). At the system level, Modi's (2002) survey locates extant water features on a digital base map and identifies hydraulic connections

Fig. 8 Dudhiya talao on a cliff edge near the top of Pavagadh Hill. (Photo by author, January 2005)

among these features. A University of Illinois workshop mapped the watersheds that supply each feature (Sinha et al. 2003). Joint efforts are planned to estimate hydroclimatic water budgets for different orientations on the hill; rainfall–runoff relations on the complex, thin-soiled terrain; water quality conditions in tanks; water use behaviors that explain water quantity and quality conditions; and the volumes, seepage and flows for different hydraulic features and social uses.

Beyond these scientific studies, the waterworks from summit to plains must be understood as a sociocultural system, as indicated by their *names* (e.g., tanks named for a milk→curd→oil series; and the familiar Ganga, Yamuna, and Saraswati river goddesses); *water uses* (ritual, as well as functional and historically strategic purposes); *technologies* (which include filtration wells, flood control channels, water warming channels, and dry-season lotus plant pools); and as yet to be discerned *cultural relationships* that guide who can use different types of waters for what purposes and with what technologies and ascribed meanings. These investigations would help generate system-wide plans that link the historical dimensions of water management with future needs, mitigate water conflicts, and set parameters for historic waterworks conservation.

Some waterworks at Champaner–Pavagadh are protected monuments, which means they must be treated as archeological features with the minimum intervention necessary to conserve their heritage values. Failure to follow this principle would aggravate professional conflict among designers, conservationists, archeologists, and tourism developers of the sort discussed earlier in the chapter, not to mention local social conflicts.

These four lines of integrative landscape design illustrate how conservation could help address the long history of social tension at sites like Champaner–Pavagadh up to the present day. The final question for this chapter is how design inquiry might also be extended to related processes of social conciliation.

Cultural Heritage Conservation and Conciliation

What difference can conservation design make for peoples and places that face various types of social conflict? Returning to the opening quotation of this chapter, can it "calm sad or angry hearts"? Many heritage projects aspire implicitly for conciliation (Aga Khan Trust for Culture 2002; Wescoat 1999; http://www.mughalgardens.org). They recognize that heritage conservation can aggravate conflict through misinterpretation, stereotyping, mythmaking, and naïve interventions that aggravate conflict focused on heritage sites and associated communities. The risks of not engaging these questions are also substantial (Das and Kleinman 2001). Social conflict contributes to the identity of places; evasion of it can perpetuate misunderstanding and leave society less prepared for recurring conflicts, especially those that invoke or appropriate cultural heritage. Evasion can also result in missed opportunities for conciliation. To identify such opportunities at Champaner–Pavagadh, it is useful to step through the six types of conflict introduced at the beginning of the chapter, in reverse order from most to least tractable, starting with conflict among professionals and concluding with violent human rights abuses.

1. *Conflict Resolution Skills for Heritage Conservationists*
As noted earlier, conflict among heritage conservationists in India is intense. These conflicts could be constructively channeled through several types of institutional development. A system of peer-review for conservation plans, comparable to procedures employed in the sciences, could help channel professional disagreement in constructive directions (Seminar 2004: 20). Publication of peer-reviewed conservation studies and critiques would focus professional conflict on substantive issues. Development of advanced professional education and certification programs would ensure that qualified specialists, e.g., archeobotanists to determine historic plantings, are engaged on heritage sites (see Conservation Architects Meet 2004). Efforts are underway to articulate heritage conservation principles that build explicitly upon inclusive provisions in the Indian Constitution (1976) and address social concerns (INTACH 2004; INTACH-AusHeritage 2004).

2. *Conflict Resolution Among Community Stakeholders*
The 1987 *Champaner: Draft Action Plan for Integrated Conservation* took an important step toward surveying community members and their interests in conservation. That study needs intensive follow-up now that the site has World Heritage status, especially as some community members have voiced concern about being displaced by conservation initiatives. Several factors complicate

community-based design. The flight of Muslim community members since 2002 poses special challenges in identifying their conservation interests and, more importantly, determining how conservation projects might create social and physical spaces for or barriers to their return. Some tribal members and grazers from the eastern hills and laborers have only temporary residences at the site that lack adequate water and sanitation. Other residents and workers have religious as well as business and family interests in the site. Visitors range from millions of pilgrims from largely rural areas to international urbane tourists, most of whom stay for short periods of several days. Conducting a fair and discerning survey of the many community interests may require collaboration with social rehabilitation organizations with expertise in postconflict reconstruction, as well as conventional survey research and participatory methods.

3. *Harmonization of Conservation and Economic Development Interests*
At a larger scale, public and private organizations will advance their interests in ways that may aggravate or ameliorate social conflict. At Champaner–Pavagadh the traditional economic sectors have included mining, forestry, agriculture, and pilgrimage services. Today, the pilgrimage economy is booming, and World Heritage status will increase active recreation (e.g., hiking, picnicking, sports events, and entertainment) as well as heritage tourism. Earlier struggles between conservationists and resource extraction industries have given way to an uneasy triad of tourism, recreation, and pilgrimage. The Heritage Trust seeks to harmonize these activities by convening representatives from various groups and striving to harmonize their views through an expanding array of planning and design proposals. Ultimately, broader institutions of civil society will be needed to respond creatively to site-specific conflicts in Champaner town and Pavagadh Hill where Muslim shopkeepers and workers were driven off.

4. *Prevention of the Intentional Destruction of Heritage*
Champaner–Pavagadh had limited architectural heritage destruction during the recent riots. World Heritage status will draw more people and attention to the site, which may increase vandalism and related problems. Training of staff in all economic sectors should include heritage protection and policing. Beyond that, school education programs must cultivate respect for diverse heritage sites and aversion to site desecration. At a time of epic struggles over ideology in education across India, this is not a simple proposition. The recent site desecration in Gujarat and invocations of earlier episodes of historical site destruction dating back a millennium must be countered with examples of expansive patronage, such as the common veneration of Kalika Mata and Pir Baba, crosscultural patronage, and the reconstruction of damaged sites.

5. *Places of Violence, and Sanctuary, as Heritage*
Fortification, siege, and conquest were major themes in the history of Champaner–Pavagadh and Gujarat, and they constitute an important aspect of its heritage. However, we also found that modern editors of medieval histories have deleted less-violent passages about the cultural landscape because these were deemed

"tedious," which supports Elise Boulding's (2000) thesis about nonviolence as the "hidden side of history." Special effort should be made to identify historical people and places that have provided sustenance for diverse culture groups and sanctuary from violence. Champaner–Pavagadh was historically a place of retreat from attacking armies. During recent strife it suffered less human rights violence than nearby towns (cf. Dreze 2003 on this point for other areas of Gujarat). Its hybrid pilgrimage and tourist sites draw together diverse peoples from the region. The dramatic natural landscape of Pavagadh Hill has an equally complex record of environmental degradation and protection.

These complex relationships at Champaner–Pavagadh – its record of violence, sanctuary, and care – may be viewed as components of an expansive approach to heritage conservation. Providing safe places and spaces for people to reflect upon this heritage, advance it collectively, and enable all to participate safely and economically in it, would consciously privilege a heritage of peace over violence.

6. Building Resilience in Places of Violent Social Conflict

Recent events in Gujarat remind us that violence can sweep through places that appear at least tenuously stable. Detailed research on patterns of communal violence reveals that some places and states have recurrent, organized violence, while others have effective resistance, resilience, and control (Brass 2003; Varshney 2002; Wilkinson 2004). As Champaner–Pavagadh appears to have a mixed record, it seems important to try to build its social resistance and resilience, along with physical infrastructure, in part through heritage conservation. It would be utterly naïve to think that landscape design could counter the "institutionalized riot machine" led by violence experts colluding with state officials in the political situations that allow extensive human rights abuses to occur. However, during the 2002 riots, some areas coped with violence better than others through peace committees; processes of rehabilitation and restitution; and effective collaboration among local, regional, national, international relief, and human rights organizations (e.g., Ahmed 2004; Bhatt 2002; Bunsha 2006: 98–100). These examples indicate that it is neither too early, nor too delicate, to strive explicitly to build resilient social relationships concurrently with World Heritage conservation.

Conclusion

This chapter has explored ways to understand and navigate the spectrum of cultural conflicts associated with landscape heritage conservation. To link the case of Champaner–Pavagadh with the symposium theme of human rights, the six types of conflict examined here may be viewed as progression from cultural rights (#1 and 2) to socioeconomic rights (#3 and 4) and ultimately to human rights *per se* (#5 and 6) (cf. chapter by William Logan *infra*). Human rights advocacy *per se* must focus on the vortices of violent conflict. However, studying those sites that prove less violent in the context of regional conflict, or whose violence takes more tractable economic and symbolic forms, can shed light on how design inquiry broadens the range of options that social groups may consider. It builds upon Rajmohan Gandhi's proposition that, "Every tree planted, or cubic foot of water conserved, is a celebration of life, a proclamation of the worth of the future. . .," by asking exactly where those trees might be planted, how water might be conserved to sustain them, and how the resultant garden might calm sad and angry hearts. Everyone can work as a designer, at the very least to do more good than harm at heritage sites, and beyond that to cultivate a vision for the future of Indo-Islamic gardens like Champaner–Pavagadh.

Acknowledgments This chapter was informed by the generous collaboration and scholarship of colleagues in India and the US, especially Karan Grover. However, it represents my personal exploration of conflict and conciliation in landscape heritage conservation, for which I alone am responsible.

References

Aga Khan Trust for Culture, 3 June 2002, *Babur Gardens Rehabilitation Project in Kabul*. Aga Khan Trust for Culture, Geneva.
—, April 2003, *Revitalization of the Gardens of Emperor Humayun's Tomb, Delhi, India*. http:// www.akdn.org/aktc/Humayun%20Brief%2004–2003.pdf (12 July 2006).
Agarwal, Arun, and Sunita Narain, 1999, *Dying Wisdom: The Rise, Fall and Potential of India's Traditional Water Harvesting Systems*. Centre for Science and Environment, New Delhi.
Ahmed, Sara, 2004, Sustaining Peace, Re-Building Livelihoods: The Gujarat Harmony Project. *Gender and Development* 12(3): 94–102.
Amin, Shahid, 2002, Sagas of Victory, Memories of Defeat? The Long Afterlife of an Indo-Muslim Warrior Saint, 1033–2000. In *Experiments with Truth: Documenta 11 Platform 2*, edited by Okwui Enwezor, pp. 97–119. Hatje Cantz, Oestfildern-Ruit.
Archaeological Survey of India and Heritage Trust (Baroda), January 2002, *Champaner–Pavagadh World Heritage Site Nomination*. Heritage Trust, Baroda.
Asher, Catherine B., 2004, Uneasy Bedfellows: Islamic Art and the Politics of Indian Nationalism. *Religion and the Arts* 3(1): 37–57.
Baxi, U., 2002, The Second Gujarat Catastrophe. *Economic and Political Weekly* 37: 3519–3531.
Bayly, C. A., 1985, The Prehistory of 'Communalism'? Religious Conflict in India 1700–1860. *Modern Asian Studies* 19(2): 177–203.
Bhatt, Sheela, 2002, *When a Town in Gujarat Refused to Burn*. Rediff. http://in. rediff.com/news/2002/jul/31spec.htm (12 July 2006).
Boulding, Elise, 2000, *Cultures of Peace: The Hidden Side of History*. Syracuse University Press, Syracuse.
Brass, Paul R., 2003, *The Production of Hindu-Muslim Violence in Contemporary India*. University of Washington Press, Seattle.
Bunsha, Dionne, 2002, Dazed, but determined: The Muslim victims of the communal violence, though still hounded out of their homes, are determined to vote. *Frontline* 19(25): 7–20 December 2002. http://www.flonnet.com/fl1925/stories/20021220007301300.htm (12 July 2006).
—, 2003, Voting for survival. *Frontline* 19(26): 21 December 2002–3 January 2003. http://www. flonnet.com/fl1926/stories/20030103008012700.htm (12 July 2006).
—, 2006, *Scarred: Experiments with Violence in Gujarat*. Penguin Books, New Delhi.

Commentary on the Hague Convention of 14 May 1954. UNESCO, Paris.

Communalism Combat, April 2003, *Special Issue: Gujarat, A Year Later*. http://www.sabrang.com/cc/archive/2003/apr03/index.html (12 July 2006).

Concerned Citizens' Tribunal, 2003, C*rime Against Humanity* [Iyer commission report], 2 vols. Citizens for Justice and Peace, Mumbai. http://www.sabrang.com/tribunal/tribunal1.pdf (12 July 2006).

Conservation Architects Meet [CAM], 2004, *CAM 2004: First Report*. http://www. intach.org/pdf/report_cam2004.pdf

Das, Veena, ed., 1990, *Mirrors of Violence: Communities, Riots and Survivors in South Asia*. Oxford University Press, Delhi.

Das, Veena, and A. Kleinman, 2001, *Remaking a World: Violence, Social Suffering and Recovery*. University of California Press, Berkeley.

Dreze, Jean, May 2003, Gujarat Revisited. *Lines Magazine*. http://www.lines-magazine.org/textmay03/dreze.htm (12 July 2006).

Elliott, H. M., 1976 reprint, Mahmud's Expeditions to India. In *The History of India as Told by its own Historians*, edited by H. M Elliott and J. Dowson. Islamic Book Service, Lahore.

Engineer, Ashgar A., 1984, *Communal Riots in Post-Independence India*. Sangam, Hyderabad.

Ferishta, Mahomed K., 1977 reprint, *History of the Rise of Mahomedan Power in India*, vol. 4, ch. 4. "History of the Kings of Gujarat," translated by John Briggs. Sang-e-Meel, Lahore.

Foote, Kenneth, 2003, *Shadowed Ground: America's Landscapes of Violence and Tragedy*, 2nd edition. University of Texas Press, Austin.

Forum Against Oppression of Women, 2002, *Genocide in Rural Gujarat: The Experience of Dahod District*. http://www.onlinevolunteers.org/gujarat/reports/rural/rural-gujarat.pdf (12 July 2006).

Freitag, Sandra, 1989, *Collective Action and Community: Public Arenas and the Emergence of Communalism in North India*. University of California Press, Berkeley.

Gaborieau, Marc, 1985, From al-Beruni to Jinnah: Idiom, Ritual and Ideology of the Hindu–Muslim Confrontation in South Asia. *Anthropology Today* 1(3): 7–14.

Gandhi, Rajmohan, 1999, *Revenge and Reconciliation: Understanding South Asian History*. Penguin Books, New Delhi.

Goetz, H., 1949, Pawagadh–Champaner. *Journal of the Gujarat Research Society* XI(2): 1–67.

Gossman, Patricia A., 1999, *Riots and Victims: Violence and the Construction of Communal Identity Among Bengali Muslims, 1905–1947*. Westview, Boulder.

Gottschalk, Peter, 2000, *Beyond Hindu and Muslim: Multiple Identity in Narratives from Village India*. Oxford University Press, New York.

Government of Gujarat, 2004, *Project: Heritage Walk at Champaner Pavagadh (Central Gujarat)*. http://www.gujarattourism.com/opportunities/Proposal_Tourism_14.html (12 July 2006).

Government of India, 1976, *Constitution*, Part IV A. (42nd Amendment 1976) Art. 51 A. "It is the fundamental duty and responsibility of every citizen of India . . . (f) to value and preserve the rich heritage of our composite culture (g) to protect and improve the natural environment including forests, lakes, rivers and wildlife and to have compassion for living creatures."

Gulbadan Begum, 1987 reprint, *Humayun-nama*, translated by A. S. Beveridge. Sang-e Meel, Lahore.

Heesterman, J. C., 1985, *The Inner Conflict of Tradition: Essays in Indian Ritual, Kingship, and Society*. University of Chicago Press, Chicago.

Heritage Trust and Archaeological Survey of India, 2002, *Champaner–Pavagadh World Heritage Nomination*. Heritage Trust, Vadodara.

Human Rights Watch, April 2002, *We Have No Orders To Save You: State Participation and Complicity in Communal Violence in Gujarat*. Human Rights Watch, New York.

—, July 2003a, *Compounding Injustice: The Government's Failure to Redress Massacres in Gujarat*. Human Rights Watch, New York.

—, 5 September 2003b, *India: Protect Gujarat Activists Now*. Human Rights Watch, New York.

—, 14 April 2004, *India Protect Witnesses in Gujarat, Conduct Investigations*. Human Rights Watch, New York.

Indian Muslim Council – USA, May 2006, *Vadodara 2006: Manufacturing Violence and the Politics of Demolition* [Compilation of articles on violence following demolition of Syed Rashiduddin Chisti Dargah]. http://www.imc-usa.org/digest/special/2006/vadodara.violence.htm (12 July 2006).

INTACH, 4 November 2004, *Charter for Conservation of Unprotected Architectural Heritage and Sites in India*. INTACH, New Delhi. http://www.intach.org/pdf/charter.pdf (12 July 2006).

INTACH-AusHeritage, 2004, *Workshop on Indian Charter for Conservation Held at INTACH, New Delhi, March 24–27, 2004; and Some Aspects of a Charter Drafted During the Aus Heritage – INTACH Workshop*. INTACH, New Delhi.

International Initiative for Justice in Gujarat, December 2002, *Interim Report*. http://www.onlinevolunteers.org/gujarat/reports/iijg/interimreport.htm (12 July 2006).

Kakar, Sudhir, 1996, *The Colors of Violence: Cultural Identities, Religion, and Conflict*. University of Chicago Press, Chicago.

Khan, Ali Muhammad, 1965, Trans, *Mirat-i-Ahmadi. A Persian History of Gujarat*, translated by M. F. Lokhandwala. Oriental Institute, Baroda.

Kotwal, Navaz, 2002, *Justice For All – Rasoolbhai's Wife*. http://www.humanrightsinitiative.org/artres/justice%20for%20all.pdf (12 July 2006).

Layton, Robert, Peter G. Stone, and Julian Thomas, eds., 2000, *Destruction and Conservation of Cultural Property*. Routledge, London.

Lowenthal, David, 1998, *The Heritage Crusade and the Spoils of History*. Cambridge University Press, Cambridge.

Mehta, R. N., 1977, *Prehistoric Champaner: A Report on the Explorations of Prehistoric Sites Around Pavagadh Hill*. Department of Archaeology and Ancient History, Faculty of Arts, M.S. University of Baroda, Vadodara.

—, [1986] 2002, *Champaner: A Mediaeval Capital*. Heritage Trust and ASI, Baroda.

Mehta, Deepa, and Roma Chatterjee, 2001, Boundaries, Names, Alterities: A Case Study of a 'Communal Riot' in Dharavi, Bombay. In *Remaking a World: Violence, Social Suffering and Recovery*, edited by Veena Das and A. Kleinman, pp. 201–249. University of California Press, Berkeley.

Midday, 2004, *Congress Takes Out Roadshow in Godhra*. http://sify.com/news/politics/fullstory.php?id=13443930 (12 July 2006).

Modi, Sumesh, 2002, Water Intelligent City: Champaner–Pavagadh. *Landscapes of Water: History, Innovation and Sustainable Design*, vol. 1, 113ff pages, edited by E. A. Fratino et al. Politecnico di Bari, Bari.

Oza, Nandini, 29 February 2004, Godhra is More than a Memory: Two Years have Passed Since the Post-Godhra Riots. The Victims and Their Families have had to Carry on with Their Lives. Today They are Grappling with a Social and Economic Boycott. *Deccan Herald*. http://www.deccanherald.com/deccanherald/feb292004/sl2.asp (12 July 2006).

Pandey, G., 1990, *The Construction of Communalism in Colonial North India*. Oxford University Press, Delhi.

People for Heritage Concern, 2001, *Cultural Resource Information System – Inventory of Built Heritage of Champaner–Pavagadh*. Heritage Trust, Baroda.

People's Union for Democratic Rights, May 2002, *Maaro, Kaapo, Baalo!: State, Society and Communalism in Gujarat*. http://www.pucl.org/Topics/Religion-communalism/2002/maro_kapo_balo.pdf (12 July 2006).

Rediff, 2006, *The Ayodhya Homepage*. http://us.rediff.com/news/ayodhya.htm(12 July 2006).

Ruggles, D. Fairchild, 2000, What's Religion Got To Do With It? A Skeptical Look at Symbolism in Mughal and Rajput Gardens, *Dak: The Newsletter of the American Institute of Indian Studies*. 4: 4–14.

Schon, Donald, 1990, *Educating the Reflective Practitioner: Toward a New Design for Teaching and Learning in the Professions*. Jossey-Bass, San Francisco.

Seminar Education Foundation, 6–9 February 2004, *Marwar Initiative. A Framework for Cooperation for Conservation, Management and Development of India's Heritage*. Sardar Samand, Rajasthan. http://www.india-seminar.com/2004/542/542%20document.htm (12 July 2006).

Sikander bin Muhammad (Manjhu), [1611] 1886 edition, Mirat-i Sikandari. In *The Local Muhammadan Dynasties: Gujarat*, edited by E. C. Bayley based on a translation by J. Dowson. W. H. Allen, London.

Sinha, Amita, 2004, Champaner–Pavagadh Archaeological Park: A Design Approach. *International Journal of Heritage Studies* 10(2): 117–28.

Sinha, Amita, Gary Kesler, and Terence Harkness, 2002, *Champaner–Pavagadh Archaeological Park, Gujarat, India*. Department of Landscape Architecture, University of Illinois, Champaign.

Sinha, Amita, Gary Kesler, D. Fairchild Ruggles, and James L. Wescoat Jr., 2003, *Champaner–Pavagadh Cultural Sanctuary, Gujarat, India*. Department of Landscape Architecture, University of Illinois, Champaign.

—, 2004, Champaner–Pavagadh, Gujarat, India: Challenges and Responses in Cultural Heritage Planning and Design. *Tourism Recreation Research* 29(3): 75–78.

Social Science Research Council, 19 December 2002, The International Initiative for Justice in Gujarat: An Interim Report. http://www.ssrc.org (12 July 2006).

Sreenivas, Janyala, 15 October 2004a, This Navratri, Gujarat does a 'Tolerant' Rewrite: Muslim Shrines . . . Unlike Last Year, Muslim Shrines, or What's Left of Them Post-Riots, Figure in its Spiritual Tourism Package. *Indian Express*. http://www.indianexpress.com/res/web/pIe/full_story.php?content_id=57003 (12 July 2006).

—, 15 October 2004b, Modi Government Goes Secular. *Express India*. http://www.expressindia.com/fullstory.php?newsid=37288 (15 January 2007).

Taneja, Nalini, 14 November 2004, Justice for Gujarat Victims: Whose Responsibility? People's Democracy. *Weekly Organ of the Communist Party of India (Marxist)*. XXVIII: 46.

Thakur, Nalini, 1987, *Champaner: Draft Action Plan for Integrated Conservation*. Heritage Trust, Baroda.

—, 2000, *The Archaeological Park as a Tool for Integrated Protecting Heritage Management with Planning Process: The Case of the Deserted 15th Century Capital Site, Champaner–Pavagadh, Gujarat*. Conference on Simplification of Urban Development Control, Goa.

—, 2002, *Champaner–Pavagadh Archaeological Park: An Integrated Approach with Comprehensive Protection and Management*. Unpublished Paper. Copy on file with author.

—, 2004, *The 'Architectural Knowledge Systems' Approach as a Solution for the Regeneration and Conservation of Indian Built Heritage*. http://www.architexturez.net/+/subject-listing/000065.shtml (12 July 2006).

Times of India, 7 October 2004, *Muslims Still Face Economic Boycott in Pavagadh*. http://timesofindia.indiatimes.com/articleshow/877252.cms (12 July 2006).

Toman, J., 1996, *The Protection of Cultural Property in the Event of Armed Conflict*.

United Nations, 1954a, *Convention for the Protection of Cultural Property in the Event of Armed Conflict*. Done at The Hague, 14 May 1954. Entered in force 7 August 1956.

—, 1954b, *X. Protocol for the Protection of Cultural Property in the Event of Armed Conflict*. Done at The Hague, 14 May 1954. Entered in force 7 August 1956.

—, 1999, *X. Second Protocol to The Hague Convention for the Protection of Cultural Property in the Event of Armed Conflict*. The Hague, 26 March 1999.

—, 2003, *Draft Declaration Concerning the Intentional Destruction of Cultural Heritage*. UNESCO, Paris.

Varshney, Ashutosh, 2002, *Ethnic Conflict and Civic Life*. Yale University Press, New Haven.

Vora, Batuk, 7 May 2004, Gujarat Relief Camps Being Closed Down. *Milli Gazette*. http://www.milligazette.com/Archives/01072002/0107200291.htm (12 July 2006).

Waldman, Amy, 2002, A Secular India, Or Not? At Strife Scene, Vote is a Test. *The New York Times*. 12 December 2002, p.18.

Wescoat, James L. Jr., 1990, Gardens of Invention and Exile: The Precarious Context of Mughal Garden Design during the Reign of Humayun (1530–1556). *Journal of Garden History* 10: 106–116.

—, 1991, Gardens of Conquest and Transformation: Lessons from the Earliest Mughal Gardens in India. *Landscape Journal* 10(5): 105–114.

—, 1992, Expanding the Range of Choice in Water Resource Geography. *Progress in Human Geography* 11: 41–59.

—, 1997, Mughal Gardens and Geographic Sciences, Then and Now. In *Gardens in the Time of the Great Muslim Empires: Theory and Design*, special issue of *Muqarnas*, edited by A. Petruccioli, pp. 187–202. E. J. Brill, Leiden.

—, 1999, Mughal Gardens: The Re-emergence of Comparative Possibilities and the Wavering of Practical Concerns. In *Perspectives on Garden Histories*, edited by Michel Conan, pp. 107–126. Dumbarton Oaks Research Library and Collection, Washington, DC.

Wilkinson, Steven I, 2004, *Votes and Violence: Electoral Competition and Ethnic Riots in India.* Cambridge University Press, Cambridge.

Chapter 4
Tourism, Cultural Heritage, and Human Rights in Indonesia: The Challenges of an Emerging Democratic Society

Christopher Silver

Introduction

Between 1997 and 2005, Indonesia was buffeted by a series of crises that had a devastating impact on one of its prime economic assets: tourism. An environmental crisis linked to the smoke and haze from the unregulated fires of large land owners in Sumatra and Kalimantan in 1997 closed airports in Sumatra and Kalimantan, and disrupted flights and sea traffic from Java to these destinations for several months. Beginning in mid 1997 and crescendoing in 1998, the Asian financial crisis wiped out banks, airlines, real estate projects, and an array of half-built or newly completed tourist-related projects throughout Indonesia. The decaying shell of a partially constructed Westin Hotel on Jakarta's main highway and adjacent to the famous Hotel Indonesia offers a continuing visual reminder of how the collapse of the capital markets impacted the tourism sector that seemed to offer limitless possibilities. Worse still, the Indonesian flag carrier airline, Garuda Indonesia, recorded a 90.3% drop in profit in 2000 owing to rising operating costs and, more importantly, huge foreign exchange losses (*Agence France Press* 21 May 2001).

Woven into the economic crisis in Indonesia was a political crisis that not only led to the fall of the Suharto regime in 1998, but also thrust Indonesia into a political maelstrom for the next 6 years, undermined foreign investments (many of which were intended to feed the tourism industry), and created the image – with abundant assistance from the international media – of a country out of control, both unstable and dangerous, and consequently unsafe for tourists (Maher 2000).

This negative image of conditions was embellished by the outbreak of ethnic/religious-based conflicts (tied to the economic and political crises but also involving longstanding local rivalries) that occurred throughout the country. These began with the attacks on the Chinese in Jakarta during the political crisis in May 1998, and spread to other areas, involving many groups. Areas affected included not only the tourism meccas of central Java in Yogjakarta and Solo, Surabaya in East Java (Indonesia's second city), portions of South and Central Sulawesi especially in remote Poso, but also the regional center of Makassar in Kalimantan (*Jakarta Post* 23 August 2000), with the indigenous Dayaks attacking the Madurese transmigrants (*The Times* 24 February 2001) and most devastatingly the emerging tourism

H. Silverman and D. F. Ruggles (eds.), *Cultural Heritage and Human Rights*.
© Springer 2007

enclaves of Lombok and Ambon in Eastern Indonesia (*Jakarta Post* 18 December 2000). In these areas of ethnic conflicts, estimates indicated the displacement of as many as 700,000 people as well as the complete cessation of tourism. These conflicts had subsided by the second half of 2001, but sporadic violence remained a problem and threatened to escalate into something bigger.

Yet just as the Indonesian economy began to recover from the fiscal crisis, and ethnic conflicts had subsided, international terrorism (with implied connections to Indonesian Muslim militants) hurled a new broadside into the recovering hulk of tourism trade. The attack on the World Trade Center in New York City, and the subsequent invasion of Afghanistan hit directly at Indonesia's tourism market (*Agence France Press* 19 September 2001). The Bali bombing in October 2002 and subsequent bomb blasts in Jakarta, which seemed to be directly linked to the jihad proclaimed in the aftermath of the 9/11 incident, thrust Indonesia squarely into the maelstrom of global terrorism (*The Economist* 6 February 2003). In addition to being identified as a nation linked to international terrorism, the Indonesian government had to deal with three notable succession/separatist movements, each related to a long-term internal struggle to create national unity in the face of powerful cultural opposition to the unitary state. These were in East Timor, which gained independence from Indonesia but at the price of a massacre, in Papua (or Irian Jaya), and in Aceh (at the northern tip of Sumatra). Charting the locus of the ethnic and political conflicts on a map shows how they reached from one end of the nation to the other, and in almost all cases involved places where cultural heritage tourism was a significant component of the local and national economy.

Conflicts, Tourism, Cultural Heritage, and Human Rights

There is a direct and powerful connection between these domestic and international conflicts and the state of tourism, cultural heritage preservation, and human rights in Indonesia. Looking at these local conflicts through the perspective of tourism, it is evident that the events of the past 8 years have put cultural heritage and human rights on a collision course in Indonesia. This collision has been exacerbated by the democratization movement underway since 1998 in the world's fourth most populous country. Some critics of democratization suggest that the changing political structure has contributed to the instability as much as anything else.

One of the underlying issues raised in this brief assessment is how Indonesia's political transformation has fueled conflict, challenged conventional notions of cultural heritage in Indonesia, and, in turn, affected human rights. The cultural clashes that have occurred throughout Indonesia since 1998 have contributed to undermining the seemingly integrated and stable multicultural society that was the bedrock of Indonesia's thriving tourism industry prior to 1997. But can and should responsibility for the demise of the tourism industry be pinned on the democratization process, or has the political transformation itself unveiled a highly localized cultural pluralism that had been submerged for decades beneath a powerful state?

In other words, the degree of integration and national stability was more a function of operation of an authoritarian state rather than the result of a national consensus. Democratic reforms and the shifting of power from the central government to the local governments fueled an intense new "localism" that has had direct implications on cultural preservation and human rights. But does this imply some sort of degenerative condition that should be balanced by reassertion of the traditional role of the state, or has the reduction of the state's control offered up new opportunities to rescue cultural tourism?

To gain perspective on this matter, it is useful to examine historically the emergence of cultural heritage tourism in one Indonesian locality to see how it developed. This can be done by briefly looking at one of the showcase areas, Bali. The case of Bali tourism shows the powerful influence of colonialism, subjugation of local culture through war, and eventually the imposition of the state over local authority.

The Case of Bali

The colonial holdings in Indonesia were aggressively managed in the twentieth century, and throughout the archipelago the impact of Europeanization was increasingly evident. At the beginning of the twentieth century the Dutch had just concluded war in the North Sumatra area of Aceh, located at the other end of the archipelago, and only the tiny island of Bali maintained resistance. Between 1904 and 1914, the Dutch colonial government focused on Bali as the last outpost refusing to come under their rule. The Balinese leadership staunchly resisted absorption in the system. When it was apparent that they could not win militarily, the royal families, rather than submit, walked into the Dutch guns in a sacrificial act known as *puputan*. The royal families of Denpasas, Badung, and then Klung Kung followed this traditional practice and the resistance to the colonial administration suddenly ceased.

While slaughtering the royal families of Bali did not square with the stated intention of the Dutch for benevolent colonialism under what was known as the "Ethical Policy," the pacification that had occurred by 1914 was followed by an effort to make Bali into a "living museum" of fourteenth-century classical Hindu-Javanese culture. At the same time, there was a heightened sensitivity to local culture and to the potential losses that would accompany Europeanization. The study of local cultures in the Netherland Indies became a major new field in Dutch universities (especially *adat* law).

Tourism in Bali is a direct result of war, local subjugation by the Dutch, and the establishment of a state enterprise. The Dutch created a new company to run tourism, Royal Paket Navigation Company, which in turn built Bali's first hotel in 1928. In pursuit of success with this new tourism enterprise, the Dutch government took a variety of measures to protect and celebrate cultural heritage.

Many years later Indonesia's first president, Sukarno (1945–1967), and his new government-sponsored company, Natour, built hotels and promoted tourism using war reparations and international loans. Sukarno's successor, Suharto (1967–1998), transformed Bali and Indonesian tourism in general from a purely state-run enterprise to project the ideal of nationalism and national pride into a cash cow for the private corporate sector. In Suharto's view, tourism was intended to be a major form of economic development for Indonesia and by the early 1990s, led by Bali's massive tourism enterprise, this sector of the national economy had become the third most important source of foreign exchange behind oil and agricultural products.

In Bali, it was the development of the 425-hectare Nusa Dua tourism development (a cluster of 5-star hotels and resorts on the southern tip of Bali) that reflected the national vision for tourism. Cultural heritage was an explicit component of the Nusa Dua approach: the design of this complex of expensive hotels incorporated local values and regulations. These posh resorts represented a hybrid of the modern, the indigenous, the Indonesian, and the Balinese. They were the foundation of cultural heritage tourism in Bali, albeit in its commodified form.

Abidin Kusno's (2000) recent study of architecture, design, and politics in Indonesia shows how the use of cultural heritage by Sukarno and Suharto extended notions of the predominance of the state and nation over the local in cultural heritage. Taman Mini Indonesia, the theme park in Jakarta promoted by Suharto's wife, sought to resurrect local culture but within the very constrained political confines of the New Order government, which demanded unity over diversity. Had not the financial crisis intervened, there would have been plans for other Nusa Dua-like complexes in other strategic tourism locations in Indonesia, all helping to push cultural heritage to the forefront of the larger effort to move the nation from developing to developed nation status. The whispers of discontent that "real" culture and heritage was being subsumed under this corporate/theme park approach were not enough to challenge this approach. It required the economic and subsequent political crises of 1997 and 1998 to thwart the movement.

Tourism in the Era of Crisis

Beginning in late 1997, the collapse of the tourism economy was prevalent throughout Indonesia, although this collapse must be seen as a multistage process. While tourism in Indonesia consists of both a foreign and domestic market, it is the level of international tourism that is a determinant of its economic impact. Available data on foreign tourists in Indonesia between 1996 and 2000 indicates that the drop in tourism from the events of 1997 and 1998 was modest and short-lived, especially given the depth and duration of the crises affecting Indonesia. A sharp drop in foreign tourism occurred between 1997 and 1998, with a loss of approximately 11% from the record 5.185 million in 1997. By 2000, however, overall foreign tourism nearly returned to the 1997 record level. Available evidence suggests that the impacts of international terrorism after September 11 produced an impact as discouraging as the foreign tourist decline in 1998. Unlike the previous crises that could be readily connected to internal matters, the impact of international terrorism on tourism had a global dimension, with Indonesia's misery being shared by many other destinations. (*Statfor GeoEconomic Analysis* 27 October 2001; Crampton 2001). Although the full impact of the September 11 incident has not been assessed, what is notable from select data is how resilient Indonesia's tourism sector was in the face of multiple crises. In the case of two key Indonesian destinations, Bali and Bantam, tourism actually thrived in the midst of the pre-September 11 crises (see *Indonesia Tourism Market Database* 2001).

From 1996 to 2000, foreign arrivals at Bali's Ngurah Rai airport grew from 1.194 million to 1.468 million persons, with a modest drop (approximately 47,000 persons) between 1997 and 1998. Batam also maintained its role as an important foreign tourist destination for those entering by sea. Unlike Bali, Batam reached its peak of 1.248 foreign arrivals in 1999, and fell off only slightly to 1.134 million in 2000. But it is important that the year 2000 figure was greater than either 1996 or 1997. It was the increase in arrivals of Singapore residents that sustained Batam's foreign tourist growth, with the number of Singaporeans increasing from 597,453 in 1996 to 742,272 in 2000. (Note the drop off after 2002: 1.5 million in 2004, 1 million in 2005).

The real victims of Indonesian crises were the urban tourism markets, notably Jakarta, Bandung, Surabaya, and Makassar, places where the political battles and ethnic conflicts were played out. In 1996, the capital city attracted 1.565 million foreign arrivals. That figure declined slightly in 1997 to 1.457 million, probably related to the effects of smoke and haze generated by the fires in Kalimantan and Sumatra. It was in September 1997 that an ill-fated Garuda flight from Jakarta crashed into the mountains near Medan because of the haze. In 1998, the number of arrivals fell to 883,000 persons, a drop of 39%. Over the next year, the Jakarta arrivals fell another 7% before picking up in 2000 to regain part of the previous loss and record slightly more than one million arrivals. It is significant that 2000 saw the Indonesian economy recover partially from the 1998 to 1999 collapse, although it was a partial and short-lived reversal. While arrival figures for other urban tourism centers in Java, Sumatra, Kalimantan, and Sulawesi are not available, available data on hotel occupancies from other urban tourism centers, especially Yogjakarta, Medan, Surabaya, and Makassar, suggest that all of these markets have been hard hit by the crises.

It is probably not coincidental that these urban areas have been featured in the international media as centers of social and political unrest. The image of urban mobs, coupled with such antitourism acts as the recent threat of "sweeps" aimed at driving foreign tourists out of the country, certainly helps to explain a part of the fall-off in foreign and domestic tourism visits (*Detikworld* 18 December 2000). It is the local environment for tourism that has become an ever more important factor under a newly implemented system of decentralization in Indonesia, and this change requires a whole new set of strategies and a dramatic orientation of the tourism industry. This is especially important now because expanded tourism, especially aimed at foreign arrivals, is recognized as a sustainable approach to economic recovery in Indonesia.

Decentralization and Democratization: The Indigenous Movement

In January 2001, Indonesia implemented two legislative acts that had been promulgated in 1999 (Law 22/99 and Law 25/99) which together greatly expanded the powers and responsibilities of district (*kabupaten*) and city (*kota*) governments. Law 22/99 consolidated central government offices with their local counterparts, including tourism (*dinas pariwisata*), ending decades of a system that had made central government the dominant player in local governance. Law 22/99 made the local governments fully responsible for developing and implementing programs, including tourism. This change in local government responsibilities occurred when Indonesia was in the throes of a severe economic crisis and on-going political instability, and so primary attention has focused on initiatives to tackle directly local unemployment and to provide basic services, with no attention to tourism. Under Law 25/99, the central government shifted the process for providing financial support to local needs from a system of targeted grants and direct payment of the costs of all government salaries to a single block grant to local governments known as the Public Allocation Fund (Dana Alokasi Umum: DAU). This new fund covers salaries, development projects, and other routine expenditures, with locally generated revenues (PAD) providing additional necessary funds. For most localities, however, locally generated revenues represent a small proportion of overall revenues, in most cases less than 30%. Indeed, what many localities discovered under decentralization is that the costs of all local employees (including those transferred from the central government offices to the local offices) coming from local revenues leaves them with far less for nonpersonnel expenditures than before (see Usman 2001; Saad 2001; Silver et al. 2001).

There are exceptions, however. For example, districts rich in resources – for example, Kutai in East Kalimantan (which recently was divided into three smaller districts) – have benefited from the redistribution of revenues derived from the extraction of gas, timber, and mining. Under the pre-2001 system, these revenues went entirely to Jakarta, but now they are shared with the localities from which the revenues are derived based upon a fixed formula. For the great majority of localities that lack these natural resources, there is a natural tendency to regard the formula for DAU as unfair and to favor a system that sends more funds to Jakarta, where they would potentially be redistributed to resource-poor areas. The real problem is not so much an unfair DAU formula but rather declining domestic revenues overall coupled with negligible locally generated revenues that in some cases had fallen in recent years. Declining tourism contributed to lost local revenues. In many of the resource-deficient areas of Indonesia, the opportunity to increase local revenues through greater tourism is more important than ever under the revised public financing processes since enactment of Law 25/1999.

Locally generated revenues from taxes were changed through tax reform legislation that was implemented just prior to the onset of the fiscal crisis in 1997. In essence, the reform removed unproductive local taxes that appeared to cost more to collect than was actually collected. The consolidation of local taxes into a smaller number of sources (the most important being land tax, hotel tax, restaurant tax, and license fees) seemed a reasonable move at the time, and was justified as a necessary modernization effort. Recent data suggest that the localities with the highest locally generated revenues are also those with the strongest base in tourism. The Badung and Giandyar districts in Bali, for example, had significantly more locally generated revenue than any other areas in Indonesia in 2001. Conversely, those areas where the tourist trade is small are able to secure far less in their own source revenues. This suggests that the strength of tourism at the local level can have a positive impact on local financial resources.

The other half of the equation – as local funding decisions replaced those of central government – was a continuing push for increased democratization of the entire political process. From 1999 through the elections of 2004, Indonesia changed from a country where all political decisions flowed from the central government without popular participation (and where there was really only one viable political party), to a system where the local legislature, the provincial and national legislatures, the major, district heads and governors, and then in 2004 the president and vice president, were elected by popular vote.

Locally Focused Tourism

How did these events affect tourism, especially in cities and towns in Indonesia? Certain internal and external factors have exerted influence, not all of which any individual locality has the capacity to control. For example, the Bali districts benefited from the overall growth in tourism in the province from 1997 to 2000 because of a combination of good value at low prices because of the weakness of the rupiah, and also because initially Bali communities avoided association with the political, ethnic, and environmental crises that so afflicted other places in the archipelago. Moreover, Bali localities had the unique advantage of receiving most foreign arrivals directly through its own airport, connecting to the large Australian and Japanese markets. During 2000, Bali hotels averaged between 85 and 95% occupancy whereas during the same period Yogjakarta star hotels were ranging between 40 and 60% occupancy, which was an increase from the average occupancy in Yogjakarta of 24.8% in 1998 and 30.45% in 1999. It is important to note that Central Java experienced some of the most vehement antiforeigner protests during this period. Cities such as Yogjakarta and Solo were among the popular tourist destinations which westerners were warned by their consulates to avoid. Although various militants had threatened to sweep hotels of foreign guests, focusing especially on the city of Solo, the threats were never carried out. But the perception of danger for foreign tourists had the effect of literally turning off the tourism faucet. In contrast, Bali resorts never experienced that problem (*Jakarta Post* 22 October 2000).

Yet Bali was decimated in the wake of the October 2002 bombing of Paddy's Bar in Kuta (Bali) which killed 200 people; virtually all tourists left immediately; and less than one-half of the number of tourists that had been anticipated in November showed up, with many hotels under 10% occupancy, and this in the face of a continuing national economic crisis that had elevated the cost of everything. The only way that Bali was able to rebuild part of its tourism base by 2003 was to offer deep discounts to Asian visitors (up to 50%) and this had mixed results since they tended, unlike westerners who had disappeared altogether, to move beyond the commercial areas into the villages and interior areas (i.e., locally based tourism). The Bali bombing rippled into Yogjakarta in Central Java, where according to the Director of the Indonesian Culture and Tourism Board, about 45% of the small shopkeepers and vendors went bankrupt after the Bali bombing incident. Later, the Marriott and the Australian embassy bombings in Jakarta kept this fear factor alive.

Expanding the tourism potential of localities is directly tied to political stability at the local and national levels, however, and political stability, as long as it is not achieved through totalitarian means, is closely linked to public welfare and ultimately human rights. As previously noted, the politics of protest since the fall of the Suharto regime have tended to include explicit antioutsider sentiments, with arguments propagated among some government critics that foreign investment is a move toward a new form of economic and political colonialism. In other words, localism has trumped globalism. Yet tourism-based economic development has also offered the greatest opportunity for local multipliers, for bringing foreign exchange with minimal loss to outflows, and strengthening local political identity. While there is evidence of some leakage in foreign exchange, displacement of labor, price inflation, and economic volatility in localities that are overreliant upon tourism (see Hall 1994), within Indonesia only Bali localities, and possibly Lombok and Yogjakarta, possess even the potential for these sorts of negative externalities. In general, the current level of reliance of other cities and districts on tourism as a component of local economic development is well below its potential to generate positive externalities. Indeed, there is much more evidence that tourism generates new small-scale enterprises that directly benefit the host community (Cushnahan 1999). But this does not mean that if localities build hotels, and advertise that they have nice beaches, the tourists will come. There are too many examples in Indonesia of government-built hotels and resorts in the 1970s and 1980s that were situated in attractive localities but remained virtually empty most of the time. Local perceptions of assets and liabilities are filtered through the cultural and political norms of that locality and may be completely out of step with potential foreign tourist markets. If marketed, these local assets may be presented to potential tourists in ways that may not adequately convey their attraction. To benefit from tourism investments, localities must understand better their market, their strengths as a destination that relate to that market, what is necessary in the way of investments to secure its market, and how tourism assets relate to those of its competitors and its natural allies in other localities.

But how is this done? First, a correction must be made, for there is one important structural impediment to local engagement in tourism outside of the destinations directly served by foreign carriers that must be recognized: The local transportation system has relatively little access to external markets. Most Indonesian cities and towns, except for Jakarta, Batam, Medan, Menado, and localities in Bali, lack direct overseas airline connections. As a result, most localities (including the cultural center of Yogjakarta) are reliant upon the domestic transportation system to provide access to the foreign tourist market. Yet under decentralization, local governments have relatively less capacity to influence directly the domestic transportation system than under the previous centralized system. Transportation services have been disrupted by the economic crises, with a fall-off in air travel and greater demands on rail and bus service. Overall, there has been a significant reduction in domestic flights to many urban destinations since 1997.

Therefore, how can cities and districts take advantage of tourism to support economic development, revenue generation, and urban revitalization under such unfavorable conditions? A necessary precondition for localities to utilize tourism as an economic development strategy is to have access to a more thorough understanding of possible markets and to devise plans to utilize local resources to make the tourism sector operate effectively. For the most part, however, local leaders do not understand what it takes to accomplish this, and the current system lacks the institutional mechanisms to make it work. Decentralization has placed tremendous new responsibilities on local government to manage the tourism sector but without any precedents to draw upon or any viable models to emulate. The logical response for local governments would be to lodge responsibility for expanded tourism in either the tourism agency (*dinas pariwisata*) or within the local planning board (*bappeda*).

But neither of these agencies alone is capable of managing the multisectoral nature of tourism, especially in growing urban areas and under such challenging political, social, and economic circumstances. A more effective mechanism would be to establish independent, quasigovernment urban tourism corporations with revenue-generating capabilities and with leadership drawn from the key local stakeholders (government, the business community, labor groups, and the transportation sector). This group would be responsible for identifying the requirements of marketing and promotion by the tourism agency, determining infrastructure and public service needs through the local planning and public works agencies, and proposing intervention that would bolster local tourism capacity, including structuring public–private partnerships for tourism-related investments.

One way to ensure a higher level of expertise among the many local novices in Indonesia's tourism trade is to establish networks of local destinations through collaborative planning and cooperative projects. Local tourism networks must respect the autonomy of cities and districts inherent under decentralization, but this can be a device to promote greater collaboration between localities that are linked within particular geographic regions through the transportation system or that offer potential synergies to attract increased tourism. The idea of *local tourism networks* offers an innovative approach to overcoming local deficiencies and strengthening the tourism component of local economic development throughout Indonesia, not just in the established tourism centers. Yet to utilize an approach such as a local tourism network requires some fundamental changes in the conception of tourism, the planning process, and local governance. Some of the changes in the local mindset necessary to utilize local tourism networks are as follows: (1) embrace the idea of localities as a tourism object in their own right; (2) treat tourism as a legitimate and key component of local economic development; (3) utilize a planning process that recognizes the interconnectivity of localities especially with regard to the infrastructure, service, and marketing components of tourism; and (4) promote a participatory planning and implementation process that enables the full range of local stakeholders to identify benefits from local tourism development.

The challenge confronting localities in Indonesia under the new system is to strengthen interjurisdiction cooperation rather than competition in tourism. In the context of Indonesia's struggle to promote overall development within a decentralized governance structure, cooperation rather than competition offers a more appropriate and viable strategy. The competitive model assumes that there is a fixed market and that local efforts should be geared toward gaining a great share.

In the case of Indonesia, the net effect of local tourism networks should not be to strengthen any one region's share of a fixed tourism market, but rather to create attractive new opportunities throughout Indonesia that will appeal to a larger segment of the global and local tourism markets. In other words, local tourism networks would expand the number and diversity of destinations, facilitate investments that would improve conditions in larger geographic areas, and help to overcome the growing separateness of localities that seems to have been engendered in the initial experiences with decentralization. Importantly, tourism development on a local basis would stimulate respect for local cultural heritage and could lead to a heritage management model whereby Indonesia's pluralism would become its signal asset. Local tourism would drive overall national tourism development rather than each locality just trying to get its share of the existing pie (Ashworth 1989).

There are some obvious and less obvious geographical configurations for potential local tourism networks in Indonesia that would expand the range of options for foreign tourists. The ten examples listed below are merely indicative of an approach that shows how local tourism networks would create new configurations that cross traditional, provincial, cultural, and political boundaries. Each is also premised on provision of an integrated transportation system to facilitate access by tourists within a designated geographical region, and that these would in turn be integrated into a national network. Moreover, each cluster would likely include a substantial larger grouping of localities than is implied by those identified in the list itself. These key actors would likely encourage other localities to play a role within the network, especially when involvement benefited all partners. The important point is that through a system of local tourism networks the potential tourist centers in Indonesia would be enlarged appreciably from the current level, that investments in public infrastructure and private facilities would be geared to a larger geographical area through coordinated efforts, and that the interaction of highly skilled tourism communities with novices in a collaborative endeavor would lead to an overall expansion of tourism in Indonesia's localities.

Local tourism networks in Indonesia, based upon a combination of geographical proximity and cultural diversity could include the following clusters:

1. Jabotabek–Baten–Bandarlampung
2. Bandung–Sukabumi–Cirebon
3. Yogjakarta–Solo–Semarang
4. Surabaya–Malang
5. Denpasar–Mataram–Maumere–Kupang
6. Padang–Bukittinggi
7. Balikpapan–Samarinda
8. Makassar–Pare Pare–Menado–Ambon
9. Medan metropolitan region
10. Batam region

Conclusion: Decentralization, Cultural Heritage, and Tourism

Decentralization and democratization in Indonesia have transformed the role of local government from that of implementing national development objectives defined largely through the central government agencies in Jakarta to one of serving local community needs as identified by local stakeholders. This is not to deny national expectations and values but rather to acknowledge that these derive from a multitude of local sources.

Under the governance and financing schemes for decentralization set forth in Law 22/1999 and Law 25/1999, localities are afforded new responsibilities to govern their affairs, provided a commitment of limited central government funding to carry out a larger share of responsibilities, and afforded the legal means to devise their own approach to meeting those responsibilities. In other words, Indonesia's approach to handling local versus national (or minority vs. majority) interests has been to move in the direction of localization. There is a clear human rights benefit here as local communities gain voice and claim the right to represent their own heritage as distinct from that of urban centers or the nation as a whole. Because of its extensive and varied assets, Indonesia represents one of the leading tourist destinations in the world. As recently as the mid-1990s, prior to the demise of the New Order regime, it was anticipated that tourism would soon overtake oil and other natural resource exports and textiles as the leading generator of foreign currency in Indonesia (Booth 1990). A powerful economic force, tourism can enable the diversity of cultural expression.

As demonstrated by the data presented above, Indonesia's tourism sector struggled under the weight of the multiple crises of an economic collapse, a massive environmental disaster, extensive political turmoil, and ethnic conflicts between 1997 and 2005. At the same time, however, localities struggled to provide for their basic needs under the new governance and finance systems, and searched in desperation for workable solutions to increasing fiscal and service provision challenges. Strengthening the involvement of localities through networking arrangements in tourism offers not only some short-term solution to local fiscal problems but introduces a new cooperative model that allows decentralization and local autonomy to flourish while knitting together into a new fabric the political and cultural diversity that is the strength and the uniqueness of Indonesia.

The end of the authoritarian regime of Suharto's New Order government and the subsequent democratic movement coincided with a severe disruption of the tourism market, and with a variety of cultural clashes throughout the Indonesian archipelago. To mitigate these circumstances, is it necessary to utilize an authoritarian or at least a centrally controlled heritage/tourism/political system to ensure that the necessary social stability is achieved? Is democracy antithetical to cultural heritage and preservation of human rights, given the abuses that have accompanied the political and economic transformation of Indonesia since 1998? The democracy movement obviously contributed to a period of political and social destabilization, but there are widespread examples of the democracy movement reinvigorating Indonesia's cultural diversity and cultural heritage, which had been submerged under a political definition of Indonesia linked to colonialism, nationalism, and modernization movements from the early twentieth century. A new paradigm of local decision making where citizen participation is not just ceremonial but substantive is one key to the transformative power of Indonesia's democratic movement and the transformation of the style and substance of cultural tourism.

A powerful new localism has emerged in Indonesia and with it the potential to create a sustainable heritage movement that is far more respectful of local tradition. But this new localism has created new points of conflict between cultural heritage, tourism, and human rights. One recent example involved a proposal to construct an art market, known as "Java World," to improve facilities at the UNESCO World Heritage site of Borobudor in Central Java. Proponents of the art market project contended that it would help to conserve the temple site by restricting vendors to a designated space separate from the monument, with parking for automobiles and buses, and where tourists could board a train to visit the site. Opponents included many local artists who objected to this commercial enterprise and also local villagers and vendors who saw the Java World project as a direct threat to the hawkers who would be removed from the site and thus denied their customary livelihood. The project leadership in the Central Java government contended that the project was "meant for public welfare," and some preservationists regarded it as a way to eliminate some of the negative environmental conditions from this revered site. Critics contended it was just a revenue generator for local government at the expense of jobs in the informal sector. The values of tourism for economic development, preservation of a cultural icon, and social justice for hundreds of poor hawkers clashed in the controversy over Java World. This was not a new circumstance in Indonesia, since many of the "megaprojects," such as the Nusa Dua complex in Bali, had also met some local resistance initially on cultural and political grounds. But what was different in this tourism development controversy was the ability of the nongovernmental organizations (NGOs) to mount a successful opposition to the project on environmental, cultural, and social justice grounds and to effectively counter the government's efforts. The new democratic localism in Indonesia had empowered the previously powerless to stand up for a different set of values around not just tourist-related developments but in a full range of new responsibilities of local government.

A commitment to safeguard human rights has emerged as one of the objectives of the new localism transforming Indonesia. It also has altered fundamentally the approach to tourism throughout Indonesia, greatly elevating the role of local interests over the previously dominant role of national governments and large corporations with government backing. As Indonesia further consolidates its indigenous democratic system, its tourist resources will be transformed as well. In what manner this transformation occurs will vary by locality. But what seems likely is that there will be a greater range of destinations where local cultural institutions are likely to be far more evident: tourist destinations that not only entertain but also educate. The result may be to transform Indonesian tourism into an institution that reflects more precisely the nation's cultural heritage and that supports human rights in new and important ways.

References

Agence France Presse, 21 May 2001, Garuda Indonesia Posts 90.3 Percent Plunge in Net Profits for 2000.

—, 19 September 2001, Asian Tourism Industry in Tatters of the Devastating U.S. Attacks.

Ashworth, Gregory, 1989, Urban Tourism: An Imbalance in Attention. In *Progress in Tourism, Recreation and Hospitality Management*, vol. 1, edited by C. P. Cooper and A. Lockwood, pp. 33–44. Wiley, Chichester.

Booth, A., 1990, The Tourism Boom in Indonesia. *Bulletin of Indonesian Economic Studies* 26(3): 45–73.

Crampton, T., 2001, Asian Tourism in Unchartered Territory. *International Herald Tribune*, 21 September 2001.

Cushnahan, G., 1999, Independent Travel and Small-Scale Tourism Development in the 21st Century: An Indonesian Case Study of Some Directions. In *Pariwisata Indonesia: Menghadapi Abad XXI*, vol. 3, edited by O. S. Santoso, pp. 64–74. Pusat Penelitian Kepariwisataan, Bandung, Indonesia.

Dahles, H., 1997, Urban Tourism and Image Management in Yogjakarta: National Development, Cultural Heritage and Presentation of a Tourist Product. In *Pariwisata Indonesia: Berbagai Aspek dan Gagasan Pembangunan*, edited by Myra Gunawan, pp. 5–28. Pusat Penelitian Kepariwisataan, Institute of Technology Bandung, Bandung.

Darling, D., March 2003, Micro-History of Tourism in Bali. *Latitudes*, 1.

Detikworld, 18 December 2000, Lasker Jihad Attack Cafés in Solo, Provokes Backlash.

Hall, Colin Michael, 1994, *Tourism in the Pacific Rim: Development, Impacts and Markets*. Longman/Wiley, Melbourne.

Indonesia, Ministry of Culture and Tourism, 2001, *Indonesia Tourism Market Database 2001*. Jakarta.

Jakarta Post, 23 August 2000, Poso Leaders Buy Hatchets for Peace Before Gus Dur.

—, 22 October 2000, Hotels in Yogjakarta, Bali See Higher Occupancy.

—, 18 December 2000, Ambonese Are Haunted by Rumors of Holiday Riots.

—, 9 January 2006, Batam Tourism in Doldrums.

Jansen, F., 1997, Urban Tourism in Bandung. In *Pariwisata Indonesia: Berbagai Aspek dan Gagasan Pembangunan*, edited by M. Gunawan, pp. 107–119. Pusat Penelitian Kepariwisataan, Institute of Technology Bandung, Bandung, Indonesia.

Johannen, U. and Gomez, J., eds., 2001, *Democratic Transitions in Asia*. Select Books, Singapore.

Kusno, Abidin, 2000, *Behind the Postcolonial: Architecture, Urban Space and Political Cultures*. Routledge, New York.

Maher, M., 2000, *Indonesia: An Eyewitness Account*. Viking, New York.

Saad, Ilyas, 2001, Indonesia's Decentralization Policy: The Budget Allocation and Its Implications for the Business Environment. SMERU Research Institute, Jakarta, 2 September.

Silver, C., I. J. Azis, and L. Schroeder, 2001, Intergovernmental Transfers and Decentralization in Indonesia. *Bulletin of Indonesian Economic Studies* 37(3): 345–362.

Statfor GeoEconomic Analysis, 27 October 2001, Declining Tourism Widespread Threat to Stability.

Straits-Times (Singapore), 9 July 2000, Special Report on Mob Violence in Jakarta.

The Economist, 6 February 2003, Lured Back to Bali: After the Bomb, Indonesia Finds a New Type of Tourist.

The Times (UK), 24 February 2001, Migrants Flee Dayak Head-Hunters.

Usman, S., 2001, Indonesia's Decentralization Policy: Initial Experiences and Emerging Problems. SMERU Research Institute, Jakarta.

Chapter 5
Transnational Diaspora and Rights of Heritage

Charles E. Orser, Jr.

Introduction

The sweep of history has witnessed the movement of large numbers of people over vast territories, beginning with the first hominid migrations. Post-Columbian history also has had its share of mass migrations, and these more recent migrational events have resulted in culture contact situations around the globe, as European superpowers have sought wealth and power in various colonial enterprises. The United States itself has seen at least four waves of mass immigration prior to the beginning of the twenty-first century. Through time, disparate peoples entered North America: colonialist northern Europeans and Iberians, enslaved Africans, Irish and Asians, and the so-called "new immigrants" from eastern and southern Europe. These migrations, stretching in time from the sixteenth to the early twentieth century, have defined the cultural history of the continent.

Scholars often refer to situations where immigrants did not necessarily choose to leave their homelands as *diasporas* to distinguish them from the more-or-less volunteer resettlements that have occurred as part of colonial projects. Africans were violently removed from their native landscapes and taken in shackles across the Atlantic; Irish immigrants were forced to move because of political oppression and food shortages; Jews fled murderous programs in eastern Europe and, ultimately, the Holocaust. Many immigrants simply fled their homelands seeking freedom from economic and cultural oppression. The precise circumstances of removal and resettlement were unique for each population – and even distinctive within each population – and accompanied by a particular set of historical push/pull factors. Nevertheless, the relevant, overarching similarity among all diasporas rests in the fact of mass population migration.

The reality of intercontinental diasporas cannot be overlooked by scholars seeking to understand the sociocultural history of the modern era. A global perspective is especially pertinent for modern-world archeologists (Orser 1996). The archeology of the nineteenth-century Overseas Chinese in western America analyzed without reference to the circumstances of then-contemporary China, for instance, would be incomplete and ultimately unsatisfactory (Orser 2007). Failure to acknowledge the trans-oceanic connections would effectively remove the Chinese Americans from their history and deny them cultural competence, history, and longevity.

H. Silverman and D. F. Ruggles (eds.), *Cultural Heritage and Human Rights.*
© Springer 2007

The occurrence of diasporas in history is important for scholars of history to recognize in their research and interpretation. Archeologists interested in cultural patrimony and heritage rights also must acknowledge and confront the difficult questions posed by diasporic history. Should members of diasporas have rights when it comes to decisions about the management and use of sites and properties in their (and their ancestors') original homeland? And if so, what are these rights? Do participants of diasporas have a stake in the heritage issues of the homeland, and if so, should such considerations extend to their descendants? If rights should have generational validity, how many generations should be "relevant"? Should third-generation diaspora descendants have a voice in the preservation and even interpretation of their ancestors' identified homesite? Each diaspora has a cultural heritage both in the homeland and created anew in the host country. The right to express and seek heritage is a fundamental, though not unproblematic, human right.

Questions such as these defy easy answers, and heritage rights scholars and archeologists have yet to consider them seriously. An example from the Republic of Ireland illustrates the complexities that may arise by the occurrence of relatively recent diasporas in which both the immigrants and their descendants – living in widely separated locales – can be identified.

The Irish Diaspora and Ballykilcline Townland

Historians of Ireland debate whether the term "diaspora" is applicable to the Irish situation, and the term has acquired a political meaning depending upon how one wishes to view the linkage between England and Ireland (Brighton 2005: 41–42). The precise nomenclature of the trans-Atlantic movement of Irish men, women, and children outside Ireland is less important than the reality that thousands of them left their homes in Ireland and traveled to the United States, Canada, Australia, and elsewhere throughout the world. Historians of American immigration tend to conceptualize the entry of the Irish in four temporally defined periods: pre-1814, prefamine, famine era (late 1840s), and postfamine (Miller 1985). At least one writer has considered "Ireland" synonymous with "diaspora," and has argued that the island is both a real and a remembered diasporic site (O'Toole 1999: 12).

The general outline of the movement of thousands of Irish out of Ireland can be written in broad strokes as a global phenomenon, but each family in the mass migration came from a distinct place. Each historical account of removal, though perhaps similar in general, was unique in its particulars. Ballykilcline townland in northern County Roscommon was one such place. The townland was only one of many removed from the landscape in the mid-nineteenth century and thus is not unique. In other ways, however, Ballykilcline is utterly special. The nature of Ballykilcline's descendant community today makes it especially unparalleled because this community's self-identified, inherited membership amplifies questions about the role of diasporic descendants in the protection and preservation of cultural heritage.

The concept of the Irish townland extends at least to the twelfth century; townlands were a common feature on the landscape by the early nineteenth century (Connell et al. 1998: 10; McErlean 1983). At the height of their existence in mid-nineteenth century Ireland – before the massive depopulation of the late 1840s – some 62,000 townlands, consisting of fields and houses, existed in Ireland. Their rural residents considered them to constitute the central point of personal reference and self-identification. Life in the rural townlands was characterized by a seasonal cycle of religious festivals and agricultural practices that promoted cooperation and cohesion (Danaher 1972; O'Dowd 1981).

At its largest size in 1845, Ballykilcline consisted of about 243 ha, and was inhabited by about 500 people. The remains of ringforts and crannogs in the townland indicate that people had lived in the area long before the nineteenth century (O'Conor 2001: 337). Two nineteenth century maps (dated 1836 and 1837) help to substantiate the longevity of settlement at Ballykilcline. The word "bally" (*baile* in Irish) in "Ballykilcline" indicates that the nineteenth century townland was probably created by the union of four quarters. Seventeenth century land divisions in the Province of Connacht, which includes County Roscommon, were usually identified, in decreasing size, as *baile*, quarter, *cartron*, and *gnive* (with 1 baile = 4 quarters = 16 cartrons = 24 gnives) (McErlean 1983: 320). The maps record three and possibly four quarters at Ballykilcline in the 1830s: Killtullyvary, or Bungariff, Aghamore, and Barravally.

Ballykilcline was one of several parcels of land leased to Nicholas Mahon in the 1650s as part of the Cromwellian colonization of the west of Ireland (Hanley 1961: 228). Mahon was an "improving" landlord who collected rents from hundreds of tenant farmers living in the surrounding countryside. These twice-yearly rents allowed Mahon to build a large Palladian mansion and to live the elite lifestyle that befitted a member of the Anglo-Ireland ascendancy (Barnard 2004). Young (1780: 184), writing in the late eighteenth century, noted that the Mahons, like many other "improvers," had planted numerous trees, bushes, and shrubs on their demesne. These plantings substantially altered the landscape and helped to transform the immediate region into an Anglo-Irish space (Orser 2004: 206).

Young (1780: 184) also described the Mahons' tenants as fairly unmotivated workers who lived in poor houses and who subsisted on "potatoes, milk, and butter." Visiting the same area a few years later, Wakefield (1812: 274) found the cabins of the tenants "most wretched." The people were "superabundant" and "miserable," and their land was segmented into "very minute divisions." Weld (1832: 317), who surveyed County Roscommon for the Royal Dublin Society in 1830, reported that conditions among Mahon's tenants were better than they had been during Wakefield's tour, though "want and wretchedness . . . are by no means obliterated entirely."

Denis Mahon, ancestor of Nicholas, lost the lease to Ballykilcline on 1 May 1834, and immediately began negotiating with the Crown for its extension. The two sides could not agree on a new arrangement, and so later that year Ballykilcline came under the direct control of the British Crown. Beginning in 1834, then, the townland was administered by His (and later Her) Majesty's Commissioners of Woods, Forests, Land Revenues, Works, and Buildings. Ballykilcline was a Crown Estate as of this date.

Upon taking control of Ballykilcline, the Commissioners' agents discovered that they would have significant difficulty collecting the rents. Agrarian unrest was nothing new in either Ireland or County Roscommon, and underground protective associations – calling themselves Threshers, Carders, Rockites, Ribbonmen, and White Boys – were present in one form or another within the county (Coleman 1999). Membership of Ballykilcline residents in such organizations is unknown, but eight members of the townland did organize a rent strike in 1835. Their actions, while perhaps not part of the agenda of a broader organization, certainly were consistent with the perspectives of such organizations.

The Commissioners sought to end the rent strike as quickly as possible, and issued notices to the tenants requiring them to surrender possession of their holdings. Fifty-two of the "74 tenancies" identified by the Crown complied and their residents were reinstated as "caretakers" with a small monthly allowance. One condition of this arrangement was that the tenants, now simply called "occupiers," were required to surrender possession immediately upon the Crown's demand. The eight original "ringleaders" of the strike, however, "absolutely refused to give up the Possession or to account with the Crown's Receivers for the Value of the Holdings in their Occupation" (House of Lords 1847: 4). When the Crown's receivers visited the tenants, most refused to surrender their homes, including many of those who had originally agreed to the caretaker arrangement.

The British government decided to institute legal proceedings against eight "ringleaders" and ordered their arrest. The tenants made a formal petition to the Commissioners asking them to forgive their actions, arguing that they had been victimized by "high, enormous rents." They further noted, however, that if the commissioners did not agree to forgive their arrears payments, they would be forced to send a petition directly to "Her most Gracious and Illustrious Majesty [Queen Victoria], tending to the Fraud and Imposition they are subjected to" (House of Lords 1847: 20).

Instead of accepting the terms of the petition, the Commissioners began to press for a legal solution to the rebellion, and in their official records they began to refer to the tenants as "Intruders on the Crown Lands of Ballykilcline." The semantic shift from "tenants" to "caretakers" to "occupiers" to "intruders" accurately charts the history of Ballykilcline in the 1830s and 1840s.

The tenants continued to resist, even though they knew that eviction was a strong possibility. After the sheriff had arrested one of the so-called ringleaders, the tenants openly rebelled and attacked the police station. The tenants continued to refuse to pay rent, and in May 1844, the bailiffs found the tenants increasingly willing to defend their homes with violence. The bailiffs "were attacked by the Tenants, and not having the Protection of the Police were obliged to retreat, after only effecting the Service of Six or Seven of the Notices, and were it not that by chance they met a few Policemen on Duty they would certainly have been killed, as it was the greatest Difficulty and fixed Bayonets that the Police could keep the Mob from them" (House of Lords 1847: 50). The tenants were "armed with Sticks, Stones, and Shovels" and used "threatening Language" against the bailiffs. The exasperated agent then sought permission to evict the tenants and either to lock or to "throw down the Houses of the refractory Tenants . . . [to] make an Example among them" (House of Lords 1847: 53).

Faced with the reality that the tenants were in a state of open rebellion, the Commissioners decided that mass eviction was the only solution to the "Ballykilcline problem." The tenants must have realized that they were out of options, because on 12 May 1846, they sent a petition to the Commissioners describing themselves as "459 Individuals of moral industrious Habits, exemplary, obedient, and implicit to their Landlady or Landlord, which is the Cause of bringing them into Contempt, but are penitent and regretful for any Misunderstanding which has occurred in the Event of the Case in question" (House of Lords 1847: 73). By this date, however, the potato blight had reached County Roscommon and, like thousands of others across the island, the tenants of Ballykilcline found it impossible to pay their rents or even to feed their families.

The Ballykilcline Evictions and Archeology

As early as May 1844, the authorities had attempted to resolve the rent strike by locking the cabin doors of the so-called "ringleaders." They used "Iron Hasps and Staples and Locks" to secure the doors, but when the evictees reoccupied their homes shortly afterward, George Knox, the Crown's estate agent, decided that a stronger alternative was necessary. He advocated leveling the houses to make them uninhabitable: "I have now ascertained that nothing short of levelling the Houses of these refractory People will ever bring them into Subjection" (House of Lords 1847: 65). In February 1847, the Attorney General for Ireland, observing that the tenants appeared to believe that "the Crown either is unable or unwilling to turn them out," asked the Lord Lieutenant to set a firm date for the tenants' removal (House of Lords 1847: 86). The tenants, acknowledging that ejectment was likely, petitioned the Crown asking either to be allowed to stay in their homes or else to be provided with the means to emigrate, in a manner "similar to that which has been lately practised by the landlords in the vicinity" (Ellis 1977: 11). In February, the authorities stated that "the Houses in which the Defendants [the "ringleaders"] reside should be levelled to the Ground and the Materials removed so as to prevent them being rebuilt" (House of Lords 1847: 88). The doors and windows thus were removed from the houses (Ellis 1977: 11). Two or three houses were repaired and renovated as police barracks, and Griffith's (1857) posteviction valuation survey indicates that only five dwellings – three houses, one "Herd's" house, and a "Police-barrack" – remained at Ballykilcline in the 1850s.

The Ballykilcline tenants were evicted in four groups, beginning in September 1847 and ending in March 1848. As of 1847, the families at Ballykilcline had been in arrears from between 9.5 and 12 years. Those families in arrears for 12 years constitute the cohort who initiated or at least originally agreed with the strike action. The Crown termed this cohort the "Defendants," and judged them to be the "most violent and dangerous ringleaders in the county, sure to cause continued unrest" (Ballykilcline Society 2001). This group was the first to be ejected. After removal, the tenants traveled to Dublin then to Liverpool; from there they embarked for New York in five ships (*Roscius*, 19 September 1847; *Metoka*, 26 September 1847; *Channing*, 13 March 1848; *Progress*, 25 April 1848; and *Creole*, 18 October 1848). In all, 366 individuals can be identified as being aboard these five vessels (189 males, 177 females). In a petition filed after eviction, but before emigration, the tenants of Ballykilcline reported that they were "deprived of their cabins, and lying out in the open air with their starvation for want of food and raiment" (Scally 1995: 94).

A plat completed in 1836 for the Crown's agents permits an analysis of the spatial realities of the Ballykilcline eviction. The first eviction emptied large plots of land in the east-central portion of the townland, as well as a medium-sized plot in the center and a small plot on the west side. Both the eastern fields and the small plot on the west side were situated at or near important crossroads that allowed access to the townland's interior. The records compiled by the Crown's agents during the rent strike indicate that they were concerned about gaining and maintaining access to the townland, and that they viewed the roads as strategically significant. The second eviction cleared the eastern part of the townland, on both sides of the road into the interior, and in the northern section at a cluster of houses. The third eviction appears to have been designed to empty those settled portions of the townland that remained along the main roads. The fourth and fifth evictions were undoubtedly designed merely to depopulate the townland of its remaining tenants.

An analysis of the demographic profiles of the five principal ships that transported the Ballykilcline evictees from Liverpool to New York, though far from perfect, provides additional information about the possible rationale that may have underlain the sequence of eviction. The demographic profile of the individuals who sailed on the first ship – the *Roscius* on 19 September 1847 – indicates that the largest category were men aged between 16 and 25; the second largest group of men were in the 26–35 age category. Women aged between 16 and 35 also constituted a large percentage of the passengers. These figures suggest that the authorities attempted to rid the townland of individuals most able to protest. The residents who sailed on the *Metoka*, the second ship, tended to be younger than those on the *Roscius*, with most of them falling in the 11–15 age range. The third eviction included families with small children, overwhelmingly male, but it also included several individuals within the 16–25 and 26–35 age groups. Calculating the mean age for each ship (from Ellis 1977: 13–21) reveals that the age profiles for both sexes steadily decreased. In short, the evictees generally grew younger with each eviction.

I conducted archeological excavations at Ballykilcline during five consecutive summers from 1998 to 2002. No surface indications suggested the presence of houses in the fields, which had been used for pasturage since the time of the evictions. The initial excavation strategy thus was designed using a combination of intensive geophysical research and cartographic analysis. The excavation centered on two houses in the southern portion of the townland in an area designated in 1836 as Kiltullvary or Bungariff. The Crown's surveyors identified the residents as Mark Nary and sons: Luke, James, and Edward. The excavation yielded thousands of artifacts from the two cabin sites (Orser 2005a,b, 2006).

The available evidence suggests that the Narys were removed from their homes during either the third or fifth evictions. If they were evicted with the third group, they would have had about five months to prepare for leaving (from September 1847 to March 1848). If they were removed in the final eviction, they would have had over a year to prepare (from September 1847 to October 1848). By March 1847, much of the eastern section of the townland had been cleared of inhabitants, including the Nary's closest relatives, 48-year-old Patrick Nary, his 28-year-old wife Mary, and their 1-year-old daughter Bridget. By October 1848, all the residents of Ballykilcline, except the informers who were allowed to stay in their homes, knew that their time at the townland was limited. After arriving in the United States, the Narys eventually made their way to central Illinois where they settled next to other Ballykilcline evictees (Orser 1998).

Posteviction Descendant Community

The history of the Ballykilcline rent strike, though barely a footnote in Irish history, retains significance as historical memory for the townland's descendants. Interestingly, however, the memory of the townland is not a facet of an active oral tradition. Rather, the memories resurfaced with the publication of a book detailing the townland's history, eviction, emigration, and resettlement (Scally 1995). Shortly after the book's publication, two of the townland's descendant community, independently researching family history, discovered one another and in the early 1990s formed "The Lost Children of Ballykilcline." This group, now called The Ballykilcline Society, includes the descendants of the evictees and represents all 49 surnames of the original families. The Society's members – truly "banished children" (Quinn 1997) – held their first reunion at the site of the townland in 1999, during the second season of excavation in Ballykilcline at the Nary cabins. The overall objectives of the Society are to gather information about the history of the townland's families and to hold annual reunions to celebrate their survival and perseverance. Over 100 men and women, mostly Americans, attended the first reunion. The Society also publishes a newsletter, called *The Bonfire*, that informs the evictees' descendant community about genealogical discoveries, news of the various families, and provides historical information about the townland. Many of the descendants are engaged in serious genealogical research, and one member of the group has written a master's thesis on the 14% of Ballykilcline evictees who settled in Rutland, Vermont (Dunn 2003).

Helen O'Neill, a writer for the Associated Press, wrote a story about Ballykilcline and its descendant community entitled "Ballykilcline's Blood" (1998). O'Neill recounts the story of a woman living in Washington State, who, while cleaning out the house of an aunt who had recently died, discovered an old trunk. Inside, the lid of the trunk had been plastered with strips of paper taken from a handwritten, nineteenth-century journal. The woman was fascinated by the puzzle presented by the strips, and spent months carefully peeling them from the trunk's lid. After deciphering them, the woman was able to piece together a sentence reading: "My Da was born in Allykilcline and so was my Ma." The woman soon learned that the author of the words was Thomas McDermott, her great-great-grandfather. Before reading Scally's (1995) history, the woman had never heard of "Allykilcline," the rent strike, or the story of the evictions. Before long, another descendant of Ballykilcline had read the book, and the descendant community was soon reconnected.

The on-going story of the Ballykilcline Society has relevance to the archeological research conducted at the townland. During the fieldwork, a student excavator uncovered a tiny, silver thimble (Fig. 1). This thimble, embossed with the words "Forget Me Not," was a variety common in the nineteenth century as a kind of commemorative object. In fact, similar examples have been found as far away from Ballykilcline as Iowa. In these examples, Native Americans have drilled holes in them and used them as ornaments (Perry 2001). The Ballykilcline thimble, though familiar during the nineteenth century, was not regarded as trivial to members of The Ballykilcline Society. Most of them viewed the thimble with a reverential awe usually reserved for the most ancient artifacts or even for religious relics. The words on the thimble were particularly meaningful because the Society had been created simply to ensure that Ballykilcline and its people were not forgotten. Most poignantly, one member of the descendant community literally broke down in tears because the thimble undoubtedly had belonged to his great-great-grandmother.

Fig. 1 Silver thimble from Ballykilcline, with inscription rolled out. Drawing by Angela Brookbank

Rethinking Descendancy in the Light of Modern Diasporic History

The shared sense of commonality experienced by the Lost Children of Ballykilcline – who had never met before 1998 (exactly 150 years after the fourth and final eviction) – was emotional and profoundly meaningful to its members. Two of the descendants, speaking independently, accurately expressed their feelings about the reassembly of the community once dispersed from Ballykilcline. Commenting at the graveside of his great-grandaunt near Ballykilcline, one descendant said: "There is no doubt that they had incredible spirit, this little group of people, the way they lived and fought against all the odds. And against all odds we are finding each other again." The woman who pieced together the fragments of the nineteenth century journal from the trunk recalled her first contact with one of the other descendants: "It was such a warm feeling. This connection with so many people from the past, this reaching to the present" (O'Neill 1998).

Comments such as these challenge archeologists and all others concerned about heritage rights to rethink our concepts of descendant community and perhaps even to reconceptualize the meaning of descendant heritage. When perceived through a diasporic lens, we can easily envision the possible weakness of viewing ancestry simply through geographical proximity. In other words, perhaps simply inhabiting a region should not automatically bestow heritage rights. Viewed through the lens of Ballykilcline, we must acknowledge that the once-contiguous townland has become a series of tiny, disconnected territories located throughout the United States. Though not contiguous, the people living in those places are cognitively linked, both within the United States and across the Atlantic to County Roscommon, Ireland. The family networks that once existed within Ballykilcline (Orser 2004: 226–234) now stretch throughout the United States. The collectivities that can be created by the shared experience of diaspora – even though experienced by ancestors generations ago – can be a powerful impetus for self-identification. As Clifford (1997: 255) notes, the sense of connection that is engendered by diaspora thinking "must be strong enough to resist erasure through the normalizing processes of forgetting, assimilating, and distancing." The Lost Children of Ballykilcline indeed had forgotten and been distanced, and their collective memory was forged only with the publication of Scally's (1995) history book.

Scholars who have examined traveling in relation to identity formation acknowledge that self- and group-sustaining identities can be created during the journey itself. Individuals "on the move" constantly renegotiate their conceptualization of their homeland and their place within it (Leed 1991). An aspect of ritual death accompanies the leaving of one's ancestral home, particularly for those who have been forcibly removed or who are fleeing racial or ethnic persecution. The Irish acknowledged the ritual death of the emigrant by holding "American wakes" (Gallagher 1982: 123–129). These "wakes" would include singing, dancing, storytelling, and all the other customs and festivities that usually accompanied the ceremony held for a deceased person (Danaher 1964).

At the same time, travelers experience the effects of entering a "new place," a sociospatial arena composed of unfamiliar, albeit often intriguing, natural and social landscapes. The act of "belonging to a diaspora" is an identity-forming process, one that serves to link "the homeland" with "the home" (Cornwell and Stoddard 2001: 7). The idea of belonging clearly serves this purpose for the Lost Children of Ballykilcline, who are united through a shared, though previously unrecognized, history that was made known only with the publication of a professional historian's study. Famine and eviction were largely taboo subjects for the Irish generation who lived through it. Scholars often remark that the horrors of the late 1840s – with its widespread starvation, mass evictions, and deadly diseases – created a silence over the landscape. In truth, however, local details of the disaster are contained in Irish-language folk tradition (Póirtéir 1995; Whelan 2001: 204–205).

The notion of diaspora is even more complicated by acknowledging that a diaspora is really a series of small journeys. These separate journeys become compressed into a "confluence of narratives" that create both individual and collective diasporic memories (Brah 1996: 183). Small journeys certainly characterize the Ballykilcline diaspora. The trips of the original evictees included travel from Ballykilcline to Dublin, from Dublin to Liverpool, from Liverpool to New York, and from New York to several other American cities and rural communities. To some extent, we may say that the diaspora continues today every time one of the descendants moves to a new locale.

The connections between the various families of the Lost Children of Ballykilcline compose what political scientist Sheffer (2003: 184) terms a "trans-state communication network." With the increased communication options and the sophisticated travel technologies of the modern era, the members of the dispersed Ballykilcline descendant community were able to find one another and once found, to develop a stable communication network that stretched from various places in the United States to rural County Roscommon, Ireland. This network of communication closed the diasporic circle by reconstituting the community. Sheffer notes that trans-state communications have been in existence since the Middle Ages, but what distinguishes them today is their democratic nature. Sophisticated communications, not being just for elites as in the past, today are available even to the descendants of uprooted tenant farmers. All members of a diaspora – no matter how dispersed in space and time – can create or join a network and in the process (re)create a descendant community.

Sheffer also notes that while the creation of trans-state networks can pull together the members of a diaspora – as it has for the Lost Children of Ballykilcline – they can also cause tension and friction between the members of the diaspora and those people who remained in the homeland. O'Neill (1998) actually makes note of this present-day tension when she writes about a descendant of one of the strike's informers. This man, still living in the Ballykilcline area, is angered by Scally's (1995) comments about his ancestor, and he threatens law suits against anyone who attempts to harm his family's name. He had little to do with the nearby reunion or with the American visitors.

The potential for friction between descendant members of diasporas and in-place nonmembers causes us to pose the question: What is the identity role of returned immigrants? In the first three decades of the twentieth century, 46,211 Irish immigrants to America left their new diasporic homes to return to their native homeland (Wyman 1993: 11). The often volatile relationships between Irish citizens and American members of the diasporic descendant community have been made famous by popular movies such as John Ford's *The Quiet Man* and Jim Sheridan's *The Field*. In both cases, the returning male Yank occupies a liminal, trans-cultural state in which he is not truly Irish but American. The American characters, however, self-identify as members of the Irish diasporic community, and each thus demands a legitimate claim to Irishness by virtue of the diasporic experience. That the characters' claims are not necessarily validated foregrounds the disjunction between the homeland community and those who are part of the diasporic, descendant community (and perhaps even one or two generations removed).

The disjunction is the point at which the most sensitive heritage issues become prominent. In addition to the roughly 500 men, women, and children evicted from Ballykilcline in 1847–1848, historians calculate that 37,286 evictions may have been ordered between only 1846 and 1849, with some 16,400 houses being leveled (Donnelly 1995: 155; Ó Gráda 1993: 103; Vaughan 1994: 230). Having been forcibly removed from their homes, should the descendants of the evictees have any voice in the preservation, protection, and study of cultural properties in their ancestors' original homeland? Should the identifiably descendant, albeit dispersed, Lost Children of Ballykilcline have any voice in the disposition and use of the lands of Ballykilcline? Modern-day capitalist nationalism answers this question quite simply "no." Not being citizens of the Republic of Ireland, and not owning land in Ballykilcline, the descendant community simply has no legal standing, even though an individual's theoretical heritage claims in fact may outweigh those of the current landowners. The thimble discovered by archeologists could be designated a family heirloom in addition to being an archeological specimen.

Such philosophical musing is not meant to suggest that Irish-Americans desire to have control over archeological properties in Ireland. No one with whom I have ever spoken has made this claim and no one is likely to make it in the future. But if we step away from our current understanding as members of nation-states and think broadly, we may propose that the rights of a descendant community should not be extinguished by the diasporic experience. When immigrant Irish men and women entered the United States, they presumably retained their heritage rights in Ireland; these were not surrendered until they became American citizens, which occurred at a much later time. But at that point, as citizens, their heritage rights became American and were spatially limited by the national boundaries of the territory of the United States. But does this fact of citizenship automatically mean that a new Irish-American citizen obtained heritage rights over Native American lands and cultural properties, or any of the heritage that had accumulated in the United States before that immigrant's arrival? In the case of displaced persons, is their heritage in the land and history that they have left behind, or in the new one where they now reside?

Questions such as these are infinitely difficult to answer, but they bear thinking about nonetheless. Once we recognize the presence of diasporas in history, and acknowledge their trans-oceanic significance in post-Columbian, global history, we cannot truly overlook such formidable questions. One possible solution to the many troubling heritage issues that arise in light of diasporas might be to adopt the concept of moral cosmopolitanism formulated by Appiah (2005). In his view, an informed, conscientious cosmopolitanism celebrates difference and unity equally. He proposes that cosmopolitanism can work because "common conversations" can be created that permit humans from vastly different places to develop dialogs and discourses. In truth, the authority grasped by the world's various nation-states probably will not allow the creation of any crossnational dialog that circumvents national boundaries. Still, we may hope that international organizations like UNESCO one day may be able to convince the world's peoples that we are all stewards of our global, cultural heritage. The historical reality of diasporas, with their mass movement of hundreds and even thousands of men, women, and children, force us to confront trans national heritage issues today. The particular case of the Irish, and even more specifically the Lost Children of Ballykicline, provides one small example to contemplate.

Acknowledgments The archeological fieldwork at Ballykilcline was conducted as a field school administered by Illinois State University. The research was performed under an excavation license issued by the Department of Environment, Heritage and Local Government (then Duchás) Dublin. My conceptions and understanding of diasporas and tenant farming communities have been enriched by the conversations with Stephen A. Brighton, Janice Orser, and many other collaborators over the years. I am also grateful to Helaine Silverman and D. Fairchild Ruggles for inviting me to the Cultural Heritage and Human Rights workshop, and for making numerous suggestions to improve this chapter. The ideas expressed herein, of course, are my own.

References

Appiah, Kwame Antony, 2005, *The Ethics of Identity*. Princeton University Press, Princeton.
Ballykilcline Society, 2001, Emigration from Ballykilcline. *The Bonfire* 3(2): 8–15.
Barnard, Toby, 2004, *Making the Grand Figure: Lives and Possessions in Ireland, 1641–1770*. Yale University Press, New Haven.
Brah, Avtar, 1996, *Cartographies of Diaspora: Contesting Identities*. Routledge, London.
Brighton, Stephen A. G., 2005, *An Historical Archaeology of the Irish Proletarian Diaspora: The Material Manifestations of Irish Identity in America, 1850–1910*. Ph.D. Dissertation, Boston University. UMI Dissertation Services, Ann Arbor.
Clifford, James, 1997, *Routes: Travel and Translation in the Late Twentieth Century*. Harvard University Press, Cambridge.
Coleman, Anne, 1999, *Riotous Roscommon: Social Unrest in the 1840s*. Irish Academic, Dublin.
Connell, Paul, Dennis A. Cronin, and Brian Ó Dálaigh, 1998, Introduction. In *Irish Townlands: Studies in Local History*, edited by Connell Paul, Dennis A. Cronin, and Brian Ó Dálaigh, pp. 9–13. Four Courts, Dublin.
Cornwell, Grant H., and Eve Walsh Stoddard, 2001, Introduction: National Boundaries/ Transnational Identities. In *Global Multiculturalism: Comparative Perspectives on Ethnicity,*

Race, and Naton, edited by Grant H. Cornwell and Eve Walsh Stoddard, pp. 1–25. Rowman & Littlefield, Lanham, Maryland.

Danaher, Kevin, 1964, *In Ireland Long Ago*. Mercier, Cork.

—, 1972, *The Year in Ireland: Irish Calendar Customs*. Mercier, Cork.

Donnelly, James S. Jr., 1995, Mass Eviction and the Great Famine: The Clearances Revisited. In *The Great Irish Famine*, edited by Cathal Póirtéir, pp. 155–173. Mercier, Cork.

Dunn, Mary Lee, 2003, *Faugh a Ballagh: Loss and Leverage in Ballykilcline and Rutland*. Master's Thesis, University of Massachusetts, Lowell.

Ellis, Eilish, 1977, *Emigrants from Ireland, 1847–1852: State-Aided Emigration Schemes from Crown Estates in Ireland*. Genealogical Publishers, Baltimore.

Gallagher, Thomas, 1982, *Paddy's Lament, Ireland 1846–1847: Prelude to Hatred*. Harcourt Brace Jovanovich, San Diego.

Griffith, Richard, 1857, *Valuation of the Several Tenements Comprised in the Union of Strokestown, in the County of Roscommon*. Thom and Sons, Dublin.

Hanley, Gerald, 1961, Nicholas Mahon and 17th Century Roscommon. *Irish Genealogist* 3: 228–235.

House of Lords, 1847, *Lands of Ballykilcline, County Roscommon. Returns to Orders of the House of Lords, Dated 16th and 19th February 1847*. Her Majesty's Stationery Office, London.

Leed, Eric J., 1991, *The Mind of the Traveler: From Gilgamesh to Global Tourism*. HarperCollins, New York.

McErlean, Thomas, 1983, The Irish Townland System of Landscape Organisation. In *Landscape Archaeology in Ireland*, edited by Terence Reeves-Smyth and Fred Hamond, pp. 315–339. BAR British Series 116, BAR, Oxford.

Miller, Kerby A., 1985, *Emigrants and Exiles: Ireland and the Irish Exodus to North America*. Oxford University Press, New York.

O'Conor, Kieran D., 2001, The Morphology of Gaelic Lordly Sites in North Connacht. In *Gaelic Ireland, c. 1250-c. 1650: Land, Lordship, and Settlement*, edited by Patrick J. Duffy, David Edwards, and Elizabeth FitzPatrick, pp. 329–345. Four Courts, Dublin.

O'Dowd, Anne, 1981, *Meitheal: A Study of Co-operative Labour in Rural Ireland*. Comhairle Bhéaloideas Éireann, Dublin.

Ó Gráda, Cormac, 1993, *Ireland Before and After the Famine: Explorations in Economic History, 1800–1925*. Manchester University Press, Manchester.

O'Neill, Helen, 1998, *Ballykilcline's Blood*. Associated Press Release, August 2.

Orser, Charles E. Jr., 1996, *A Historical Archaeology of the Modern World*. Plenum, New York.

—, 1998, *A Report of Investigations for the First Season of Archaeological Research at Ballykilcline Townland, Kilglass Parish, County Roscommon, Ireland*. Report submitted to Duchas, Dublin.

—, 2004, *Race and Practice in Archaeological Interpretation*. University of Pennsylvania Press, Philadelphia.

—, 2005a, An Archaeology of a Famine-Era Eviction. *New Hibernia Review* 9: 45–58.

—, 2005b, Symbolic Violence, Resistance, and the Vectors of Improvement in Early Nineteenth-Century Ireland. *World Archaeology* 37: 392–407.

—, ed., 2006, *Unearthing Hidden Ireland: Historical Archaeology at Ballykilcline, County Roscommon*. Wordwell, Bray, Ireland.

—, 2007, *The Archaeology of Race and Racialization in Historic America*. University Press of Florida, Gainesville.

O'Toole, Fintan, 1999, *The Lie of the Land: Irish Identities*. Verso, London.

Perry, Michael J., 2001, A Territorial Period Site in Dubuque. http://www.uiowa.edu/~osa/learn/dubuque/tps1.htm (16 August 2006).

Póirtéir, Cathal, 1995, *Famine Echoes*. Gill and Macmillan, Dublin.

Quinn, Peter, 1997, In Search of the Banished Children: A Famine Journey. In *Irish Hunger: Personal Reflections on the Legacy of the Famine*, edited by Tom Hayden, pp. 143–156. Roberts Rinehart, Boulder, Colorado.

Scally, Robert J., 1995, *The End of Hidden Ireland: Rebellion, Famine, and Emigration*. Oxford University Press, New York.

Sheffer, Gabriel, 2003, *Diaspora Politics: At Home Abroad*. Cambridge University Press, Cambridge.

Vaughan, William E., 1994, *Landlords and Tenants in Mid-Victorian Ireland*. Clarendon, Oxford.

Wakefield, Edward, 1812, *An Account of Ireland, Statistical and Political*. Longman, Hurst, Rees, Orme, and Brown, London.

Weld, Isaac, 1832, *Statistical Survey of the County of Roscommon, Drawn up Under the Direction of the Royal Dublin Society*. R. Graisberry, Dublin.

Whelan, Kevin, 2001, "Born Astride the Grave": The Cultural Effects of the Great Irish Famine. In *The Famine Lectures: Léachtaí an Ghorta*, edited by Breandán Ó Conaire, pp. 204–217. Roscommon Herald, Boyle.

Wyman, Mark, 1993, *Round-Trip to America: The Immigrants Return to Europe, 1880–1930*. Cornell University Press, Ithaca.

Young, Arthur, 1780, *A Tour of Ireland with General Observations on the Present State of that Kingdom made in the Years 1776, 1777, and 1778*. T. Cadell and J. Dodsley, London.

Chapter 6
Performing Slave Descent: Cultural Heritage and the Right to Land in Brazil

Jan Hoffman French

Introduction

"Cultural heritage and human rights" is a counterintuitive pairing. Nevertheless, despite its inherent tension between the particular and the universal, cultural heritage and human rights have come to seem a natural marriage of terms. As an indication of the growing recognition that local "aspects of human achievement" have "universal significance" (Cleere 2001: 22) in the post-World War II era, the 1972 UNESCO World Heritage Convention was supplemented in 2003 to include intangible cultural heritage and in 2005 to protect diversity of cultural expressions. These important additions to the World Heritage Convention were intended to implement the 2001 UNESCO Universal Declaration on Cultural Diversity, whose Article 4 designated cultural diversity as a human right: "The defense of cultural diversity is an ethical imperative, inseparable from respect for human dignity."

Scholars have debated definitions of the terms and implementation of the policies involved in cultural heritage work over the years in many settings. Their interventions range from discussions of conservation, preservation, destruction, and reconstruction of cultural heritage (Hufford 1994; Layton et al. 2001) and its use as a tourist destination and receptacle for history and memory (Bruner 2005; Clifford 1997; Handler and Gable 1997), to its role in funding and choosing sites for archeological research (Ashmore and Knapp 1999; Funari et al. 1999). Moreover, the considerable attention paid to the problematics and contradictions inherent in the juxtaposition of the bundles of meanings associated with "human rights" and "cultural heritage" has led to new scholarship that proposes bridging mechanisms and alternatives to the quandaries created by heretofore dichotomous approaches (Cowan 2006: 21). To understand how the two concepts intersect, I would suggest that we ask the following question: *What does cultural heritage add to the notion of "rights" and rights-based claims to recognition and redistribution?* Such an inquiry is entirely in keeping with Jane Cowan's (2006: 21) call for "empirically grounded studies of rights and culture [that] confront us with – and force us to grapple with – the messiness, contradiction, ambiguity, impasses, and the unintended consequences [that arise] when demands are recognized or accommodated."

H. Silverman and D. F. Ruggles (eds.), *Cultural Heritage and Human Rights.*
© Springer 2007

In this essay, I will provide a window onto the "social life of rights" (Wilson 1997), defined as "the social forms that coalesce in and around formal rights practices and formulations, and which are usually hidden in the penumbra of the official political process" (Wilson 2006: 78). I will accomplish this through an examination and analysis of a particular performance of rights, literally through a play produced and performed by adolescents in a backland northeastern Brazilian village in celebration of its recognition as a descendant of a fugitive slave community. By tracing the permutations of the story that have become the play, this essay will shed light on the productive role that legislating cultural heritage can play in the demand for land rights. A close consideration of the processes in this essay supports Wilson's (2006: 82, n. 5) admonition to be open to all the ways that local appropriations of rights "are neither about domination nor resistance vis-à-vis the state, but, instead, serve as an outlet for the expression of local identities, intracommunal feuds, family, [and] personal conflicts."

Situating Brazil and its Quilombos in a Cultural Heritage System

Well before the UNESCO declaration and convention, Brazil included in its first democratic constitution (1988), after more than two decades of military rule, a prescient articulation of the UNESCO declaration in two provisions in the "Social Order" title of the constitution. Article 215 guarantees "cultural rights" and specifically protects "manifestations of popular, indigenous, and Afro-Brazilian cultures," while Article 216 defines "Brazilian cultural heritage" as both "material and intangible assets" that "bear reference to the identity, action, and memory of the various groups that form Brazilian society," including "forms of expression" and "modes of living" in addition to buildings, objects, documents, and "sites of historical, natural, artistic, archeological, paleontological, ecological, and scientific value."

The advanced character of the Brazilian view of cultural heritage is not surprising when placed into the historical context of twentieth century Brazilian legal history. As early as 1937, President Getúlio Vargas "promulgated a decree-law instituting one of the world's most advanced preservationist codes" (Williams 2001: 90). Rather than being a mere paper decree, "nearly half of all entries into Brazil's official registry of national heritage . . . were completed before 1945" (Williams 2001: 90), the year UNESCO was established.

The democratic constitution of 1988 contains two other provisions that together have been used to advance the struggles of rural black communities for rights to land they have occupied for generations. The provision that has received most attention is a one-sentence clause granting land rights to "descendants of runaway slave communities," known as *quilombos*. About 5 years after the constitution was enacted, the Brazilian government began recognizing some rural black communities as quilombos, and 5 years after that, it issued land titles to a handful of those communities under the other, less publicized, constitutional provision – Section 5 of Article 216, which declares as cultural heritage "documents and sites" associated with historical quilombos.

Mocambo, a small village on the banks of the São Francisco River in the semiarid backlands of the Brazilian Northeast in the state of Sergipe, and the site of my research, was one of the quilombo communities that received such title.[1] Motivated by new legal rights, access to land, and the possibility of improvements in their living standards, residents of Mocambo had embarked on a campaign in 1993 to gain quilombo recognition (achieved in 1997), even though it would mean identification with a much-derided category associated with oppression and slavery – *negro*. Since then, the residents of Mocambo have experienced a cascade of changes in their lives, relationships, and self-conceptions. At the same time, those transformations have been guided by, and continue to be associated with, practices, beliefs, and worldviews about race, color, ethnicity, and religion that were salient prior to the invocation of the "quilombo clause" and that remain embedded in newly configured narratives.

This essay is about one such narrative and the changes it reflects and has generated. In the pages that follow, I chronicle the transformation of a family story into the foundational narrative of those in Mocambo who have come to identify themselves as black people descended from fugitive slaves. I also examine the parallel process of how Mocambo, a 90-family village of landless rural workers, has become a modern-day "quilombo" with title to more than 5,000 acres that had belonged to residents' former employers.[2]

---

[1] Mocambo is the real name of the first recognized quilombo in Sergipe, the smallest state of Brazil. Both *mocambo* and *quilombo* are African-derived words (Castro 2001: 285; Schneider 1991: 251; Schwartz 1992: 125). In English, escaped slaves were referred to as "maroons," derived from the Spanish *cimarrón*, "based on an Arawakan (Taino) Indian root" originally meaning "domestic cattle that had taken to the hills in Hispaniola" (Price 2002: 8) and subsequently applied to American Indian slaves who had escaped bondage. By the 1530s, *maroon* was being used to refer to African slave runaways in the English colonies, whereas in the Spanish colonies, groups of maroons were called "palenques." As *cimarrón* did in the Caribbean, *mocambo* first referred to runaway cattle in the backlands of Brazil. In fact, the village of Mocambo in Sergipe was named for a nearby stream where cattle would gather (Arruti 1998).

[2] When the government delivered land title to Mocambo in July 2000, it did so without addressing the already existing titles of 42 private landowners. This produced a complex legal situation: One large parcel was in the process of land-reform expropriation; the strip along the river used by residents for planting was officially owned by the federal government as land on the banks of rivers flowing through more than one state (*terra marítima*); and the largest parcel was owned by the former governor of the state, João de Seixas Dória, who was sympathetic to the cause of his former employees (he had been arrested on the day of the military coup in 1964 and imprisoned for a year because of his support for land reform). He did not contest the granting of title but did insist on compensation, part of which he received when he appealed to his friend, the former president of Brazil. Technically, Mocambo has been recognized as a "remanescente de quilombo" community. Nevertheless, I use the term *quilombo*, even though it is an anachronism, because the people themselves have come to refer to their village as a "quilombo" and the national quilombo movement has also adopted the shortened form. Ideologically, removing the modifier *descendant* reinforces the militant aspect of resisting slavery – historical or metaphorical.

In the case of rural Brazil, with the advent of the quilombo clause, villages previously considered "rural black communities" have begun to associate themselves with representations of an imagined African past. Some authors and activists have come to consider such communities' indispensable inspirations for the twenty-first-century black consciousness movement (Linhares 2004; Pereira and White 2001). Just as some anthropologists have argued for a connection between Brazil, as a nation, and African sensibilities as a result of the large number of Africans brought as slaves until the mid-nineteenth century (Segato 1998), others have pointed out a certain romanticization of Africa in the context of quilombo recognition (Véran 2002). In this essay, I mean to complicate further the connection between "Africa" in the imagination of Brazilians and modern-day quilombos that have come to represent "myth and history" (Hill 1988) as well as the past and future of what it means to be "black" in the "African diaspora" (Gomez 2005). In that regard, I follow David Scott's (1991: 278) proposal for a "theoretical repositioning" of the place of "Africa or slavery" as events whose reality can be traced through time to a particular group, to "Africa" and "slavery" as tropes associated with those events. Like Scott, I am concerned with the "rhetorical labor" such tropes perform in the construction and assertion of identities. To aid in explaining the mechanics of this process, I draw on the concept of "constrained refashioning" (Wilson 1995). By showing that new elements in cultural practices are forged "in the shadow of the past" (Fuoss and Hill 2001), I propose that assuming a black identity in rural Brazil does not preclude multiple identifications drawn on local, national, and international discourses.

In the next section, I provide background about the enactment and interpretation of the quilombo clause. Then, I describe briefly how Mocambo came to be recognized as a quilombo. Finally, I recount the family story and trace its transformation by village storytellers and teenage actors into the foundational narrative of Quilombo Mocambo under the influence of government officials, anthropologists, lawyers, local Catholic Church, and black-movement activists.

Constitutional Right to Land for "Quilombos"

As the military regime began to cede ground to a civilian government in the 1980s, Brazil entered a phase of democratic transition. The first civilian president since the coup in 1964 took office in 1985, and then, in preparation for the adoption of a new constitution, a constituent assembly met regularly during 1987. In the context of the constituent assembly, black-consciousness-movement activists, a few of whom were delegates, proposed that land be guaranteed to rural black communities that could claim lineage from quilombos. This has been viewed as a compromise – a concession made by those in the black movement, who wanted all rural black communities to be given land (Linhares 2004: 823). Compared with the level of lobbying and demonstrating in the streets of Brasília conducted by indigenous activists, there was relatively little public manifestation of concern regarding rights of Afro-Brazilians. Black activists, however, argued that establishing the category of "remanescente de quilombo" with an attendant right to land was appropriate because 1988 would also be the centenary of the abolition of slavery.[3]

Moreover, a movement had begun in the 1970s to introduce to the public the figure of Zumbi of Palmares, the king of the largest and longest-lasting quilombo in Brazilian history. Palmares has been termed "an African State in Brazil" (Kent 1965). In existence for almost the entire seventeenth century, Palmares had a population estimated at 11,000 (Schwartz 1992: 123). The Palmares quilombo was celebrated by nineteenth century writers and was appropriated and publicized in the twentieth century by Brazilian black movement activists, such as Abdias do Nascimento (1980), who developed the "quilombismo" ideology, relating modern black activism to "the spirit of resistance of the ancient quilombos" (Véran 2002: 20).

By 1988, the Palmares quilombo and its king had obtained a place in the official history of Brazil. In fact, Palmares was declared a national heritage site in 1985. Zumbi, as a "living presence in the resistance" by oppressed black people in Brazil, was identified as an "ongoing source of inspiration for the political actions of contemporary Black Brazilians" (Pereira and White 2001: 137).[4] With the 20 November 1995 celebration of the 300th anniversary of the death of Zumbi and the destruction of Palmares, the quilombo came to symbolize "the privileged space of an ideal of freedom by means of which the slaves preserved their human dignity, inserted themselves in a sociocultural memory, and organized forces to challenge the system that oppressed them" (Pereira and White 2001: 137). Since then, November 20th has been adopted by the government as Zumbi of Palmares or Black Consciousness Day.

When the quilombo clause was enacted in 1988, providing that "survivors of quilombo communities occupying their lands are recognized as definitive owners, and the State shall issue them titles to the land" (Linhares 2004: 818) and Article 216 added quilombos to sites of cultural heritage, few expected that they would have much effect. Nevertheless, the Palmares Cultural Foundation, established as an agency of the Ministry of Culture in 1988, began to identify quilombos throughout rural Brazil. Since then, on the basis of various inventories, between 743 and 1,296 quilombos have been identified in 22 states (Linhares 2004: 819). At least one source charts 61 properties encompassing 119 quilombo communities that have been titled

---

[3] Over 3.5 million Africans were imported to be slaves in Brazil beginning in the mid-1500s. Today, the largest number of African-descended people outside of Africa live in Brazil.

[4] The representation of runaway slave communities as symbols of modern resistance can also be seen in Spanish-speaking countries, such as Venezuela, where *cimarronaje* is used not only to refer to escaped slaves living in hidden places with African cultural manifestations (Price 1983) but also to denote a "living tradition still determined to resist the domination of a European ruling class" through "re-Africanizing" or "cimarronizing" festivals that have been appropriated as celebrations of mixture (Guss 2000: 49, 50).

by federal and state governments since 1995, including Mocambo.[5] Another source predicts that more than 3,000 descendants of quilombos will be identified (Linhares 2004: 819). As of May 2005, the Center of Geography and Applied Cartography of the University of Brasília had identified 2,228 quilombo communities, and 70 had been officially registered by the federal land reform agency.

In the immediate wake of the enactment of the quilombo clause, some government officials assumed that the legal meaning of "remanescente de quilombo" would be determined by historical evidence, whereas others, tied to the black movement, advocated a broader definition. This was important, they argued, because land and birth records were sparse and many rural black communities denied any relation to slavery or claimed that their ancestors had escaped from slave vessels on arrival in Brazil. Groups of slaves also sometimes received land through gifts from their owners or the Catholic Church (Almeida 1989; Baiocchi 1983; Magno da Silva 2000; Vogt and Fry 1996). Therefore, over the years since the enactment of the quilombo clause, the Palmares Cultural Foundation (2000) has adopted the view that "quilombo" signifies a "space of freedom, of refuge. . . . Currently, the historiography redefines the concept, not to cling to only the flights and escapes but the autonomous forms of living, with the pattern and model of common use."

Requirements of proof have expanded and contracted since the early 1990s, with almost every quilombo recognized under slightly different criteria. Some themes, however, have remained constant. Communal land use in a rural setting was initially, and has remained, a key factor in quilombo recognition proceedings. Until 2003, anthropologists were required to visit communities making claims for quilombo recognition.[6] They looked for communal land usage, elderly residents who could recount memories of talk about a slave past, physical markers of long-term

---

[5] See Comissão Pro-Índio n.d. The titles issued by the Palmares Foundation in 2000 that involved privately owned properties, including Mocambo, are legally problematic in that they were issued without expropriating or indemnifying the private landowners. Because of these problems, the Palmares Foundation has issued no further titles since 2000. All titles since then have been issued by state land agencies. In 2003, the Partido dos Trabalhadores (Workers Party, or PT) government of Luiz Inácio Lula da Silva published new rules for recognizing and titling quilombos that, in addition to eliminating the requirement of anthropological reports for recognition, moved responsibility for demarcating and titling quilombo land to the land reform agency, the Instituto Nacional de Colonizaçao e Reforma Agrária (INCRA), thus taking that power away from the Palmares Foundation (Decree 4887/03 and Normative Instruction of INCRA, No. 16). The titles issued by the Palmares Foundation without indemnification, according to one INCRA official, are considered valid and will not be reissued by INCRA but can be challenged in court. At the end of 2004, INCRA had not yet issued any titles to quilombos but had "initiated more than 100 proceedings and already had in its data bank more than 1,500 quilombo communities" (Claudio Rodrigues Braga, INCRA official, e-mail to author, 16 November 2004).

[6] The 2003 rules eliminated the prerequisite of an anthropological report for recognition. This has caused consternation among anthropologists, some mediating agents, and members of the quilombos. Although the purpose of the new rules is to allow communities direct access to the government, the repercussions at this point are unknown. For example, a second quilombo has been recognized in Sergipe, on the new basis of self-identification alone. When the community reached the stage of land demarcation, however, leaders expressed concern that without an

occupation of the land, and cultural practices that could be construed as ethnic markers. Another crucial element of the black movement's argument in favor of the quilombo clause and its advocacy of an expansion of the clause's application, as well as in the subsequent public discourse about quilombos, had to do with an asserted connection to Africa. Therefore, despite anthropologists' efforts to restrict the identification of quilombos to rural black communities who cultivated land communally, the mass media continued to present these communities as "authentic and archaic African tribes in the midst of contemporary Brazil" (Véran 2002: 20).[7]

In considering the appeal of Africa as a historical reference for Brazilians of all colors, it is instructive to turn to Rita Segato's formula for locating Africa "within the equation of the nation" (1998: 129). Segato proposes that the articulation of blackness and discourse about Africa "varies according to national framework" (1998: 130). Unlike the situation in the United States, "traditions" in Brazil, such as Afro-Brazilian religions, which are practiced by people of all colors and classes, "have inscribed a monumental African codex containing the accumulated ethnic experience and strategies of African descendants as part of the nation . . . this codex operates as a stable reservoir of meaning from which flows a capillary, informal, and fragmentary impregnation of the whole of society" (Segato 1998: 143). In explaining the state's role, Segato (1998: 144) observes that the hegemonic view of Brazilian national formation (intermingling of the three "races" – Portuguese, indigenous, and African), which incorporates individuals of any origin, serves as a "re-creation of Africa in Brazil" and was adopted by a weak state that was not consolidated enough to impose an erasure of Africa. Segato argues that this inability to erase Africa from the Brazilian imaginary must be placed in the context of "the existence of a virulent racist attitude and feeling in Brazil against people of black color" (1998: 148). Because of the "peculiar processes that lie behind the Brazilian form of racism," in her view, the state was forced to "share this encompassing . . . function with black enclaves that actively produce and expand African culture through the nation and beyond" (Segato 1998: 148, see also p. 145).

Tied to the discourse about African survival, however, a certain element of "folklorization of blackness" (Godreau 2002; Hanchard 1994) may also be involved in the government's quilombo recognition program. Connecting quilombos to a romantic notion of agricultural practices in Africa (Geipel 1997; Pereira and

---

anthropologist to help elicit their history and the boundaries of their land, they would receive less land than they should. Situations like this one also raise the question of how knowledge production about quilombos, up to now imbricated with the production of anthropological knowledge, will change as the new rules are implemented. In mid-2005, recognizing the need for help in demarcating the quilombo lands, INCRA submitted a request to the Associação Brasileira de Antropologia (ABA) for a list of 120 anthropologists who could be engaged for that purpose (ABA vice president Peter Fry, personal communication, 17 September 2005).

[7] Articles published in the mainstream Brazilian media bore such titles as "Forgotten Africa: Remnants of ancient quilombos, 511 black communities live isolated in the interior of the country" (Veja 1998) and "The Heirs of Chico Rei" (Istoé 1998; Chico Rei, a slave born in Africa, was reputed to have been a king there and was captured with his entire entourage).

White 2001: 136) creates a "special distancing of blackness," relegating it to communities that are isolated and "different," often through an attempt to "document the prevalence of African cultural traits or survivals" (Godreau 2002: 293). In Brazil, the primary enunciated goal of both the government and black movement activists is to guarantee that impoverished rural black communities are inserted into the nation with full citizenship rights while their way of life and cultural practices are protected – a goal of a newly conceived multicultural, pluralistic Brazilian society (Pereira and White 2001).[8] Nevertheless, even if unintentional, an effect of these efforts has been a form of folklorization, particularly when African cultural survivals are invoked to support quilombo claims. Moreover, the desires of the members of quilombo communities may not entirely mesh with the images of them as a link to the past (Véran 2002). For them, government recognition brings the promise of modernization – electricity, running water, better roads, technical assistance for agricultural production, and health care – all of which are part of the implicit promise that comes with recognition and land. The implementation of those promises does not necessarily comport with the expectations associated with the folkloric aspects of the requirements for recognition and can create a gap that is often filled with feuding, disgruntlement, and the exacerbation of factional fighting within the quilombos, as was the case in Mocambo.

Quilombo Recognition: Becoming Black in the Eyes of the State

In 1992, four years after the quilombo clause was adopted, a group of about 20 families from Mocambo became embroiled in a dispute with a neighboring landowner over their right, as sharecroppers, to plant on her property. They were subsequently expelled from the property. The dispute arose because the neighboring Xocó Indians (a related group of African- and indigenous-descended rural workers who were recognized as a tribe in 1979) had enlisted the help of some Mocambo families in their bid to add that piece of land to their indigenous reserve (see Arruti 2002; French 2003, 2004). The expulsion by the landowner was especially difficult for the Mocambo families because the land they had been planting was part of the last rice lagoon remaining after the construction of hydroelectric dams upriver. Out of concern for the plight of the families, the parish priest called in a lawyer nun, who introduced to the Mocambo families the idea of petitioning for federal

---

[8] Although the constitutional provision does not mention race or color, it has come to be interpreted by activists not only as granting a right to land but also as recognizing quilombo residents as subjects of economic, social, and political rights. They see quilombo recognition as a way to promote full "citizenship." The notion of citizenship in Brazil has come to include all of the rights just listed and is often used to denote going beyond a bare-bones notion of "political citizenship" (see Paoli 1992).

recognition as a quilombo. Although it was an untried method of acquiring land (a few quilombos had been recognized, but none had yet received land and some were involved in judicial disputes that would go on for years), a majority of Mocambo residents decided to pursue quilombo status.[9]

Thus began a campaign to prove to government visitors, including the anthropologist who came to research the validity of their claim, that the Mocambo families were descended from fugitive slaves. At first, the government ignored their request because they had no records and the architecture of their village did not meet the standards of the patrimony commission. According to the patrimony commission architect, Mocambo had no "buildings that dated from before the beginning of the [twentieth] century"; neither were there "traces of Afro-Brazilian religions" (Arruti 2001: 246).[10] After 60 Mocambo families illegally occupied the neighboring disputed land and were expelled by court injunction in 1993, the villagers and their lawyer turned their attention again to pursuing quilombo recognition. By that time, the requirements associated with the quilombo clause were being relaxed, at least in part because government investigators and anthropologists had learned that historical evidence of the existence of fugitive slave communities was often impossible to document. At many identified quilombo sites, investigators could find evidence only of communal land cultivation, memories of having lived in the same location for multiple generations, and typical backland cultural practices rooted in Iberian folk Catholicism with the addition of music and dance influenced by the indigenous and African background of almost all backlands residents. As anthropologists became more involved in quilombo recognition cases, concepts associated with the ethnicity theory of Fredrik Barth (1969; i.e., self-definition and boundaries defined against other groups in an attempt to organize difference) began to trump strict historical evidence consisting of architectural, archeological, and documentary proof. Long-term occupation of rural land by black people, communal planting, and some manifestation of undefined "black culture" became the trinity of requirements settled upon.

At this point, the Mocambo villagers were in a better position to prove their status. Although there is little doubt that some of the people who live along the São Francisco River are descended from enslaved people (Africans, Indians, or both), no direct evidence indicates that they are descended from a community of runaway slaves. Mocambo residents, in fact, did not talk about slavery at all before the quilombo clause entered the picture. Once it did, as I discuss below, "slavery" became a metaphor for the suffering of their great-grandparents at the hands of the landowners for whom they had toiled at the end of the nineteenth century, when

---

[9] The complexities of this decision-making process, including the role played by the Xocó, the various legal strategies, and the increasing levels of mobilization, as well as the role of the Catholic Church's Pastoral Land Commission are described in French 2003.

[10] Richard Price, a renowned expert on maroons in the Americas, strongly criticized the first anthropological studies that identified quilombos in Brazil. In an oft-cited article published in Brazil, Price (1999) stressed that the anthropologists' reports were based on an imprecise characterization of black peasant communities as quilombos.

the institution of slavery was being abolished.[11] The anthropological expert who authenticated Mocambo as a "remanescente de quilombo" has written, "This is the moment, and not before, that narratives [in Mocambo] point to as the 'time of slavery'" (Arruti 2001: 238).

Almost from the beginning of the quilombo movement and at the same time that recognition proceedings were wending their way through the federal bureaucracy, several families in Mocambo were opposed to pursuing recognition. In hindsight, now that a large swath of land has been declared the property of Quilombo Mocambo and the political shift to the left at the national and state levels has brought more attention to the plight of the rural poor in Brazil, it seems difficult to imagine why people living under the impoverished circumstances of the early 1990s in Mocambo would have opposed a move that would eventually provide such rewards. When an untried law is invoked, however, people consider potential risks as well as rewards. In this case, both residents who were for and those who were against the quilombo path thought their route was the better way to achieve an improved life with running water, electricity, bathrooms, refrigerators, and paved roads. The problem from the point of view of those opposed (known as *contras*), and perhaps the irony, was that to get such modern improvements they were being asked to identify themselves with a premodern sensibility, a slave category, and a racial category that had been reviled since the moment their ancestors arrived in Brazil.

Approximately two-thirds of the 90 families living in Mocambo were participants in the quilombo movement and the other one-third belonged to the contra faction. This faction included people who could have qualified as *quilombolas* (on the basis of their heritage and long-term residency) as well as relative newcomers to Mocambo – families who were forced to move when the land they lived on was expropriated for the Xocó reserve. The contras and their allies had determined, from the early days of the struggle that it was to their benefit to remain loyal to local politicians who, for years, had been the only source of promised services. Favors were provided in exchange for political support at election time, leaving many people, particularly those who preferred the losing candidates, with practically no access to resources such as agricultural technical assistance, irrigation equipment, seeds for planting, and legal help with claiming pensions and resolving disputes. The federal untried promise did not seem as certain as the local political configurations, which were at least predictable, if often unfair or unjust.

A strong element of competition also existed between the leader of the contras and some of the leaders of the quilombo movement, who were first cousins. Within

---

[11] In 1850, a law was enacted declaring that land previously considered open for indigenous peoples to live on would henceforth be available for purchase (Indians were deemed to be fully assimilated in the Northeast). The land in Mocambo's county was redistributed to the local elite, who turned it into cattle ranches. The so-called blacks from the foot of the high plateau (*negros-do-pé-da-serra*), ancestors of some of the current residents of Mocambo, were pushed into three residential nuclei, including Mocambo, and became day laborers and sharecroppers of the landowners.

the first three years of the struggle for recognition, this had developed into a full-scale family feud. The moment most identified with a hardening of positions was the disagreement in late 1995 over whether the already-constituted community association, whose president was to become the official leader of the contras, could be used to hold title to the quilombo land. This was a crucial issue because Brazilian land law has no provision for collective ownership and the Palmares Foundation required that title be held in the name of an association formed expressly for that purpose. Over the objection of the contras, a new association was formed to hold the land and was given the name Antônio do Alto Association, a reference to the new foundational story of Quilombo Mocambo.

Only residents who supported the struggle for recognition were permitted to become members of this new association and, hence, to have indirect land ownership when the title was finally given to the association in July 2000. Quilombo leaders' definition of who could be a member of the new quilombo association contradicted the discourse of the federal attorney, who insisted that all the black residents of Mocambo were entitled to the land. "Black" did not refer only to shades of skin color but was primarily a shorthand term for all but a few families who had lived in Mocambo since its inception. Ultimately, the test for membership was commitment to the struggle, self-identification as black, and loyalty to the cause. Consequently, once the land was titled in the name of the new quilombo association, the contras, even though they were considered black and descendants of fugitive slaves by the government, were excluded from working on the land by the group of Mocambo residents who had fought for quilombo recognition. As can be imagined, the atmosphere in Mocambo remained tense throughout the entire decade of quilombo mobilization.

The Story of Antônio Do Alto Becomes the Foundational Narrative of Mocambo

As a brief introduction, the play mounted by the Mocambo teenagers and examined here enacts the story of Mocambo's most renowned ancestor, Antônio do Alto and his unfortunate end. The basic elements of the original story are as follows: Antônio do Alto, the great-grandfather of an elderly resident of latter-day Mocambo, had a love affair with the powerful landowner's niece; when the landowner learned that his niece was pregnant, he had Antônio do Alto buried alive. My analysis of the elaboration and transformation of this story into the quilombo's foundational narrative runs along two axes – one of change that shifts in response to perceived legal exigencies tied to cultural heritage definitions and renders the story persuasive in the context of the quilombo clause, and the other of representational stability. The aspects of the story analyzed along the second axis render it comprehensible and credible by retaining preexisting structural elements of power, sexuality, family, and patronage. Through variations in the family story and its appropriation by a group of Mocambo teenagers, the story became a play about slavery that is performed twice a year in the village. I will now discuss the story in detail.

In September 1995, almost 2 years after Mocambo's pursuit of recognition began, the Palmares Foundation sent the anthropologist José Maurício Arruti to investigate Mocambo's claim to quilombo status. While in the village, Arruti got to know an elderly, soft-spoken, dark-skinned man named Antônio Lino dos Santos, known to all as "Sr. Antônio." From the beginning, members of the quilombo movement and its supporters considered Sr. Antônio to be the best person for the task of "historical recuperation." For this reason, he was elected to the coordinating committee of the new quilombo association and eventually became its president. As the leader and as a man with an acknowledged talent for recounting the past, Sr. Antônio was designated to show Arruti the markers of old houses, corrals, and boundaries and to explain how the village had become consolidated as the surrounding land was turned into cattle-raising pasture in the previous century. Sr. Antônio's reputation for having more historical knowledge than anyone else in Mocambo was founded on his undisputed talent for storytelling. In fact, respect for Sr. Antônio's leadership was enhanced when Arruti memorialized one of Sr. Antônio's stories in his report to the Palmares Foundation justifying Mocambo's recognition as a quilombo.

Sr. Antônio's mother had told him the story about her grandfather's fate many years before. Arruti included the story of the great-grandfather for whom Sr. Antônio had been named in his report in the following broadest outline:

> Antônio do Alto fell in love with the niece of the landowner for whom he worked and having found that the girl returned his interest, they maintained a relationship until the landowner discovered them. When he learned of the affair he was so enraged that he had Antônio do Alto killed, and so that the punishment would be of the same magnitude as his fury, he had him buried alive. [Arruti 1997: 43]

A notable detail about this first-recorded rendition of the story is the absence of any mention of slavery or of fleeing from slavery, even though Arruti was using the story as evidence for Mocambo's claim to quilombo status. In fact, no evidence exists that Antônio do Alto or his father were slaves or that the landowner was a slaveholder, as I explain further below. Another significant omission from this first rendition was any reference to the race or color of any of the protagonists, a detail whose importance rapidly became clear to the Mocambo storytellers and in later versions was remedied. This first version, rather than being a story about slavery and race, was most likely a story about social status and kin relations in the backlands. As Sr. Antônio was encouraged to retell the story of his great-grandfather, and as others who also claimed descent from Antônio do Alto took up the story, these and other details changed. The naming of the new community association after this ancestor, shortly after Arruti's visit, was a crucial step toward enshrining the story as the foundational narrative of Quilombo Mocambo.

Before I describe and analyze this first and the subsequent versions of the Antônio do Alto story, I will review when and how often the story has been told and presented as a play. Village teenagers first performed a play based on Sr. Antônio's story in May 1997, when the president of the Palmares Foundation came to Mocambo from Brasília to celebrate quilombo recognition.[12] For each of the Black Consciousness Day celebrations following quilombo recognition, the play has been performed in a manner reminiscent of the kind of pageant well known in the tradition of rustic folk Catholicism.[13] The play has also been featured at each of Mocambo's annual patron saint festivals since quilombo recognition. The performance I witnessed on Black Consciousness Day in 2000 was mounted to celebrate the land grant. In addition to witnessing the play, I encountered four versions of the Antônio do Alto story during my year of fieldwork that culminated in my dissertation on law's instigation of new northeastern Indian and quilombo identities (French 2003). I heard Sr. Antônio tell the story to a self-identified black Palmares Foundation lawyer in April 2000. I also collected two transcribed versions: one was taken from a videotaped workshop on black culture for Mocambo schoolteachers led by a black activist from the state capital, and the other, Sr. Antônio's narration, was transcribed at my request by a staff member of the nongovernmental organization that had helped with the recognition and land-grant process. Partial versions of the story were told to me by several Mocambo residents, who all claimed to be descended from Antônio do Alto. Through retellings by Sr. Antônio, the recording of the story by anthropologists and activists, and the production and performance of the play, Antônio do Alto had come to be considered the founder of the quilombo.

Although Sr. Antônio was a direct descendant of Antônio do Alto and was the village storyteller, his stature as a leader had diminished significantly over the

---

[12] The teenagers were encouraged to take charge of the story and the play by the parish priest, who continued to advise and aid the quilombo movement in Mocambo. The local Catholic Church was, and continues to be, dedicated to keeping young people within its fold and engaged with the church's projects. Inspiring the teenagers, however, was their interest in the evening soap operas (*telenovelas*) shown on television. Since electricity had come to Mocambo in 1997, they had been spent hours watching soap operas, which in Brazil are often historically based. So the possibility of being a "star," if even for only one night, was part of the thrill of preparing for and performing the play. For example, in the version of the play that I saw, when Antônio do Alto's mother learned of his fate, she cried and railed against the injustice committed against her son. While Antônio's mother, who had been given the name Xica, was wailing, the other participants in the play giggled each time her name was used. I thought this might have been because of a well-known story of a slave woman, Xica da Silva, who was said to have seduced a powerful white colonial official and become his imperious and pampered mistress. The story was the basis for one of the most-watched soap operas. Xica da Silva is an iconic figure in Brazilian popular culture, hence, the giggles. The teenagers' decision to insert the reference to another, but opposite, cross-racial seduction as a joke contributed to the frisson of the play.

[13] Pilgrimages and pageants are descended from rural folk Catholic practices brought to Brazil from Portugal in the first years of colonization during the sixteenth century (Queiroz 1976). The ludic nature of those practices is the legacy of Portuguese folklore (Marques 1999). Throughout the northeastern backlands, dances such as the samba de coco, conjectured to have African slave roots, and the *toré*, or *torem*, reputed to have indigenous ancestry, are also performed. In Mocambo, the main index of African descent "proving" quilombo status is the dancing of the samba de coco on special occasions.

years. In mid-2000, he stepped down as president of the association to run for county office, only to be disqualified because he was illiterate. A younger man took over as association president and often boasted that he was more capable than Sr. Antônio because he had traveled and knew how to relate to government officials and movement organizers in Brasília. As in the case of the "culture-conscious Brazilian Indian" discussed by Suzanne Oakdale (2004), one of the ironies of this sad situation for Sr. Antônio was that he, as the guardian of Mocambo's history was considered less capable of leading the quilombo than the younger man, who had spent time in the city and had traveled more than the average Mocambo resident. Even though quilombo supporters benefited from the younger man's literacy, they nevertheless respected Sr. Antônio's family story, which had become the dominant foundational narrative of the quilombo.

The continuing respect for Sr. Antônio's family story, as it became the quilombo's foundational narrative, was evident during my visit to the village in mid-2004, when Mocambo was on the verge of gaining legal right to use the strip along the river and finalizing the expropriation of the neighboring land on which the struggle had begun. Reflecting the influence of cultural heritage on this most local of levels, the quilombo association had turned an unused, one-room school building owned by the state into a museum and library named for Sr. Antônio's mother, the granddaughter of Antônio do Alto. The museum housed pictures of Sr. Antônio's ancestors and items from his parents' house. Sr. Antônio, although upset and disaffected from the governance of the quilombo, sparkled as he showed off his family as the root from which the quilombo sprouted. Speaking with great solemnity, authority, and ceremony, Sr. Antônio described each museum item and how it related to his family history. His family, because of the Antônio do Alto story, has come to represent the "history" of Mocambo.

The story of Antônio do Alto is not simply a tale with some historically accurate elements. It has entered the "mythic-historical consciousness" (Hill 1988: 9) of the quilombolas and the general public in surrounding areas and the capital who have heard the story and attended performances of the play. Myth and history are not necessarily mutually exclusive categories and in some circumstances may be inseparable. In the former plantation zones of northeastern Brazil, for example, stories abound about slaves being punished with death for having relations with wives and daughters of their masters. Even today in the backlands of the neighboring state of Bahia, guides relate such stories and show visitors the places were slaves were buried alive.[14] If one considers the Antônio do Alto story as a merging of history and myth, it provides a rubric that allows one to examine how it has

---

[14] Another myth is belied by such stories – the assertion espoused by Gilberto Freyre (1986) in the 1930s that slavery in Brazil was more benign than in the United States. Freyre, considered a pioneer in the sociology of the Brazilian Northeast, and often considered the originator of the "myth of racial democracy," was born in the northeastern city of Recife in 1900, the son of a former slaveholding family. He received a B.A. from Baylor University and an M.A. in 1923 from Columbia University (where he worked with Franz Boas) and is best known for his work on slavery. He taught at Stanford University for a few years in the early 1930s while he finished his

changed and why certain elements remain unchanged. The particular "organization of clues" (Silverstein and Urban 1996: 5) I propose here allows for an analysis while retaining respect for Sr. Antônio's family story as part of the history of the area that has been preserved through oral narration for three generations and is now being transformed into a "living tradition."

I analyze the elements of the versions of the story of how and why Antônio do Alto was buried alive along two axes. Along one axis are those elements that shifted in response to perceived legal requirements and expectations of quilombo supporters, including black-movement activists. Along the other axis are the elements that remained within the structure of the story's origins as a backland tale of power, sexuality, family ties, and patronage. The play, conceived of and performed by village teenagers, although based on Sr. Antônio's renderings, contains important "facts" introduced by the performers. Because the play has become the public version of the story, it has been most instrumental in consolidating the specific, locally grounded, form of quilombo identity experienced in Mocambo.

Axis of Change: Cultural Perspectives on Legislative Categories

Recall the broad outline of the Antônio do Alto story as it was told by Sr. Antônio in 1995: Antônio do Alto fell in love with the niece of the landowner. She returned his affection, and they maintained a relationship until the landowner discovered them. He became so enraged that he had Antônio do Alto buried alive. Three aspects of the story were transformed over time that signal changes traceable to perceptions of legal requirements and expectations of outside supporters. The following three

research for *Masters and Slaves*, first published in 1933. In that book, Freyre reacted against the legal segregation and racism he had seen while going to graduate school in the United States. He differentiated slavery in Brazil from US slavery on the basis of differences between Portuguese and English colonizers (Freyre 1986). His book became a bestseller and gave form to a preexisting powerful belief in the difference between the two societies that had circulated for many years. Freyre's iteration became so widespread that Brazilians, on a regular basis, continue to repeat his assertions: that Brazilian slavery was more benign and that this had led to better relations between black and white people in Brazil by allowing for miscegenation and strong kinship bonds across racial lines ("racial democracy"). On the positive side, Freyre was a vocal opponent of theories of scientific racism and with his book strove to lay to rest the belief that the Brazilian national character had been perverted by African "blood." For Freyre, and for the revised national ideology from the 1930s onward, black people from Africa had, and their descendants continued to have, a positive influence on the country's history, culture, and national identity. "By the 1960s, however, Freyre's arguments were being subjected to criticism. Historians were finding evidence of cruelty to slaves" (Wright and Wolford 2003: 118). The legacies of slavery clearly had produced inequality between darker- and lighter-skinned people in Brazil. Even though there is an "ethos of cordiality that floats on the surface" (Wright and Wolford 2003: 118) and many white Brazilians insist that everyone is descended from Africans, the discrimination that African-descended Brazilians suffer has been shown to be highly correlated with skin color (see, e.g., Telles 2004).

components were introduced in the subsequent versions: slavery, race or color, and a trip to the Afro-Brazilian cultural center of Bahia by the child born to the niece after Antônio do Alto's death.

When Sr. Antônio told the story to the black Palmares Foundation lawyer, he began by asserting, "Antônio do Alto was a slave." This is the only explicit mention of slavery. In fact, none of the versions casts the landowner as a "master" but, instead, all refer to him by his historical name, Captain Zezé Dória, or, as in the play, by the generic title denoting power and patronage in the Northeast, *coronel*.[15] The implication, however, that a form of slavery was the backdrop for the story was emphasized by Sr. Antônio in late 2001 when he added a detail that had not appeared in any of the earlier versions: Captain Zezé had seized the land on which the black people of the area had lived at least since the mid-nineteenth century, when the Brazilian emperor, Dom Pedro II, on his trip up the São Francisco River, purportedly bequeathed the neighboring land to the indigenous inhabitants. After seizing the land, Captain Zezé forced the "blacks" to build a house for his son in a single day. Thus, Sr. Antônio concluded, the family of Antônio do Alto had "come to be enslaved" by the captain.

Research conducted by the parish priest when quilombo recognition was first considered failed to locate a listing for Captain Zezé in the baptismal books as the owner of slaves, even though calculating back from the birth date of Sr. Antônio's mother (1907), Antônio do Alto would have been born sometime in the 1870s, when slavery was still legal.[16] If the family had been slaves, Sr. Antônio's grandfather would have heard about it and more than likely would have passed that information along to his grandson. Captain Zezé, like most of the other landowners in the area, used sharecropping labor and did not own slaves (Arruti 2002: 220). In fact, Antônio do Alto's father was always referred to as a "cowhand" of Captain Zezé. In the northeastern backlands where Sr. Antônio and his ancestors lived, the primary economic activities were raising cattle, growing rice and cotton as cash crops when there was enough rainfall to sustain them, and subsistence farming. Landowners often lived in a county seat and hired local families to care for their cattle and oversee their property, as Captain Zezé had done with Antônio do Alto's

---

[15] Coronel is a title derived from the National Guard (founded in 1831), which issued honorary posts to wealthy landowners and political bosses. Even after the guard was abolished, and apart from those who actually held the rank, the style of address was used by the rural population for any political leader or man of influence (Leal 1977: xv). From that title comes the concept of "coronelismo," a system associated with the rural Northeast, of favor exchanges and control over the local populace that was "a compromise, an exchange of advantages between public power, progressively invigorated, and the decadent social influence of the local bosses, particularly the landowners" (Leal 1977: 20). Coronelismo places the coronel as a key broker who consolidated his position through loyalty from the peasants who lived on his land and through control over municipal revenues. Coronels competed for political power, leading to a warlike environment in the small towns of the rural countryside.

[16] The "Free Womb" Law of 1871 provided for the registration of all slaves and their children and specified that all children born of slaves after 1871 were to be free. When the child was eight, the slave owner could receive a government payment or enjoy the labor of the child until age 21.

family. The sensibility advanced by Sr. Antônio when he referred to his ancestors as "slaves" was a result of what he had learned about the history of "true" quilombos as fugitive slave communities. Moreover, the "slavery" being referred to, implicitly or explicitly, in each of the versions of the story could just as easily have been a form of virtual slavery that many backland peasants experienced. By calling it "slavery," Sr. Antônio fulfilled what he perceived as a requirement of black activists and the government while stating, what was, for his family, a general truth of their economic circumstances.[17]

Even more explicitly than slavery, skin color became an increasingly salient aspect of each of the versions of the story. Indicating that the niece was "white" became a theme as did the use of the word *black* not only to describe Antônio do Alto but also to refer to his fellow villagers who were ordered to bury him alive when the captain discovered his niece's pregnancy. The teenagers added the most significant "fact" involving the color of the protagonists in their dramatized version of Sr. Antônio's family story. As noted above, I witnessed a performance of the play on 20 November 2000, at the end of the Black Consciousness Day pilgrimage across the land that Quilombo Mocambo had been awarded earlier that year. The Catholic priests who had helped organize the event hoped that this show of unity would convince some of the quilombo opponents to change their minds. In the tradition of backland folk Catholic practices, the long walk included cross-bearing and stops to dance and sing along the way; in the new quilombo "tradition," some men wore skullcaps meant to identify with Africa, made by a Mocambo resident who was the uncle of one of the black priests.

When the group of pilgrims arrived in Mocambo, the crowd went to the end of one of the two streets in the village, where the church, built in 1950, stands. Significantly, the church stands at the end of the street where many of the contras and their allies live. Quilombo supporters had constructed a stage in front of the church, and about a hundred people were in attendance for the event. It began with singing and recitations by Mocambo schoolchildren about black heritage and then proceeded with a play based on the story of how Antônio do Alto was buried alive. After the usual opening depicting the romance between the slave and his master's niece, played by a young woman who was chosen for her relatively light skin and "white" facial features, the coronel forced her to reveal the name of the baby's father. The niece replied, "I will go to the city and wait to see if the baby is born

---

[17] Until abolition in 1888, African-descended Brazilians occupied a variety of status positions, in many increments ranging from slave to free. Free people of color were at an advantage legally, with the power to make contracts, dispose of property, defend themselves against their employers, and testify against other freemen. Economic distinctions between free men and slaves were less apparent. Some slaves grew their own food, marketed the surplus, held skilled occupations, could accumulate money to buy freedom, and could work in the cities, living and working on their own and paying a portion of what they earned to their masters. At the same time, some free people suffered discrimination and received little for their labor, such that the distinction between slave and free labor is not very helpful in understanding economic and social relations. "If slaves acted like peasants and peasants were treated like slaves, then the distinctions begin to lose their meaning" (Schwartz 1985: 252).

white." When that turned out to be the case, the niece returned, baby in her arms, and held the child out to her uncle. She said, "Just as you wanted." The coronel agreed to raise the baby girl in his household so long as she was never told the identity of her biological father, Antônio do Alto. This attempt to racialize the story still carries within it the seed of ambiguity toward race and color prevalent in the northeastern backlands and Brazilian society, more generally.

The effects of this discursive racial polarization was beginning to be felt beyond stories and plays in the everyday life of Mocambo. As previously mentioned, some families had relocated to Mocambo after they were moved off their own land when it was converted to an indigenous reserve in the early 1990s. These "outsider" families were allied with the contras. I am reluctant to endorse the appellation of *outsider* for those families, even though quilombo supporters often referred to them that way, because substantial intermarriage occurred between them and both local Xocó Indians and Mocambo residents. Even though none of the "outsiders" would have been, or had ever before been, classified as "white," as the feuding intensified, quilombo supporters, including children, began referring to them as "the whites," thus, ratcheting up the potential racial element of the fractured community life of Mocambo. This is not to suggest that the quilombo movement created factionalism in the village. In the shifting of emphasis to race and color and giving it a name, however, lines of difference became hardened and contributed to a reframing of the concept of "community" for all the residents of Mocambo. People previously assumed to be part of the Mocambo community were now being considered "outsiders."

The third element added to the story, by Sr. Antônio possibly to provide an allusion to African-based religious observance, involved Maria, the grown daughter of Antônio do Alto and the white niece. Significantly, this addition was emphasized in the versions told in the presence of urban-based black activists, who had organized the workshop for Mocambo's elementary schoolteachers to give them the background in Afro-Brazilian heritage they needed to teach the quilombo's children. In these versions, after Captain Zezé died, Maria learned that Antônio do Alto had been her father. She traveled to Salvador, Bahia, the center of Afro-Brazilian religion and culture, and went to a *candomblé* temple (*terreiro*) to participate in that African-based religion's practice of speaking to the dead. Maria saw her father, who revealed himself by possessing the body of the "father of saints" (*pai de santo*), the religious leader of the terreiro. Speaking through the pai de santo, Antônio do Alto confirmed that Maria truly was his daughter, lending an alternative reading to the notion of being "buried alive." This added element further mythologized Antônio do Alto by making him powerful enough to return to this world. When the black lawyer from the Palmares Foundation asked, "What did Antônio do Alto say to his daughter?" Sr. Antônio responded, "He said he had suffered for her by being buried alive." By adding this element, Sr. Antônio was also adding a hint of subversion to the story. Maria's trip to Salvador to see her father undermined her uncle's plan to erase Antônio do Alto completely. As the revised tale goes, he may have been buried, but he remains alive as do his black identity and legacy.

These additions to Sr. Antônio's family story are part of a process of incorporation of reified images of slavery, previously unexpressed antagonism between black and white, and the place of Afro-Brazilian religion in the politics of quilombo recognition. As such, through the revised narrative, they are defining black identity for others (Oakdale 2004: 61) – for the contras and their "white" allies within the village and for people who live in the area but are not aware of the new ways of being "black" and "quilombola" in the northeastern backlands. In Mocambo, where the "traditional" and the "modern" are intertwined, embodiments of folk Catholicism (pilgrimages and pageants) serve as vessels through which quilombo identity is transmitted and reshapes the social space through which these cultural practices move (Urban 2001: 24, 55).

Mocambo quilombolas have self-consciously formulated their stance vis-à-vis rights, activists, and the transnational world (Abercrombie 1998: 156) through the retelling of the story and regular productions of the play. These additions have been self-consciously appropriated to improve Mocambo's standing on a national scene that has come to value descent from runaway slaves and rural black identity as part of Brazilian national cultural heritage. Even with the land grant, much is still at stake in the field of quilombo recognition, including food aid, agricultural technical assistance, irrigation, health care, education, and credits for cooperative farming, all of which has been promised but most of which have not yet arrived.

Axis of Representational Stability: Anchoring Mythohistory in Narratives of Slavery

Each of the three story elements that were changed or added could be viewed as a potential simplification of "ideas about blackness and whiteness into Manichean binaries that are easily readable to a wider audience and can move in global circuits of commoditized images" (Wade 2002: 18). Wade and others (e.g., Agier 2002; Hoffmann 2002), however, discussing parallel instances of rural black community recognition on the Pacific coast of Colombia, point out the crucial need to consider the deep-seated complexities of race and color in the region before jumping to the conclusion that people vying for recognition as "black" are engaged in the reification of categories historically viewed with suspicion by rural backlanders. In this section, I examine elements of the Antônio do Alto story that are anchored in the specificities of the region. The alterations in self-identification wrought through an engagement with legislative categories (such as "quilombo") and activists' expectations, could only have been possible against the backdrop of, and in dialogue with, existing perceptions and customary modes of thinking. The story's twists and turns reveal some of the particular ways race, color, sexuality, family, and power are conceptualized in Brazil, specifically in the backlands of the Northeast.

Four key elements of the story remain within the structure of its local and national origins. The first element, fundamental to the foundational aspect of the narrative, is a surprising twist at the end of the play and in all versions of the story. After the protagonist has been buried alive and his daughter has been accepted by the white landowner's family, it is revealed to the audience that Antônio do Alto had a wife in Mocambo with whom he had two sons before his affair with the master's niece. One of those sons was Sr. Antônio's grandfather; hence, the historical and genetic tie of Antônio do Alto to the residents of Mocambo who would, 100 years later, celebrate Antônio do Alto as the community's founder. Reflecting the sexual politics of the backlands, Antônio do Alto's stature as the founder of Mocambo is not sullied by his unfaithfulness to his black wife. Significantly, her name is not recalled, just as the name of the master's niece and Antônio do Alto's mother's name have been forgotten, even by Sr. Antônio. The story reflects the gendered nature of life in the rural interior of Brazil, where men are powerful and women nameless.

The second element, added by the teenagers in the production of the play, reflects the youths' grounding in a place where racial categories remain mutable and malleable. In a performance that has elements of racial polarization tied to a new black identity, as discussed above, a moment occurs when the narrator of the play describes Antônio do Alto's two sons by his Mocambo wife. They are referred to as "caboclos." This is a revealing choice of nomenclature because *caboclo* in the north-eastern backlands, and even more clearly in the Mocambo area, most often means a person with indigenous ancestry. Therefore, at the point in the play at which the biological link is made between Antônio do Alto and Mocambo as a site of black identity, the direct ancestors of the man most identified as black among village residents, Sr. Antônio, are referred to by a term that denotes racial mixture.

The third element of the story, added by the teenagers and discussed in the previous section, involves the niece's plea to her uncle that she be permitted to see if the child is born "white," in which case it can be raised in the landowning family. In this case, an element that represents change – a new polarization based on racial identity – contains a twist that also makes it an element representing stability, grounded in local assumptions and cultural understandings. The upshot of the story is unquestioned: that a black slave man and a white woman could have a child born white and free. The niece's gamble, added by the teenagers, albeit with added emphasis on race, remains within their life experience, because they live in a society in which black parents can have white children and vice versa and in which white children can have black siblings from the same parents. The teenagers and the audience did not find it problematic that the "white" daughter of Antônio do Alto could lead a privileged life, whereas her dark-skinned half-brothers would live as "slaves" in Mocambo.[18] Once the child, Maria, learned of her parentage, she was incorporated into Antônio do Alto's Mocambo family, and, according to Sr. Antônio, she married a state police commander and moved to the state capital to be near her half-brother, Sr. Antônio's grandfather, one of the black children of Antônio do Alto.

This theme of racially inclusive families resonates in the lives of other Mocambo residents and even in Sr. Antônio's immediate family. His daughter-in-law, one of the most militant quilombo activists in the village, had light-skinned relatives, including cousins who lived across the river and were the employers of her parents. She was

---

[18] Even in such a family, the darker-skinned children are often afforded fewer opportunities in Brazilian society. See Telles (2004).

proud that these relatives did not call her parents "employees" and that they invited them to parties, unlike other people with black relatives who do not even acknowledge them, introducing them as belonging to the darker side of the family, euphemistically calling them "moreno" (a term used for physical types ranging from olive to dark-brown complexions). In fact, this important leader of the quilombo struggle referred to herself as "morena" (and not "negra") and said of her own grandparents, "Each side had a light-skinned one with straight hair marrying a black one with bad hair." This example of the not-uncommon coexistence of a new black identity alongside the acceptance of negative assessments of darker-skinned relatives and compatriots allowed a militant black quilombola to speak unself-consciously in terms that contradicted her militancy. In another example, Sr. Antônio has proudly explained that he had white relatives in the city who were policemen and who protected him in his youth when there was trouble at parties. He could even carry a gun without it being confiscated (Arruti 2002: 315).[19] These anecdotes only hint at the numerous situations in which family trumps race, color, and class in the backlands.

Even though the ideology of "racial democracy" has been dealt serious blows in the last few decades, with official and public recognition of racial discrimination (including measures outlawing it) and a new racial quota system in higher public education in many states and the federal district, the hegemonic worldview that underpins race and color consciousness in Brazil continues to inform peoples' everyday lives (Sheriff 2001). "'The blood is the same,' . . . Racism is repugnant [and] un-Brazilian. It poisons what is closest to the shared heart, the common spirit of Brazil . . . to call [racial democracy] a mere myth-as-smokescreen is to miss the extent to which it is also a series of heteroglot narratives that . . . implicitly direct themselves to the future as well as to the past" (Sheriff 2001: 220). Consequently, through this essay's brief analysis of the nodal points at which the Antônio do Alto play retains the structure of the continuing racial politics of Brazil, one can see that certain conceptualizations of race and color remain intact, even with the assumption of a new black identity. This transformation of identity within existing structures has been termed "constrained refashioning" (Wilson 1995: 13), in which an underlying set of assumptions permits the group to be anchored while it initiates and experiences change (Wilson 1993). New elements are forged "in the shadow of the past. [The 'something new'] is a palimpsest on which the past is written over but not entirely erased . . . simultaneously present and absent, ineffable yet palpable" (Fuoss and Hill 2001: 113 n. 4). In Mocambo, assuming a black identity does not necessarily preclude simultaneous racial logics.

The fourth element of the story, again an aspect of the tale that has dual meanings in the context of change and stability, is the reported journey of Maria to "talk to her

---

[19] Adding a certain symmetry to the relationship between the landowner's niece and Antônio do Alto, in that same generation, Sr. Antônio's great-grandmother on the other side of his mother's family had a relationship with the landowner's son, with whom she had two "white" sons who went to live with their father in the city. These were the grandfathers of the white side of Sr. Antônio's family to which he was referring. This information, in conjunction with the Antônio do Alto family story (before it became a foundational narrative), reveals just how common these kinds of relationships were in the backlands.

father" in an Afro-Brazilian religious ceremony. This was most likely added under the influence of the black-activist organizer of activities designed to raise black consciousness in Mocambo. This activist was a long-time follower of candomblé (D'Acelino 1999). In another cultural innovation in Mocambo, also in connection with the black activist, the quilombolas began performing their signature dance dressed in the white clothes and turbans worn by elderly black female adherents of candomblé, even though neither the quilombolas nor anyone else in the area practices the Afro-Brazilian religion. At the same time, no one was surprised that Antônio do Alto's daughter, Maria, a "white" woman, would go to a ceremony associated with Afro-Brazilian cultural practices. Adherents represent every class and racial self-identification – from senators and authors to maids and metalworkers (Johnson 2002: 100).

At the intersection of these two axes of analysis – one of change, the other of stability in representation – the nature of identity transformation is clarified through the play's development from a family story and its performance to reinforce celebration of quilombo recognition and Black Consciousness Day. Observations made with respect to other rural black communities in Brazil shed light on the importance of the play in the process of quilombo identity formation. As part of a recent oral history project, Karina Cunha Baptista (2003: 13) has produced a sensitive analysis of interviews with known descendants of slaves in a variety of locations in Brazil. Like the Mocambo residents before quilombo recognition, interviewees were silent with respect to any kind of racial identity, insisting only that they were peasants. Baptista concluded that, particularly when there was no memory of slave ancestry or contact with "African cultural practices," racial identity was diluted, allowing peasant identity to predominate. Moreover, she found that when the matter of racism was raised by interviewers, the "assimilationist" ethos of Brazilian national identity ("we are all one people") emerged as the primary social identity among rural Afro-Brazilians. Acting out the foundational narrative of what has become Quilombo Mocambo, although reminiscent of religious pageants and pilgrimages, is not about holy intervention. Metaphors notwithstanding the act of struggle to achieve some degree of autonomy as it combined with an opportunity provided by the state through cultural heritage legislation has drawn on local understandings and worldviews to create a racial self-identification tied to a history previously untold.

Conclusion

Brazilian anthropologist Neusa Maria Mendes de Gusmão (1996: 9) has observed that land defines who quilombolas are. The struggle for land in the context of the quilombo clause, Gusmão explains, is not just a confrontation between legal ownership of land and other forms of possession but is also a matter of "individual and group definition as subjects – blacks of this or that place" (Gusmão 1996: 10–11). "Land as territory is the fruit of social narrative in the context of tension in which diverse groups confront each other" (Gusmão 1996: 10). In Mocambo, Sr. Antônio's family story, reconstructed as a play, is an integral component of the social narrative associated with the transformation of newly acquired land into the territory of a quilombo.

Although one is tempted to place the greatest emphasis on the land grant as instrumental in identity formation, I have tried to show in this essay that land should not overshadow the role of cultural forms and practices in the formation of new ethnoracial identities and self-identifications made possible by legal provisions. Most significant is the crucial role that "Africa" and assuming a black identity (and how those two phenomena are linked) have come to play in the transformation of social relations in rural communities in the Brazilian backlands, historically considered to be neither white nor black in racial terms. In this essay, I have striven to make the indispensable connection between the reworking of self-identification and public self-representation by the people doing the work. In the case of Mocambo, that self-representation was conceived and performed by members of a community in the process, and under the stress, of exploring the intersection of multiple discourses meant to improve their lives.

One of the key factors in the reconfiguration of backland as quilombo identity is the law that provides protection to cultural heritage. Thus, we can see that international conventions and declarations, designation as world heritage sites, and national laws designed to preserve cultural heritage have proven to be both protective and productive. Since cultural preservation is most often associated with solidly material things, such as buildings (Azcona and Zanirato 2005), it may be easy to forget that both "culture" and "heritage" are in a constant state of flux, creation, and re-creation. The stories told in this essay about a play conceived and performed by a new generation of quilombolas, a legal category of heritage that has existed for only a little more than a decade, reveal the productive effects of cultural heritage laws, particular with respect to "intangible cultural heritage."

Just as this essay has investigated the notion of "constrained refashioning" (Wilson 1995) in relation to the self-identification of members of Quilombo Mocambo, a set of similar concepts may be noted with respect to "culture as patrimony" (Gonçalves 2005). Brazilian anthropologist José Reginaldo Santos Gonçalves brings to life terms such as "resonance, materiality, and subjectivity" to remind us of the tangible intangibility of cultural heritage. To become accessible as "heritage" practices must "encounter resonance with its public" (Gonçalves 2005: 19). Heritage is situated somewhere between history and memory, as the story of Antônio do Alto reveals. The "truth" of the story lies in its resonance with desires and struggles existing in the present. Because the access to the past that heritage makes possible is, in part, dependent on chance, and cannot be planned, the role of laws and conventions protecting cultural heritage may or may not be successful (Gonçalves 2005: 20). However, if heritage is a mediating force between aspects of "culture" – self-perfection as in a work of art or drama and the "expression of a collective soul" (Gonçalves 2005: 28) – it may also be an ideal mediator between the particular and the universal, the conundrum with which I began this essay. Finally, crucial to appreciating the importance of the concept of cultural heritage is the recognition that the imposed, official division between tangible and intangible is illusory, as the materiality of the play in Mocambo reveals. The aim must be to avoid ossification by remembering the inextricability of the two.

Acknowledgments   Funding for this research was provided by the International Dissertation Field Research Fellowship (IDRF) program of the Social Science Research Council (SSRC), a Fulbright Dissertation Grant (USIA), a National Science Foundation Dissertation Improvement Grant, and travel grants from the Duke University Latin American and Caribbean Studies Center. A Rockefeller residential fellowship at Northwestern University and a postdoctoral fellowship in Latin American Studies at the University of Maryland, College Park, provided venues for presentation of this research at earlier stages. Substantial portions of this essay first appeared in *American Ethnologist*, Vol. 33, No. 3 (2006). That paper was revised and reframed for the Collaborative for Cultural Heritage and Museum Practices international workshop generating this volume on cultural heritage and human rights.

References

Abercrombie, Thomas, 1998, *Pathways of Memory and Power: Ethnography and History among an Andean People*. University of Wisconsin Press, Madison.

Agier, Michel, 2002, From Local Legends into Globalized Identities: The Devil, the Priest and the Musician in Tumaco. *Journal of Latin American Anthropology* 7(2): 140–167.

Almeida, Alfredo Wagner Berno de, 1989, Terras de Preta, Terras de Santo, Terras de Índio-Uso Comum e Conflito, na Trilhados Grandes Projetos. In *Cadernos NAEA 10*, edited by C. a. H. (orgs). Gráfica e Editora Universitária UFPA, Belém.

Arruti, José Maurício Andion, 1998, Mocambo/Sergipe: Negros e Índios no Artesanato da Memória. *Tempo e Presenço* Suplemento Especial (March/April 1998): 26–28.

—, 2001, Agenciamentos Políticos da 'Mistura': Identificação Étnica e Segmentação Negro-Indigéna entre os Pankararú e os Xocó. *Estudos Afro-Asiáticos* 23(2): 215–254.

—, 2002, '*Étnias Federais': O processo de identificação de 'remanescentes' indígenas e quilombolas no Baixo São Francisco*. Ph.D., Museu Nacional, UFRJ, Rio de Janeiro.

Ashmore, Wendy, and Arthur Bernard Knapp, 1999, *Archaeologies of Landscape: Contemporary Perspectives*. Blackwell, Malden, MA.

Azcona, Emilio Luque, and Sílvia Helena Zanirato, 2005, La Gestión del Patrimonio Cultural: Políticas de Intervención en el Nordeste de Brasil y Andalucía. *Estudos Ibero-Americanos* 31(2): 155–175.

Baiocchi, Mari de Nasare, 1983, *Negros de Cedro (Estudo Anthropológico de um Bairro Rural de Negros em Goiás)*. Atica, São Paulo.

Baptista, Karina Cunha, 2003, O Diálogo dos Tempos: História, Memória e Identidade nos Depoimentos Orais de Descendentes de Escravos Brasileiros. *Primeiros Escritos de Laboritório de História Oral e Imagem (LABHOI)* 11: 1–23.

Barth, Fredrik, 1969, Introduction. In *Ethnic Groups and Boundaries: The Social Organization of Culture Difference*, edited by Fredrik Barth. Little, Brown and Company, Boston.

Bruner, Edward M., 2005, *Culture on Tour*. University of Chicago Press, Chicago.

Castro, Yeda Pessoa de, 2001, *Falares Africanos na Bahia (Um Vocabulário Afro-Brasileiro)*. Academia Brasileira de Letras Topbooks, Rio de Janeiro.

Cleere, Henry, 2001, The Uneasy Bedfellows: Universality and Cultural Heritage. In *Destruction and Conservation of Cultural Property*, edited by Robert Layton, Peter G. Stone, and Julian Thomas, pp. 22–29. Routledge, London.

Clifford, James, 1997, *Routes: Travel and Translation in the Late Twentieth Century*. Harvard University Press, Cambridge.

Cowan, Jane K., 2006, Culture and Rights After Culture and Rights. *American Anthropologist* 108(1): 9–24.

D'Acelino, Severo, 1999, *Memorial do Curso: Resgate da Memória Cultural do Mocambo*. Secretaria Estadual da Educação, Desporto e Lazer, Aracaju.

French, Jan Hoffman, 2003, *The Rewards of Resistance: Legalizing Identity among Descendants of Índios and Fugitive Slaves in Northeastern Brazil*. Ph.D. dissertation. Department of Cultural Anthropology, Duke University, Durham.

—, 2004, Mestizaje and Law Making in Indigenous Identity Formation in Northeastern Brazil: 'After the Conflict Came the History.' *American Anthropologist* 106(4): 663–674.

Freyre, Gilberto, 1986, *The Masters and the Slaves: A Study in the Development of Brazilian Civilization*. Second English Language Revised Edition. University of California Press, Berkeley.

Funari, Pedro Paulo A., Martin Hall, and Sian Jones, 1999, *Historical Archaeology: Back from the Edge*. One World Archaeology, 31. Routledge, London.

Fuoss, Kirk W., and Randall T. G. Hill, 2001, Spectacular Imaginings: Performing Community in Guatemala. In *Global Multiculturalism: Comparative Perspectives on Ethnicity, Race, and Nation*, edited by G. H. Cornwell and E. W. Stoddard, Rowman & Littlefield, Lanham.

Geipel, John, 1997, Brazil's African Legacy. *History Today* 47(8): 18–24.

Godreau, Isar P., 2002, Changing Space, Making Race: Distance, Nostalgia, and the Folklorization of Blackness in Puerto Rico. *Identities: Global Studies in Culture and Power* 9: 281–304.

Gomez, Michael Angel, 2005, *Reversing Sail: A History of the African Diaspora, New Approaches to African History*. Cambridge University Press, Cambridge.

Gonçalves, José Reginaldo Santos, 2005, Ressonância, Materialidade e Subjetividade: As Culturas como Patrimônios. *Horizontes Antropológicos* 11(23): 15–36.

Gusmão, Neusa Maria Mendes de, 1996, Da Antropologia e do Direito: Impasses da Questão Negra no Campo. *Palmares em Revista* (1): 1–13.

Guss, David M., 2000, *The Festive State: Race, Ethnicity, and Nationalism as Cultural Performance*. University of California Press, Berkeley.

Hanchard, Michael George, 1994, *Orpheus and Power: The Movimento Negro of Rio de Janeiro and São Paulo, Brazil, 1945–1988*. Princeton University Press, Princeton.

Handler, Richard, and Eric Gable, 1997, *The New History in an Old Museum. Creating the Past at Colonial Williamsburg*. Duke University Press, Durham.

Hill, Jonathan David, 1988, Introduction: Myth and History. In *Rethinking History and Myth: Indigenous South American Perspectives on the Past*, edited by J. D. Hill, pp. 1–17. University of Illinois Press, Urbana.

Hoffmann, Odile, 2002, Collective Memory and Ethnic Identities in the Colombian Pacific. *Journal of Latin American Anthropology* 7(2): 118–139.

Hufford, Mary, 1994, *Conserving Culture: A New Discourse on Heritage*. University of Illinois Press, Urbana.

Istoé, 1998, *The Heirs of Chico Rei, May 20*. http://www.terra.com.br/istoe/politica/149424.chtm (19 April 2005).

Johnson, Paul Christopher, 2002, *Secrets, Gossip, and Gods: The Transformation of Brazilian Candomblé*. Oxford University Press, Oxford.

Kent, R. K., 1965, Palmares: An African State in Brazil. *Journal of Negro History* 6: 161–175.

Layton, Robert, Peter G. Stone, and Julian Thomas, eds., 2001, *Destruction and Conservation of Cultural Property*. Routledge, London.

Leal, Victor Nunes, 1977, *Coronelismo: The Municipality and Representative Government in Brazil*, translated by J. Henfrey. Cambridge University Press, Cambridge.

Linhares, Luiz Fernando do Rosário, 2004, Kilombos of Brazil: Identity and Land Entitlement. *Journal of Black Studies* 34(6): 817–837.

Magno da Silva, Rosemiro, 2000, *A Luta dos Posseiros de Santana dos Frades*. Editora UFS, Aracaju.

Marques, Núbia N., 1999, *O Luso, O Lúdico e o Perene*. Imago, Rio de Janeiro.

Nascimento, Abdias do, 1980, *O quilombismo: documentos de uma militância pan-africanista*. Vozes, Petrópolis.

Oakdale, Suzanne, 2004, The Culture-Conscious Brazilian Indian: Representing and Reworking Indianness in Kayabi Political Discourse. *American Ethnologist* 31(1): 60–75.

Palmares Cultural Foundation, 2000, Document prepared for the UN Third World Conference to Combat Racism, Discrimination, Xenophobia, and other forms of Intolerance, held in August 2001 in Durban, South Africa. Palmares Cultural Foundation, Brasília.

Paoli, Maria Celia, 1992, Citizenship, Inequalities, Democracy and Rights: The Making of a Public Space in Brazil. *Social and Legal Studies* 1: 143–159.

Pereira, Edimilson de Almeida, and Steven F. White, 2001, Brazil: Interactions and Conflicts in a Multicultural Society. In *Global Multiculturalism: Comparative Perspectives on Ethnicity, Race, and Nation*, edited by G. H. Cornwell and E. W. Stoddard, pp. 123–141. Rowman & Littlefield, Lanham.

Price, Richard, 1983, *First Time: Historical Vision, Afro-American People*. Johns Hopkins University Press, Baltimore.

—, 1999, Reinventando a História dos Quilombos. Rasuras e Confabulações. *Afro-Ásia* 23: 239–265.

—, 2002, Maroons in the Americas: Heroic Pasts, Ambiguous Presents, Uncertain Futures. *Cultural Survival Quarterly* 25(4): 8.

Queiroz, Maria Isaura Pereira de, 1976, *O Campesinato Brasileiro: Ensaios sobre Civilização e Grupos Rústicos no Brazil*, 2nd edition. Editora Vozes Ltda., Petrópolis.

Schneider, John T., 1991, *Dictionary of African Borrowings in Brazilian Portuguese*. Libertas, Hamburg.

Schwartz, Stuart B., 1985, *Sugar Plantations in the Formation of Brazilian Society: Bahia, 1550–1835*. Cambridge University Press, Cambridge.

—, 1992, *Slaves, Peasants, and Rebels: Reconsidering Brazilian Slavery*. University of Illinois Press, Urbana.

Scott, David, 1991, That Event, This Memory: Notes on the Anthropology of African *Diaspora* in the New World. Diaspora 1(3): 261–284.

Segato, Rita L., 1998, The Color-Blind Subject of Myth; Or, Where to Find Africa in the Nation. *Annual Review of Anthropology* 27: 129–151.

Sheriff, Robin E., 2001, *Dreaming Equality: Color, Race, and Racism in Urban Brazil*. Rutgers University Press, New Brunswick.

Silverstein, Michael, and Greg Urban, 1996, *Natural Histories of Discourse*. University of Chicago Press, Chicago.

Telles, Edward Eric, 2004, *Race in Another America: The Significance of Skin Color in Brazil*. Princeton University Press, Princeton.

Urban, Greg, 2001, *Metaculture: How Culture Moves Through the World*. Public Worlds, vol. 8. University of Minnesota Press, Minneapolis.

Veja, 1998, Forgotten Africa: Remnants of Ancient Quilombos, 511 Black Communities Live Isolated in the Interior of the Country. May 20, pp. 80–81.

Véran, Jean-François, 2002, Quilombos and Land Rights in Contemporary Brazil. *Cultural Survival Quarterly* 25(4): 20.

Vogt, Carlos, and Peter Fry, 1996, *Cafundó: A África no Brasil*. Ed. da Unicamp, Companhia das Letras, São Paulo.

Wade, Peter, 2002, *Race, Nature and Culture: An Anthropological Perspective*. Anthropology, Culture, and Society. Pluto Press, London.

Williams, Daryle, 2001, *Culture Wars in Brazil: The First Vargas Regime, 1930–1945*. Duke University Press, Durham.

Wilson, Richard Ashby, 1993, Anchored Communities: Identity and History of the Maya-Q'eqchi'. *Man, New Series* 28(1): 121–138.

—, 1995, *Maya Resurgence in Guatemala: Q'eqchi' Experiences*. University of Oklahoma Press, Norman.

—, 1997, *Human Rights, Culture and Context: Anthropological Perspectives*. Anthropology, Culture, and Society. Pluto Press, London.

—, 2006, Afterword to 'Anthropology and Human Rights in a New Key': The Social Life of Human Rights. *American Anthropologist* 108(1): 77–83.

Wright, Angus, and Wendy Wolford, 2003, *To Inherit the Earth: The Landless Movement and the Struggle for a New Brazil*. Food First Books, Oakland.

Chapter 7
Historical Disruptions in Ecuador: Reproducing an Indian Past in Latin America

O. Hugo Benavides

> Do you know why people like me are shy about being capitalists? Well, it's because we, for as long as we have known you, were capital, like bales of cotton and sacks of sugar, and you were the commanding, cruel capitalists, and the memory of this is so strong, the experience so recent, that we can't quite bring ourselves to embrace this idea you think so much of. As for what we were like before we met you, I no longer care. No periods of time over which my ancestors held sway, no documentation of complex civilizations, is any comfort to me. Even if I really came from people who were living like monkeys in trees, it was better to be that than what happened to me, what I became after I met you.
>
> (Kincaid 1997: 36–37)

Introduction

In the first wedding ceremony ever held at the pre-Inca site of Cochasquí, near Quito in the north highlands of Ecuador, the local shaman made an incantation to the indigenous genealogy of the Ecuadorian bride that gave her the right to marry her foreign (Russian) husband in this land, rightfully hers. This native appeal is more telling when you take into consideration that the bride neither had direct ties with any contemporary Indian community nor had lived in the country for over a decade. Both she and her husband had flown in from Miami, where they lived, to get married at Cochasquí. She chose Cochasquí as the place from which to justify her Indian genealogy/ Ecuadorianess, which were called into question by her living outside of the country and marrying outside of the national fold.

As I participated as a guest at the wedding, held on the summer solstice of 1997, I sensed, in the inherent quality of the ritual activities held at Cochasquí, an urgency to connect to a national sense of belonging that maintained (and also questioned) what being a native signifies. The bride had come back to reclaim her Ecuadorianness, to "invent" it; her getting married at Cochasquí accomplished that. The wedding service was full of symbolic appeals to Incas, other Indian communities, and Andean deities without any actual concern for historical or geographical truths. Rather, the essentializing celebration expressed a constant need to reaffirm a symbolic truth that wove all of these indigenous elements into a common fabric, and allowed all the guests present to claim the site as Ecuadorian.

H. Silverman and D. F. Ruggles (eds.), *Cultural Heritage and Human Rights*.
© Springer 2007

Echoing Foucault (Miller 1993: 250), the symbolic truth at Cochasquí was not and did not necessarily have to be true – that did not make it less real nor did it have less actual implications on performers and spectators alike.

I use this wedding metaphor to introduce the present chapter on the politics of heritage identity in Ecuador today. This question of identity politics is large, containing within it greater issues of human rights in our globalizing existence, entertaining what it means to be a native, what is the role of the environment in this political enterprise, and ultimately what are the boundaries of local/global enterprises in the current discourse of development and political struggle.

The Indian movement is a particularly good place to interrogate these issues of belonging because Native Americans, or Indians, in Ecuador today are the best example of a postmodern identity and, in that sense, of the inherently localized manners in which the global gets constituted in localized fashion. It is this global/local dynamic that has allowed the Ecuadorian Indian movement (CONAIE/Confederation of Indian Nationalities of Ecuador) to become the largest social movement in the country in the last decade, paralyzing the nation several times during week-long strikes, ousting two democratically elected presidents, and even facing off the International Monetary Fund (IMF). And yet: who is Indian or not? What role do the environment and the past play in this identity enterprise? And what are the daily impacts of survival? These are looming questions that are far harder to answer than one would initially assume.

For the last 10 years I have spent a considerable amount of energy and time working on and researching the political implications of the past in the contemporary nation-state of Ecuador. As part of my research endeavor I have also assessed the relationship of the archeological past to one of the leading Indian movements in the continent, that of the CONAIE, and I grapple with the immediate relationship of notions of heritage to the construction of a more just and democratic society. During this time, I also have had to reconsider and negotiate my own troubled relationship to the research subject since, as an Ecuadorian national myself, these issues are anything but academic, and are intimately related to why I decided to become an archeologist/ anthropologist 20 years ago.

My passion for archeology was determined by my political ambition to contribute to the construction of a more coherent and congruent Latin American history, one in which the glories of the Indian past would not be alienated and distanced from the contemporary oppression of their descendants. In this manner, I (and comrades, both faculty and students) saw archeological research as a way of righting a profound historical wrong and allowing the native Indian communities to finally have their rightful place in the historical record, and, even more importantly, to be able to use this historical legitimization to ensure a political capital that could transform their livelihoods and with them revolutionize our understanding in order to make a more humane and Indian nation than our governments and elite would want us to believe Ecuador was capable of.

Twenty years after that youthful archeological imperative and 10 years after my initial considerations of the larger conundrums of historical production, I feel able to provide some insights into the enormous obstacles that not only Ecuador but also many other postcolonial nation-states face in the new global order. This endeavor also necessitates assessing the pitfalls of a cultural heritage and human rights agenda that many times leaves its constituency behind in an effort to achieve lofty goals that depart from their original blue-prints.

In the following pages I will limit myself to what I believe are the biggest issues in terms of heritage and human rights in Latin America: (1) the challenge of creating congruent national histories where historical periods have been marked by rupture and colonial domination; (2) the politics of the Amazon within the shadows of a global ecological movement; and (3) understanding the relationship between heritage and development, and the limitations of generalizing a Western discourse beyond its initial ideological boundaries. It is these issues, I argue, that are essential in assessing the elements of political domination contained within the projects of heritage and historical production. And yet, as in all cultural projects and endeavors, from that of development to living our own lives, the challenge is not to regress to a utopian period that never existed but hopefully to provide some level of agency within the restricted structure of modern capital and postmodern forms of identity production.

Historical Disruptions and Congruent Narratives: Getting One's History Wrong

As I rapidly assessed from my ethnographic work at the pre-Inca archeological site of Cochasquí, there is nothing natural or congruent about national histories. Quite the contrary, national narratives by the state, local communities, or even the Indian movement were consistently put together from the same loose and jagged remains of the pre-Hispanic past and used to legitimize each one's political claim and cultural survival. The narratives I looked at changed as a result of a shifting kaleidoscope of images, memories, and evidence that served to construct and maintain differing notions of power.

And although each proclaimed its truthfulness in authentic terms, their main difference was not afforded by either the narratives or elements themselves but rather by the epistemological and hermeneutical devices used to define the narratives in the first place. It was this "proof of burden" that defined what was or was not considered evidence, which was what ultimately provided the most defining understanding of the character of each historical narrative. In this manner, while the CONAIE's narrative incorporated oral history as a valid form of historical heritage, national newspapers believed that scholarly (and popular public) opinions were most important in defining what was true about the past, and therefore deemed part of real history.

As many scholars have argued, history is never linear nor does it inherently express causality by itself but rather, it is our own renderings of it, as defined by the hermeneutics of historical production, that structure historical accounts (Foucault 1991). In this sense, archeological interpretations without exception are incorporated into master narratives that reinterpret and meaningfully connect the nation's present with the past. In doing so, the narratives overlook the breaks and discontinuities that make smooth transition lines impossible and that would therefore delegitimize the whole national historic enterprise.

The need for historical continuity is particularly explicit in colonial settings, where the new leaders are keen to present themselves as the natural inheritors of the dominated group and territory (Kuklick 1991: 165). Colonialism always implies an artificial and violent break from the immediate past and a necessary legitimization of the new order as natural and ever-constant. In this enterprise, archeological interpretations are used to obliterate the break and present a new unproblematic extension of the archeological past to the political present. Ecuador is no exception to this postcolonial conundrum. The nation-state elaborates a complex discourse of colonial conquest: first, by the Incas over a thousand years ago; second, by the Spaniards less than five centuries ago; and most recently, a current white/*mestizo* elite that is continuously reinforced in its position of political and social privilege.

In this manner national histories homogenize cultural diversity by "permanently removing generations of (local) history from the landscape and create a national historic rootlessness under official state sponsorship" (Patterson and Schmidt 1995: 20). All historical versions, in their own fashion and for their own gain, strive to overlook the discontinuities in their own archeological rendering of the past. National archeological narratives, official or not, are always about presenting: a *smooth* history where there are only accidents; a *continuous* subject where there is only discontinuity; a *homogenous* nationality where there is heterogeneity of communities; and historical *truth* where there is only subjugated knowledge.

Therefore, while on the one side we have a pervasive production of national narratives that are vying for differing levels of acceptance and effects of power, we also have been privy to the struggle of a powerful Indian movement that has gone beyond any initial expectation and/or predictions in terms of its range of cultural influence and political power. However, quite dramatically, the growth of the CONAIE has not only demanded a new redefinition of who is Indian and who is not, but also of who represents Ecuador, and what role the archeological past and cultural heritage plays in that representation. What is even more interesting (and telling) in this regard is the almost complete absence of an archeological discourse or heritage agenda within the CONAIE's successful reclaiming of its past and political present.

Contrary to what many (including myself) would have ventured, the Indian movement today in Ecuador has a limited relationship with reclaiming ancient sites and archeological objects from what they deem their own original communities. Interestingly enough, the battlefield for the Indian's (and the nation-state's) past is fought within the political arena of the national congress, presidential elections, and nation-wide strikes and marches, not in the limited theaters of ancient sites and museums. This is not to imply that sites or museums do not play an essential political role in the national hegemonic imaginary but, rather, that the CONAIE's political process might give us insights (and hopefully short-cuts) to the destabilizing role through which heritage claims and human rights concerns might be better served.

The cold relationship between Indian and archeologist has a long tradition not only in Ecuador, but also throughout the Americas. The re-burial issue in the US and the commodification of the sites of Chichén Itza in Yucatan and Machu Picchu in Cuzco all point to the alienating role of archeology and archeologists in the reclaiming of original homelands. It is a difficult relationship that, as Deloria (1979) has keenly assessed, frankly reflects the colonial legacies within the discipline. Archeology and archeologists are still invested in fulfilling their patriarchal and dutiful role as the guides and givers of heritage to localized communities that should thank our endeavor. However, as the CONAIE's successful strategy indicates, many original descendent communities may be implementing historical plans different from our anthropological/archeological ones, and of even greater hegemonic implications.

Therefore, I strongly believe that in postcolonial settings such as Ecuador there is an overriding necessity, even an obsession to construct a congruent national narrative precisely because one never existed. It is this maddening Western historical imaginary ideal that pushes individuals and communities to vie for contrasting national narratives that will only fail in better ways (a la Beckett) to represent a national whole that does not exist. It is because of this postcolonial impossibility of national representation that some political strategy and plain human savvy might be the least harmful road to take. Why not forget about representing a whole (in this case, "Ecuadorianness") and, rather, articulate limited historical ethnic identities (as the case of Indian in Ecuador) that themselves are the result of a Western capitalist expansion that decimated and ultimately transformed not only the Americas but Europe as well. It is because of this eventual inherent relationship between global and local sites of contestations and identifications that much more dynamic and historically congruent forms of heritage and human rights need to be articulated and implemented.

In this manner, perhaps one of the most essential elements of the heritage project that must be analyzed is the role of Europe (and the US itself) in this global cultural enterprise. As I argue below, I believe that there are quite specific relationships between heritage production and development endeavors that make these issues of historical recovery one of the political domination and hegemonic implications. But even before formulating the necessary Western legacy contained within both the global heritage and human rights agendas, there is an even more pervasive and essential relationship between the Americas and Europe (and the US) contained within what Quijano (1993) refers to as "colonialities of power." It is these pervasive neo/postcolonial relationships that continue to reshape, epistemologically speaking, old mechanisms of historical appropriation that define what is even deemed recoverable history and what is not.

As an Ecuadorian who has been constituted as such by living most of my life outside of Ecuador, I am – in an intimately painful manner – well aware of the mechanism through which the local is inherently defined as such from a global vantage point. In this manner it is not surprising that it is Europe and transnational NGOs, not Ecuadorians (and, worse, the Ecuadorian government), that have fueled the political project of the CONAIE and served to revindicate the same historical subjectivity that they (Europe and the US) so brutally vilified centuries ago. Yet, as Kincaid (1997) would have it, there is a world of things in this, this silence and apparent contradiction in terms of Indian ethnogenesis, legitimization of a pre-Hispanic archeological past, and ultimately the struggle for a human rights agenda for the continent.

But how does one begin to unravel not only the definition of history, but also – even worse – the recovery of a mutilated historical subject that is not unitary or unified other than in its imaginary proportions? Again, the project seems daunting, if not for the fact that it is carried out every day both in small and large political endeavors that allow postcolonial societies, like Ecuador, to struggle on with visions of a more prosperous and cohesive future. It is this same project that both the CONAIE and government are invested in, as is every single person who tries to define his/her livelihood against such terrifying uneven odds – perhaps with different understandings and outcomes but, ultimately interested in constructing a congruent narrative that will legitimize the advancement of the nation, however differently that may be defined and understood.

In these contested sites of historical narratives, the heritage and human rights agenda enters, not really as an outside/Western interruption, but rather as an inherent constitutive device of the colonialities of power that have defined the Latin American (and Ecuadorian) subject from the very beginning. Therefore, the struggle in a more realistic approximation is less about what history recovers and why, and more about why it is that we are invested in such a global project of local definitions, what political purposes it serves, and ultimately how that same venture defines and produces history in the process. After all, just like the Ecuadorian government and the CONAIE, academics and transnational cultural agencies have already entered the fray of producing history, with the added terrifying quality denial that we are doing so.

Historical Disruptions and the Greening of the Amazon's Past

Now that there is peace between Ecuador and Peru,[1] only Brazil, of the Amazonian countries, makes use of the Amazon in an explicit or direct manner to boost or define their own national identity (see Jan French's paper in this volume). Yet the fact that no direct or explicit relationship is established between the official state rhetoric and the regional historical complexes does not negate that even greater forms of subtle hegemonic discourses are being elaborated between the historical past and political present. Therefore, how does the Amazonian past enter into the political debate of the Andean nations in a time when the transnational discussion of native rights, ecological concerns, and even the rise of ecotourism enters the

---

[1] During the 1980s, as border tension continued between Ecuador and Peru, official Ecuadorian stationery was emblazoned with the slogan: "El Ecuador Fué, Es, y Siempre Será Un País Amazónico," referring to Ecuador's claim for Peruvian Amazonian territory down to Iquitos.

global imagination within specific national concerns as well as that of specific transnational corporations, particularly that of oil companies?

The Amazon has become one of the main representatives of ecological promise (represented as either paradise or decimation, depending on one's viewpoint) and the struggle for indigenous rights. These dual discourses, of ecological production and indigenous livelihood, are in stark contrast with the more traditional representation of Amazon land exploitation, either that of rubber trapping/cattle-herding or oil extraction. It is in this particular political scenario of daily struggle and global forces that Amazonian Indians struggle and archeological research is carried out. It is not lost on anybody, especially archeologists, that the last decade has seen an increase of archeological research in the area, funded by the same foreign oil companies that are responsible for decimating the region.

Similar to other regional arguments, such as the reburial issue, archeologists in the Amazon once again are faced with the serious dilemma of being seen as siding (and realistically so) with precisely the same global forces that they hope their own work would oppose. On the one hand this is not a new dilemma, but rather a clear and coherent corollary of the colonial legacy of the West's scientific (and humanistic) enterprise. Social knowledge production in the Americas has always been produced and utilized by those in power, in terms of both race and class, and even the most democratic of its development meets structural limitations that reemphasize the uneven distribution of cultural knowledge in the continent. In the Amazon this particular dilemma is expressed in the co-option of valuable intellectuals who, as experts of the past, align themselves with precisely those who are destroying the human and natural resources that the experts wish to save.

This reality is further complicated by a large and significant group of activists, both nationals and not, who are increasingly aligned with ecological conservation movements as well as with the Indigenous Amazonian communities who are fighting transnational corporations for their daily and cultural survival. At the same time these urban activists themselves are seen as foreign allies to the Amazonian communities and equally provide a much needed support coming from foreign international agencies and NGOs. Therefore, to present a picture of local natives fighting foreign global forces is in itself inaccurate, since at this point in time, native local identity production is as clearly contingent upon global support as it has been for the last five centuries (Benavides 2004).

It is also in this complex framework that the archeological research carried out in the Amazon seems rather insignificant in the production of regional identifica-tions, national legitimization, and fodder for the globalization players throughout the world. The complex history of archeological research of the last 100 years has gone from seeing the Amazon as a cultural backwater to the original locus of high Andean civilization, but this seems highly irrelevant in the explicit political reconfigurations currently being worked out in the region or even being played out in the national imaginary of their Andean counterparts. Unfortunately, out of this archeological engagement – or more accurately, the lack of direct archeological engagement – two serious fallacies arise that are an impediment to a more accurate discussion of the Amazon's cultural problematic and its representation, and that as an impediment also play an active part in the current problematization of the region.

The first fallacy in this regard is the belief, particularly by archeologists of the region, that a serious consideration of their findings would serve to make right most of the political and cultural wrongs. These experts think that if they were taken more seriously, and if their work were funded less by business concerns, and if they were given more cultural authority in the area, then the Amazon's problems would be seriously and positively reconfigured. This naïve and pervasive professional position is not new in archeology, and it characterizes development discourse as a racist and colonial legacy of our Western origins. Instead, it could be argued that experts are the ones who need to engage themselves more seriously with the sociopolitical reality of the regions and not vice versa.

The second fallacy is to believe that archeological knowledge does not already play an important part in the region and each nation-state's national imaginary simply because no explicit or direct link is made. On the contrary, archeologists and archeological knowledge are already playing an important part in the problematic distribution of the Amazon's productive resources, both cultural and economic. The fact that archeologists are seen as part of the problem for the development of native rights is not a misassumption by indigenous communities but rather a reality that most archeologists pretend not to see.

But archeological knowledge *is* readily used when it comes to the Amazon, particularly if it can provide a simple and unproblematic rendering of the region as a green natural paradise destroyed by western capital expansion. Of course, this panacea is also a rhetorical political tool, into which social knowledge easily falls. Therefore, it is not a surprise that recent books such as Tierney's (2000) *Darkness in El Dorado: How Scientists and Journalists Devastated the Amazon* have a wide popular appeal. In many ways, his and other similar works are doing nothing more than giving empirical support for rhetorical ideas and discourses that 100 years of archeological research have already put into people's heads. If anything, it is quite interesting how archeology suffers from its own discourse against foreign intrusion.

In this sense, it is important to wonder about the manner in which archeology has been able to carry out this pervasive rhetoric in the region, and what the contemporary power-effects of archeology's effusive regional production are, rather than to advocate for an audience that it already has captivated. It is necessary to question the discourse that has "greened the past" and naturalized native rights; it is also necessary to be skeptical about the politics of transnational exploitation that fund archeological research. This awareness will permit a more realistic picture of the Amazon and the Andean nation-states. It is also in this charged environment that the future of the Amazon, national imaginaries, Indian communities, and archeological research will continue to embody the differing local and global forces at play in the region.

Historical Disruptions and Heritage: A History
of Development

One of the most disturbing elements of the heritage and human rights global agenda
is its eerie similarity with the development project. Perhaps as the Mexican Nobel
Laureate, Octavio Paz, stated, anthropology is the conscience of the West; that in
one way or another, these are all internal mechanisms of capitalism that surface to
attempt to alleviate the system's unethical destruction of peoples and environment
for capital accumulation and surplus. Although ironic, as an anthropologist I am
even less hopeful than Paz.

As I have outlined elsewhere in terms of my research in Ecuador, the CONAIE
is itself one of the most successful development projects to date (Benavides 2004).
It has been able to muster financial and symbolic support from international NGOs,
and its environmental and human rights agenda supports its critical positioning
within contemporary global relationships. However, it is also in this fashion that the
Ecuadorian Indian movement faces an enormous challenge – for in this alternative
Indian version there is an embryonic element, by necessity, that seeks to represent
its own version as a hegemonic history in similar terms but with a different context
to the official version being contested (Wylie 1995; Chatterjee 1986).

The Indian movement finds itself on a political tightrope: at one level it strongly
opposes the IMF and the World Bank's structural adjustment policies, yet at
another level it consistently supports the development project being funded and
planned by the World Bank. The movement continues to relate to the double nature
of the World Bank's economic agenda without explicitly entertaining the idea that
the development funds so badly needed by the country originate from the unequal
globalization processes that overwhelmingly limit and dominate the third world's
economic production.

At the same time, the recent Indian identity espoused by the movement is itself
partly a result of modern capitalist globalization processes (Benavides 2004). Only
this political and economic reality would justify the Indian movement's support by
foreign NGOs and other First World institutions. This same "westernization" support
of Indian identity makes the movement's relationship with its historically constituted
enemies, the Catholic Church and the military, much more understandable. After 500
years of painful evangelization, the Indians have finally come full circle and are making use of the very religious institution that was initially implicated in the ethnocide
and genocide of Indians (Native Americans) throughout the continent.

History and heritage enable Indians today in Ecuador to employ an ethnic
identity that was the cause of their domination. Therefore, Indians are able to parlay
their ethnic oppression as cultural capital to obtain funds, political recognition, and
other resources from First World nations, many of which were once (and still are)
perpetrators of their own cultural destruction. Native struggles, development
schemes, and democratization plans are entangled retransformations of old uneven
political alliances between First and Third World forces (Hall 1997). To this degree,
the Indian movement is not a representative of some pristine cultural authenticity

but rather a "reconversing" of previous social symbols and meaning in contemporary terms (García-Canclini 1992).

In this complex reality, the Indian movement is the most modern, or even postmodern, signifier of Ecuador's contemporary political struggle – a struggle that is now also fought beyond the country's national borders. This particular global context places the Indian movement's financial support and identity in a very fragile context. If the counterhegemonic demands of the CONAIE are met – and this could only occur in a global reordering of the economic order – the movement would pretty soon find itself with no more First World NGOs and development projects to fund it, and perhaps more dramatically without a cultural global understanding in which Indians could translate their identity in such a positive manner. After all, it is instructive that Indian groups have taken this long to find a cultural context that enables their political projects. It is clear that Indian uprisings and protests are not new; only their current national success.

However, since a global economic reordering seems highly unlikely – the IMF, World Bank, and First World nations are not on their own going to invert the current uneven socioeconomic relationships – the Indian movement may have to face its own hegemonic reordering. Although the CONAIE consistently expresses itself as an instrument for the greater democratization for itself and the nation, it is plausible that the opposite might ensue. That is, since current unequal global conditions are continuously transforming, CONAIE will probably be co-opted into a hegemonic enterprise before the Ecuadorian state experiences any kind of democratic dissolution.

Few scholars, and even fewer anthropologists for obvious disciplinary reasons, have been willing to elaborate on the hegemonic constraints that the Indian project presents. As a singular exception to this reticence, Muratorio (1998) has expressed how the CONAIE is beginning to constitute itself as a hegemonic community along Western notions of gender, language, ethnicity, and class. It is not surprising to realize, as Muratorio points out, that the head positions of the movement are mostly occupied by academically educated Indian men with membership in the larger Quechua/Spanish speaking ethnic communities. Ironically, the movement's options are limited on both sides: on the one hand a more democratic reordering of the global order would signify its demise; and on the other hand its national success would secure its own form of political/gender domination and that of other racialized groups. . . . Although as the work of Hall (1997), García-Canclini (1992), and Foucault (1991) indicates, capitalism and social discourse are reconfigured in quite power-full and truly unpredictable ways.

Conclusion: The Politics of Forgetting

As Renan ([1890]1990) outlined over a century ago, part of being a nation is getting your history wrong. This is also relevant for national movements like the CONAIE, the development discourse, environmental NGOs, as well as other transnational interests such as the global heritage and human rights agendas.

Rather than pointing a finger at one or several of these institutions, endeavors, or projects, I think it more worthwhile to ponder some of the larger structural discourses on which these globalizing assumptions are built and from which the current production of a native identity is fabricated.

One of the essential elements in this regard is the understanding that the native is not an independent element counter to any globalizing force. Quite the contrary. *The native is the most global identity being produced under the subterfuge of local struggles.* Modern (and cyber) capital are in desperate need of natives and, unlike centuries ago, political governmentality is no longer afforded through the extinction of difference but rather through difference itself: transnational capitalism and its effects of power depend on difference as part of its hegemonic stronghold. Interrogating the native should make us realize that we are all natives and that this is an important element that modern capital seeks to hide and history to forget. But again, it is telling how both heritage agendas and human rights agendas target some people as natives, over others, and define them as more authentically native in their liberating enterprise.

This interrogation of a native identity also demands the interrogation of boundaries, not only in a physical and symbolic sense but also as constitutive elements of identity production. The boundary in which I am most interested is that fictitious or invented one (in Benedict Anderson's sense) between global and local enterprises; i.e., to understand the contemporary world as that of a (local) global with enormous effects of power that serve to reinsert differing forms of hierarchical differences since colonial times. What Stuart Hall refers to as old new forms of colonial exchange. At the same time it is important to interrogate how the Other continues to be essential in this globalizing enterprise of cultural and human heritage.

Why is it that the interrogation of the native other, whatever it might be (in this case Indian, but also women, black, and/or homosexuals) is still used to sustain an idea of globalization that might be new, even though the phenomenon is not? How is it that we have come to assess globalization as a worthwhile empirical phenomenon at the precise moment when fewer commodities are being exchanged than centuries ago? Why is it that interrogating the Other still serves to sustain the ultimate otherness of a reified white male Christian heterosexuality that seems as engrained in different forms of political and socioeconomic control as ever? As Kincaid (1997: 80–81) states:

> ... eventually, the masters left, in a kind of way; eventually, the slaves were freed, in a kind of way. Of course, the whole thing is, once you cease to be a master, once you throw off your master's yoke, you are no longer human rubbish, you are just a human being, and all the things that adds up to. So, too, with the slaves. Once they are no longer slaves, once they are free, they are no longer noble and exalted; they are just human beings.

Acknowledgments I would like to thank University of Texas Press, *Critique of Anthropology*, and the Interdisciplinary Seminar on Globalization and Identity at Fairleigh Dickinson University where some earlier version of these ideas have appeared and/or were discussed. Particular thanks to all of the members of the workshop on cultural heritage and human rights held at the University of Illinois in 2006 for the discussion and enlightening political exchange. As always, much thanks to Gregory Allen for his support and love, always essential in the constant struggle for a committed scholarship and life.

References

Benavides, O. Hugo, 2004, Anthropology's Native Conundrum: Uneven Histories and Developments. *Critique of Anthropology* 24(2): 159–178.

Chatterjee, Partha, 1986, *Nationalist Thought and the Colonial World: A Derivative Discourse.* Zed Books for United Nations University, Tokyo.

Deloria, Jr., Vine, 1979, *Custer Died for Your Sins.* Avon, New York.

Foucault, Michel, 1991, *Remarks on Marx.* Semiotext(e), New York City.

García-Canclini, Nestor, 1992, Cultural Reconversion. In *On Edge: The Crisis of Contemporary Latin American Culture*, edited by G. Yudice, J. Flores, and J. Franco. University of Minnesota Press, Minneapolis.

Hall, Stuart, 1997, The Local and the Global: Globalization and Ethnicity. In *Culture, Globalization and the World-System: Contemporary Conditions for the Representation of Identity*, edited by A. King. University of Minnesota Press, Minneapolis.

Kincaid, Jamaica, 1997, *A Small Place.* Farrar, Straus, and Giroux, New York City.

Kuklick, Henrika, 1991, Contested Monuments: The Politics of Archaeology in Southern Africa. In *Colonial Situations: Essays on the Contextualization of Ethnographic Knowledge*, edited by G. Stocking, History of Anthropology, vol. 7. University of Wisconsin Press, Wisconsin.

Miller, James, 1993, *The Passion of Michel Foucault.* Anchor Books, Doubleday, New York.

Muratorio, Blanca, 1998, Indigenous Women's Identities and the Politics of Cultural Reproduction in the Ecuadorian Amazon, *American Anthropologist* 100(2): 409–420.

Patterson, Thomas C., and Peter R. Schmidt, 1995, Introduction: From Constructing to Making Alternative Histories. In *Making Alternative Histories: The Practice of Archaeology and History in Non-Western Settings*, edited by Thomas C. Patterson and Peter R. Schmidt. School of American Research Press, Santa Fe.

Quijano, Aníbal, 1993, América Latina en la Economía Mundial. *Problemas del Desarrollo* 24: 5–18.

Renan, E., 1990, What is a Nation? In *Nation and Narration*, edited by Homi Bhabha. Routledge, London.

Tierney, Patrick, 2000, *Darkness in El Dorado: How Scientists and Journalists Devastated the Amazon.* W. W. Norton, New York City.

Wylie, Alison, 1995, Alternative Histories: Epistemic Disunity and Political Integrity. In *Making Alternative Histories: The Practice of Archaeology and History in Non-Western Settings*, edited by Thomas C. Patterson and Peter R. Schmidt. School of American Research Press, Santa Fe.

Chapter 8
Plains Indians and Resistance to "Public" Heritage Commemoration of Their Pasts

Larry J. Zimmerman

Introduction

Colonialist cultures readily and even painstakingly have commemorated events from their own histories. Historic landmarks and statues mark battles where their militaries celebrated glorious victories and even where their soldiers were gallant in defeat against overwhelming odds. They also have preserved and interpreted for posterity key nonmilitary events or places in their historical master narrative. As they moved toward a postcolonial position, some have been willing to memorialize episodes and places where those they colonized valiantly resisted conquest, indeed, where the colonizer even may have committed atrocities. As Ševčenko (2004) observes:

> Around the world, people instinctively turn to places of memory to come to terms with the past and chart a course for the future. From makeshift roadside memorials to official commemorations, millions of people around the world gather at places of memory looking for healing, reconciliation and insight on how to move forward. . . . It's here, through the process of preserving the past, that evidence of human rights violations is maintained and made public, issues this evidence raises are debated and tactics for preventing it from happening again are developed.

For Ševčenko, doing so seems entirely reasonable and important, but hers may be a peculiarly colonialist view. Surprisingly, even when commemorations openly admit guilt and regret, those who seek to commemorate such events and places sometimes find the victims to be uncooperative and, not uncommonly, actively resistant to the plans for these sites of conscience.

The reasons they resist are the subject of this chapter, and are not at all simple, ranging from who gets to tell the story to the occluding language of commemoration and preservation. The primary examples will be American Indians,[1] and from

---

[1] I am fully aware of the variations of names used for American Indians and their political ramifications. I will use several terms interchangeably in this chapter, but mostly just Indian. Similarly, I am aware of preferred terms for Indian nations and the names they call themselves, but will use the more common terms by which they are known. No disrespect is implied; communication is the primary concern.

H. Silverman and D. F. Ruggles (eds.), *Cultural Heritage and Human Rights*.
© Springer 2007

the Great Plains, but a final example will be cross-cultural. At the core of resistance is the view that the past is somehow a public heritage, an idea against which Plains Indian people have struggled.

A Public Heritage? Lessons From Archeology and Repatriation

That the past is a public heritage seems to be a value held primarily by members of dominant societies and rarely one held by indigenous peoples. As in many things colonial, master narratives overwhelm counternarratives by subsuming them and seeking to change the meaning of the counternarrative. The idea goes something like this: "What's ours is ours and what's yours is ours too!" There are numerous examples ranging from the control over and interpretation of particular archeological remains to control of and access to sites.

There are few better examples than that of the Kennewick/Ancient One skeleton. Even the names that people give the skeleton suggest the divide. Dominant society members and archeologists use the name of the place where the remains were discovered in 1996, an archeological convention for naming archeological sites; however, the Umatilla tribe uses the name "Ancient One" to indicate the personage of the remains and their cultural connections and responsibilities to them, which they claim to know through oral tradition. Found along the Columbia River near Kennewick, Washington, investigators initially thought the remains were those of a Euro-American pioneer based on skull features that seemed to be Caucasoid. When an ancient spear point was found embedded in a hip and radiocarbon dates indicated a date approximately 9,200 years old, contemporary archeological ideas about the early occupation of the Americas were challenged. Osteologists ascertained that skull characteristics statistically did not seem to be like those of the ancestors of modern American Indians and hoped to study the remains in detail. The Umatilla demanded the repatriation of the remains under the Native American Graves Protection and Repatriation Act (NAGPRA) of 1990 and did not wish to allow study of the remains. Eight scientists used the legal system to stop the repatriation and to demand time to study the remains. Nearly a decade of legal wrangling eventually resulted in a Ninth Circuit Court of Appeal's opinion that the Umatilla could not prove cultural or biological descent, even to the point of saying that Umatilla oral tradition was inadequate as evidence. The court would not declare the Ancient One to be Native American (see Zimmerman (2005) for a discussion of the court's decision and its impacts).

A near frenzy of the media ensued when a reporter misinterpreted the term Caucasoid as Caucasian, and the first scientist to investigate the skeleton imagined him to look like the British actor Patrick Stewart (who starred in the *Star Trek: The Next Generation* series). This played into a centuries-old desire for a European heritage for the Americas – the Moundbuilder Myth – which was especially popular in the 1800s. The myth was that an unknown race was on the American continent before the Indians and that they built the earthworks that Euro-American explorers and settlers discovered as they moved west. One speculation was that they were "white," perhaps survivors of the Atlantean deluge or descendants of the Lost Tribes of Israel. Though scientifically discounted, the Moundbuilder Myth has hardly died out, and with Kennewick it saw resurgence. Whether Kennewick was purposely used by the scientists to bolster public support for their case or just a byproduct of the Moundbuilder Myth, the media turned it into a science-versus-religion, us-versus-them, archeologist-versus-Indian struggle over control of history (see Thomas (2000) for a discussion of the historical roots of the struggle).

Nowhere is this issue more clear than in exchanges between dominant society members about Kennewick Man in a CBS Television *60 Minutes* segment aired in 1998. Lesley Stahl, the interviewer, queried Douglas Owsley, a Smithsonian osteologist, about the potential impact of repatriating Kennewick Man:

> Douglas Owsley: "If there is no opportunity for us to look at [Kennewick and other similar remains], we'll never answer our questions."
> Lesley Stahl: "We're talking out *our* history?" [tonal emphasis]
> Douglas Owsley: "We're talking about *American* history, yes." [emphasis mine]

Later in the program Stahl also raised the matter with James Chatters, the first archeologist to examine the remains:

> Lesley Stahl: "Is this an attempt by the Indians to control history?"
> James Chatters: "In a word, yes."

When Stahl interviewed Armand Minthorn, a Umatilla representative, and asked if he was curious about what the scientists might find, he replied that the Umatilla did not want study done because it was not necessary. Their traditions provided all they needed to know about the Ancient One.

The importance of these exchanges is no small matter. They reflect the belief on the part of the dominant society that the past is a human history and not that of a particular group, while the indigenous group considers the past to be theirs and intrusion by others to be unnecessary and unwelcome. A related idea is that dominant society members seem to believe that unless sites are publicly accessible and interpreted scientifically, indigenous heritage is a "lost" heritage. In the case of reburial of human remains, this is almost a cliché, with reburial likened to burning books or stating that the past will be lost unless archeology is done, noting, as Clement Meighan did early in the repatriation discussions, that "[i]f archeology is not done, the ancient people remain without a history and without a written record of their existence" (1986: 6–7). Even in the *60 Minutes* segment, Owlsey was asked about the loss of important information if the remains were reburied, and he replied that the information would become "as narrow as a grave." At base, what this implies is exactly what the old truism states: "the victor writes the history," which colonized people usually resent deeply.

The Damaging Vocabulary of Public Heritage

Even when such histories attempt to be fair, their vocabulary can be alienating. An effort on the part of the colonizer to "save" or "write" the past of a colonized people can be portrayed as an important, even noble, undertaking as in the Ševčenko quotation above. Protecting and interpreting heritage certainly is important to colonized people, but their views about how it should be done may be very different. Even the words used to describe sites or events from these peoples' pasts can be interpreted differently and misunderstood. Colwell-Chanthaphonh and Ferguson's (2006) cautions about using the word "abandoned" are instructive. They note that "to abandon" means to give up with the intent of never claiming a right or interest. Archeologists commonly use "abandoned" to describe sites or regions as if the people completely disappeared and were no longer around to use a place. The descendants of those who once lived on a site or used a place may see the place in a way very different from dominant society members intent on interpreting or preserving a site. Their reality may be that use, reverence, and a concept of sacredness remain, though usage and access have changed.

Jeffers Petroglyphs provides an example. Located in southwestern Minnesota on a site the Minnesota Historical Society preserves and interprets, Jeffers has more than 2,000 petroglyphs pecked into an outcropping of Sioux Quartzite. Some glyphs may be as much as 5,000 years old (Callahan 2001). The tendency for many is to think of the site as part of the archeological past rather than as a site of more or less continuous usage into the present by several tribes. Even during the 1800s when intense pressure was put on the Dakota, who lived (and still live) near the site, to relinquish their religion in favor of Christianity, Dakota people would sneak onto the property to pray. The religious observance at Jeffers did not figure in official discourse but it occurred. Although they no longer make petroglyphs at Jeffers, the site still sees intensive use by Dakota people and other tribes. There is no evidence over the past 5,000 years that the site was abandoned.

Other people see their "archeological" sites in the same way. At the 2002 "Toward a More Ethical Mayanist Archaeology" Conference in Vancouver, British Columbia, a Mayan scholar, Lix Lopez, raised several commonly used archeological terms as troublesome. Paraphrasing him, he challenged those of us who were archeologists by saying, "When you use words like that, what you are telling us is that our culture no longer exists or is in ruins or that we ourselves are gone." One word he complained about was "ruins," which he noted could be interpreted as the remains of something that had been destroyed, disintegrated, or decayed. The Mayan reality, however, was that the usage of these sites had just shifted in a reorganized landscape. He also did not like his people being described as "vanished," which implied they were no longer in existence and their sites no longer in use. The reality is that his people certainly were still there, and these places, though changed, are still there and often still used. Similarly, he disliked "disappeared," indicating that something had ceased to be. The reality was that most groups or places continue. He hated the term "Mayan collapse," which could be an abrupt loss of perceived value or an abrupt failure of function, when the reality is that most places retain their function and value.

Another word might be added: "preserve." *The Free Dictionary* (2007, http://www.thefreedictionary.com/preserve) defines "preserve" as "to maintain in safety from injury, peril, or harm; to protect; a domain that seems to be especially reserved for someone." When dominant society preservationists say that they wish to preserve a site, an implication might be that descendant communities are incapable of caring for their own heritage and that the dominant society can do it better, suggesting the implicit right of the dominant society to access a place while in some way restricting access by a descendant community. There is the fear that descendant community members will somehow damage a site or will not be as concerned about the place as those seeking to preserve it.

Miscommunication relating to these words has consequences that can prove difficult. The result can be a profound distrust by a group of indigenous people about all aspects of what scholars say about them and their pasts. Some even see it as an attack on their own beliefs. As a Prairie Potawatomi man, Chick Hale, asked at a reburial meeting in Iowa in 1980, "[W]hy do archaeologists study the past? Are they trying to disprove our religion?" (Anderson et al. 1980: 12). Most archeologists would reject this, but perhaps they *are* trying to disprove indigenous beliefs if they take the approach advocated by archeologist Ronald Mason (1997: 3):

> [Archaeology,] by its very nature must challenge, not respect, or acknowledge as valid, such folk renditions of the past because traditional knowledge has produced flat earths, geocentrism, women arising out of men's ribs, talking ravens and the historically late first people of the Black Hills upwelling from holes in the ground.

Stories told by archeologists may be different in substance and tenor from those of indigenous people, and for indigenous people to accept dominant society archeological or historical constructions of the past as true, they must alter or even relinquish their own stories and cultural identity. Their views of commemorative sites may be similarly affected. If they accept dominant society stories told about these sites, their own versions of what happened there may be compromised. They also may feel that their emotional needs regarding the site are subsumed by the emotional needs of the dominant society.

The relevance of these ideas about control of heritage and miscommunication regarding preservation of sites is not limited to sites from the more distant past, but extends into the present. When preservation of sites of conscience is at issue, the problems seem abundantly clear. Three examples from the Great Plains from the time of the Indian Wars of the late 1800s demonstrate the range of responses and problems.

The example of Ft. Robinson and Dull Knife shows what happens when a site of conscience is developed and the stories of the colonizer and colonized differ. Wounded Knee shows the collapse of plans to develop a site of conscience when there is an almost complete breakdown of communication. Sand Creek shows that sites of conscience can be mutually developed if there is respect for the stories of the victims.

A One-Sided Site of Conscience: Ft. Robinson
and Dull Knife

Located in the northwestern corner of Nebraska, Ft. Robinson was a focal point for the domination of Plains Indians in the late 1800s during what commonly has been labeled "the Indian Wars" of 1876–1890. The fort initially was a camp meant to oversee the Red Cloud Agency of some 13,000 Lakota (Sioux), named for the Lakota chief who had been victorious over the US Army, a decade earlier. Ft. Robinson is also where the famous Oglala warrior Crazy Horse was murdered in 1877. One of the most poignant stories is that of the Northern Cheyenne chief, Dull Knife (also known as Chief Morning Star).

Dull Knife, Little Wolf, and their bands were not involved in the Greasy Grass battle, more commonly known as the Battle of the Little Bighorn or Custer's Last Stand. Although the Lakota and some Cheyenne were victorious in wiping out Custer's Seventh Cavalry units in late June, 1876, Dull Knife and Little Wolf realized that the US Army would take vengeance on any Sioux or Cheyenne, whether involved in the Custer battle or not. Eventually, Dull Knife and Little Wolf's people were taken into custody and removed from the Northern Plains to the Darlington Agency in Oklahoma Indian Territory. Conditions on the way were horrible, and on their arrival were no better. Therefore, after a few months of poor conditions, poor medical care, and several deaths, they left the agency. Pursued by the military, they fought a 1,300-mile running battle, successfully evading the soldiers until they reached northwest Nebraska. With winter coming, Little Wolf led his band to hide in the Sand Hills region. Dull Knife hoped to winter with Red Cloud's people, but on arriving at the agency found that it had been moved to Pine Ridge. Soon captured by the military, his people were taken to Ft. Robinson where they were told they had to return to Indian Territory. This they refused to do, and they were incarcerated in military barracks. Held initially without food for about 10 days, they still refused to go to Oklahoma, and then were refused water and heat. Preferring death to a return to Oklahoma, on the moonlit night of 9 January 1879, they broke out of the barracks in the hope of making it back to their lands in Montana.

The stories of the Northern Cheyenne and military are in agreement up to this point. The military's account is that Dull Knife led his people across the parade ground and up into the surrounding bluffs near the fort, but the Cheyenne story is that he sent out a few of his Dog Soldiers to draw the guards away, escaping out the back of the barracks, down to a stream mostly hidden from view, and then up into the bluffs away from the fort. The stories come into agreement when the soldiers catch up with the escapees well north of the fort and kill 64 of them in a buffalo wallow where they had taken refuge. Dull Knife and his family found a cave and were able to escape death. From the time they left Oklahoma, their story was presented by the Eastern newspapers as one of courage and honor in the face of harsh and unfair treatment by the government. After the attempted escape from Ft. Robinson, under pressure from public opinion, the government allowed Dull Knife, Little Wolf, and the other survivors to return to Montana and to have a reservation on their traditional lands.

The Cheyenne "outbreak" now has been absorbed into the master American narrative about the atrocities committed against Indians, and was made popular by Mari Sandoz's novel *Cheyenne Autumn* (1953) and John Ford's film of the same title (1964). The Nebraska State Historical Society (NSHS) has commemorated the event at Ft. Robinson with markers, conducted archeological excavations on the barracks, and even reconstructed it in 2003, using the military's report of the escape. There can be little doubt of the sincerity of the historical society in their wish to make the fort a site of conscience commemorating the ill-treatment of the Cheyenne. However, the Northern Cheyenne have problems with it, which on first glance seem trivial, but on closer examination are not at all so, and the problems go to the very core of their self-image.

In 1988, I was privileged to be invited by the Northern Cheyenne to be involved in a project in which they sought to challenge the military and NSHS story of the escape from the barracks. My team worked closely with the Northern Cheyenne doing archeological testing to check the feasibility of their story (McDonald et al. 1991). They had been given a tract of land adjacent to Ft. Robinson that contained the escape route that their oral history recognized; they intended to use the land to build their own memorial to counter the NSHS story. Their contention was that the NSHS story violated the memory of Dull Knife, asking how it was that a man who had been able to elude the military in his flight, with ill and injured people, for 1,300 miles would do something as improbable as to move his people across an open area and put them in immediate jeopardy. Rather, Dull Knife used his Dog Soldier decoys to draw the army away from the actual escape. What the military and NSHS had done was to accept a version of the story that tarnished the memory of a man who essentially was a Northern Cheyenne culture hero. The Northern Cheyenne refused to accept this construction, despite the fact that the dominant society believed the variation of their oral tradition from the military story to be relatively minor and unimportant. They do not participate in the site of conscience because it does not recognize their oral tradition and the character of one of their culture heroes.

Almost a Site of Conscience: Wounded Knee

A decade after Dull Knife's "outbreak," about 50 miles from Ft. Robinson, Wounded Knee, South Dakota, saw what most historians consider the final encounter of the Indian Wars. Misrepresentation of what happened at Wounded Knee began almost before the 1890 "Battle of Wounded Knee" ended. The one assured fact is that the "battle" was a massacre of more than 150 mostly unarmed members of Bigfoot's band of Minneconjou Lakota Ghost Dancers, but even that number is uncertain. Some state the number at 150 while others assert that it was more than 300 men, women, and children. Twenty-five soldiers died, probably from friendly fire. Twenty soldiers received Congressional Medals of Honor. Some hailed them as heroes, while others heavily criticized the Seventh Cavalry soldiers and their commander, Colonel James Forsyth, for their actions. Forsyth later was brought up on charges, which were dismissed with only a criticism of his tactics. From the beginning, some people saw the battle for what it was, a massacre that marked the end of military resistance by the Indians. As the truth came out, the "battle" became a massacre, and over the years the dominant society in the United States has come to see Wounded Knee as a symbol of the many atrocities committed against Native Americans, standing as a heinous example of the brutality of America's westward expansion.[2]

The site has few markers indicating its importance in American history, but not for want of trying. Efforts to commemorate the site go back to at least the 1940s. For decades, however, only the mass grave of the victims and an associated cemetery, along with a small church, marked the site. The site's symbolism as a point of Indian resistance has gained additional meaning since the 71-day siege by the government after the takeover of Wounded Knee by the American Indian Movement in 1973. Since the early 1970s, the site has become a major tourist destination for people from all over the world. Many stop to read the sign and take the short walk to the mass grave.

In the late 1980s, local Lakota worked to build a cultural center, now used as a small museum and place for the sale of crafts. Other than that, only a large green sign at the edge of the nearby road explains the events of the massacre. A few tourists stop in the now-dilapidated cultural center, and some stop to buy crafts for sale there.

A century after the massacre, when the state of South Dakota sponsored a Year of Reconciliation (1990), the United States, which had never apologized for the massacre, finally sent regrets to the Sioux (Senate Congressional Resolution 153/House 386, 101st Cong., 2d Sess.). Two years later, the proposal for what would become the 1995 Chief Bigfoot National Memorial Park and Wounded Knee Memorial Act surfaced in Congress (US Senate 1995), promoting an 1,800-acre Wounded Knee National Tribal Park. After study, the National Park Service (NPS) recommended several alternatives, the third selected for discussion in the bill. This alternative for the park had a unit on the Cheyenne River Reservation where Bigfoot's band had traveled to Wounded Knee, with a trail following that route, and a larger unit on Pine Ridge Reservation with an interpretive center. Buildings not present at the time of the massacre were to be removed. A 17-member Advisory Commission would oversee the park, with representatives from districts on both reservations, representatives from the Wounded Knee Survivors Associations from both reservations, the Secretary of the Smithsonian, and the governors or their State Historic Preservation Officers from South Dakota and Nebraska. Management of the units would be through the tribes. On the surface, the park appeared to be a good idea, with lots of input from the American Indian

---

[2] Ethnographer James Mooney (1991) was at the site only days after the massacre. Reprinted many times, his book gives what is probably the most complete account of the massacre and the Ghost Dance.

nations concerned, but it died due to objections from those mostly closely associated with land around the site.

Wanbli Sapa (1996) provides an account of the problems on a website generally supportive of activist Native American causes. The article focuses primarily on the lack of representation and consultation of those who owned the land or lived on the areas that would be turned into the park. Apparently, there were many vested interests in having the park and memorial built, including those of the tribal councils and even the Wounded Knee Survivors Association, which the author claims now do not represent the views of the majority of survivors. The main source of objection came from the Wounded Knee Landowners Association (WLA), and also comprised many members of the Survivors Association, which claimed its members were not consulted about the bill or invited to the Congressional hearing. Most members were those whose lands and homes would be directly affected. Many would have lost their land to the new park, their homes removed to clear it of structures.

In a letter responding to the bill, the Wounded Knee Landowners Association (1995a,b) raised a list of 75 objections. The letter title called the proposal a "*wasichu* proposal," that is, a white man's proposal. There were several objections to the bill's historical description of the massacre, ranging from calling the massacre an "incident" and assessing no blame for it, to the constant reference to Chief Spotted Elk as Chief Bigfoot, the latter apparently a derogatory name given by the military. Other objections seemed more damaging, claiming that the WLA members were not consulted in the feasibility study and implying that the proposal was another ploy by the government to reclaim valuable Lakota treaty lands. One objection asked about responsibility for damage to the sanctity of the site by contractors or tourists. Another worried about the contemporary cemetery, which is still being used, adjacent to the mass grave of the Wounded Knee victims, and whether it would be moved. The letter (WLA 1995b) concluded with the following:

> No other ethnic group in this country has had to address concerns that the Native Americans have had to address. No other ethnic group has continually had their burial grounds desecrated. No other ethnic group has been continually played against one another as the Native Americans have. No other ethnic group has had to be violently confronted on its home ground and have the government lie continually in order to get what it feels is the best of the poor Indians. No other ethnic group has been shunted to unwanted areas, forced to live in extreme poverty, been denied by law to practice its religious [sic] (even voodoo was never outlawed), had its children kidnapped by the government and taught to hate their ethnicity.

What is apparent from these concluding remarks is that at least some Lakota see the proposed commemoration and park as yet another attempt by the government to harm them. In the WLA view, the government got the story wrong, told lies, attempted to take Indian land, and planned to turn sacred ground into a tourist destination. With these objections, the park proposal collapsed.

A Site of Conscience: Why Sand Creek Became
a National Historic Site and Wounded Knee Did Not

The Wounded Knee Massacre was horrendous for the taking of innocent lives by an out-of-control military, but the Battle of Sand Creek, as it was initially labeled, might have been worse because of the grotesque mutilation of the corpses, even those dying yet still alive. Sand Creek stands as one of most horrible massacres of the Indian Wars.[3] The gold and silver rush of the 1850s–1860s brought thousands of miners into Colorado, which put pressure on the hunting territories of the Cheyenne and Arapaho people. Some chiefs, who had gotten along with whites, were forced to sign an agreement that did not have the approval of most of their people. People objected to the treaty and refused to live on reservations or sell their land, and violence erupted, which sometimes has been called the Cheyenne–Arapaho or Colorado War of 1864–1865.

Black Kettle and his band of Southern Cheyenne and some Arapaho were told they would be safe and could camp along Sand Creek about 40 miles from Ft. Lyon in eastern Colorado. On 29 November 1864, Reverend John Chivington, an officer in the Colorado volunteer militia, attacked Black Kettle's camp with about 700 men. Black Kettle was a known peace-seeker, a fact fully known to Chivington. Accounts of numbers of soldiers and Cheyenne vary, as well as the exact course of events. As the massacre began, Black Kettle raised the American flag and a white flag over his lodge thinking they would be recognized as peaceful, just as he had been instructed to do if he met troops. The attack continued without mercy under Chivington's reported order, "Kill and scalp all the big and little; nits make for lice." Initially reported as killed, Black Kettle escaped, and his wife, although she survived, was shot many times. Others were less fortunate. Pregnant women had their fetuses cut from their womb, babies were bayoneted, and many victims were savagely mutilated. Soldiers were said to have removed skin and pubic hair of women and wore them as bloody trophies stretched around their hats. Other body parts, especially scalps, eventually made their way back to Denver with the soldiers where they were exhibited for an admission price in a theater. More than 150 Cheyenne and Arapaho died. A sad irony is that almost 4 years to the day later, Black Kettle and other Southern Cheyenne people were massacred on the Washita River by George Armstrong Custer's Seventh Cavalry, the dead also mutilated by soldiers.

But soon the event began to unravel. Within a month, word came that the attack would be investigated by a Congressional committee. By March of 1865, the

---

[3] Numerous books about the Sand Creek Massacre provide a range of detail, sometimes in contradiction with others, but most are useful for descriptions of basic events. One of the earliest books on the subject is by Hoig (1961). For a list of others and for images of original documents, see the Tutt Library collection at Colorado College, available online at http://www2.coloradocollege.edu/LIBRARY/SpecialCollections/ Manuscript/SandCreek.html (Viewed 18 November 2006).

committee was taking testimony,[4] most of it extremely damaging. Chivington faced a court martial but could not be punished because he was no longer in the US Army. He was forced to resign from the Colorado militia, could not be involved in politics, and could not campaign for Colorado statehood. His guilt followed him until his death in 1892. Interestingly, the Methodist Church, for which Chivington was a minister, formally apologized to the Cheyenne and Arapaho in 1996.

Under the National Museum of the American Indian Act of 1989, the Northern Cheyenne sought repatriation of remains collected from the massacre site by the US Army, at the time stored in the Smithsonian's National Museum of Natural History (1992). The Northern Cheyenne formed the Northern Cheyenne Sand Creek Descendants in 1995 and by 1998 had worked to put forward a Senate bill to establish Sand Creek Massacre National Historic Site. Later that year Public Law 105–243, the Sand Creek Massacre Site Study Act[5] authorized formal study of the site. Following the study, Colorado Senator Ben Nighthorse Campbell, a Northern Cheyenne tribal member, proposed the Sand Creek Massacre National Historic Site Act, which became Public Law No: 106–465 in November of 2000. Thus, the United States authorized the site of the Sand Creek Massacre as a National Historic Site. Since then, the NPS, which will administer the site, has been acquiring land for the site through purchase, gifts, and trust agreements. The site will open in 2007.

During the time Sand Creek was under consideration as a National Historic Site, concerns of the Southern Cheyenne, Arapaho, and Northern Cheyenne have differed considerably from the kinds of concerns expressed by the Northern Cheyenne about Ft. Robinson and the concerns of many Lakota about Wounded Knee. The feasibility study by the National Park Service (2000) notes on its cover that the study was "[p]repared by the National Park Service in consultation with the Cheyenne and Arapaho Tribes of Oklahoma, the Northern Cheyenne Tribe, the Northern Arapaho Tribe, and the State of Colorado." The 1998 study act required the consultation,[6] and about 20 tribal members and others attended the first tribal consultation meeting in Denver. There were "nine consultation meetings . . ., numerous conference calls, letters to tribal officials, tribal representatives and interested tribal members, and discussions with interested tribal organizations. In addition, nine information meetings were

---

[4] Some of the testimony of participants, including Chivington, is available online at http://www. snowwowl.com/swolfscmassacre4.html. Viewed 7 October 2006. Their words are both revealing and horrifying. The original testimony is from the Joint Committee on the Conduct of the War, Massacre of Cheyenne Indians, 38th Congress, 2nd Session (Washington, 1865), pp. 4–12, 56–59, and 101–108.

[5] The full text is available at http://www.sandcreek.org/project_pubLaw105–243.htm. Viewed 12 November 2006. The Northern Cheyenne provide an excellent web site containing many documents and a timeline of events at http://www.sandcreek.org/. Viewed 6 December 2006. Other useful documents are available at the NPS's Sand Creek Massacre web site at http://www.nps. gov/sand/historyculture/people.htm. Viewed 6 December 2006.

[6] Consultation was required by other federal mandates regarding tribal consultation and dealing with tribes on a government-to-government basis.

held" on the reservations (National Park Service 2000: 13). Cooperative agreements with the tribes (the Southern Cheyenne declined) allowed $10,500 per tribe to collect oral histories. Yet despite consultation and participation, the tribes expressed concerns throughout the process about issues of sacredness at the site: They wanted areas set aside for tribal religious use, repatriation of human remains, and burial of the remains of Sand Creek Massacre descendants. Many felt that the consultation was not done properly and that tribal protocols had not been followed. As well, they felt that the NPS had not listened to the tribes' concerns and had not given oral tradition the same authority as scientific evidence.

Yet despite all these concerns, the Sand Creek National Historic Site is nearing completion, while that at Wounded Knee is dead and the Ft. Robinson project has gone ahead without the Northern Cheyenne story being told. Why should this be, especially when the factual and emotional content of the sites is so similar? The reasons are several and complex, and some are historical. The US government almost immediately investigated and condemned the massacre at Sand Creek, and although there was no formal apology, there was open recognition of the atrocities. Whereas at Wounded Knee several soldiers were honored as heroes, Chivington was admonished and essentially banished from Colorado. One major difference is that with Sand Creek, much of the initiative for the project came from the Cheyenne and Arapaho themselves, not from an outside entity. In part, the reason they became involved was that the National Museum of the American Indian Act was in place, and the Cheyenne were able to bring back remains of some who died in the massacre, which had the effect of augmenting the already sacred nature of the site. That the authorizing legislation was sponsored by a Northern Cheyenne Senator had no small symbolic significance. Indians were speaking for themselves on the matter.

The tribes saw the project as one in which they had real ownership. The idea was not forced onto them, a fact that was in marked distinction to the way that some Lakota felt the Wounded Knee commemoration would be and that the Northern Cheyenne felt the commemoration of Dull Knife's escape was. Even though there were complaints about the consultation process, consultation with the NPS did occur, whereas at Ft. Robinson there was none, and at Wounded Knee, at least one important group felt left out. Even though some in the tribes felt that the oral tradition evidence surrounding Sand Creek was not treated on par with science, at least oral histories were collected. Ultimately, the reason the site succeeded was that the Sand Creek National Historic Site was about them, their history, and their loss. The site was not primarily about the dominant society and its needs for a site of conscience. Yet the site still can serve conscience as a way to remember and perhaps to find reconciliation.

Healing and Reconciliation for Whom?

Repeating a line from the Ševčenko quotation at the start of this chapter: people seek to "gather at places of memory looking for healing, reconciliation, and insight on how to move forward." The descendants of victims, however, might say that there can be no healing or reconciliation short of apology and the passage of time. They often choose to reject even the history of the event as it gets told at places of memory, because the story is seen as false or incomplete. As American Indian Movement activist Bill Means put it in a speech commemorating the Martin Luther King, Jr. holiday: "We do not need your past! We know what our lives mean" (personal observation, ca. 1988). As Tuscarora writer Richard W. Hill (1999) put it regarding Wounded Knee, "[T]hey say it is a wound that will not heal . . . [A]s long as museums refuse to tell the truth, the wound created over one hundred years ago will continue."

Are sites of conscience meant to keep alive the memories of atrocities so that they will not be repeated, or are they built to salve the conscience of the society that committed them? As is apparent from the three sites discussed here, sites of conscience take on qualities of the sacred, perhaps most evident in battlefield commemorations, to which the massacres may be related (see for example, most of the chapters in Linenthal (1993), especially the chapters on the Alamo and the Little Bighorn). Following van der Leeuw (1986: 52–53), every establishment of a sacred place is a conquest of space, made powerful because a place is appropriated and owned by some entity. One way to certify the sanctity of the site is to set up boundaries that keep some people out, that is, as he says, sacred places practice a "politics of exclusion." For Ft. Robinson and Wounded Knee, what this means is that the sites essentially were appropriated by non-Indians as their own sites of conscience, and in the case of Wounded Knee, this meant taking land to do it. Though some Lakota supported the site, other Lakota saw the basis of that support as a way to "line the pockets" of those in tribal government through the tourism the site would bring to Pine Ridge Reservation. Although they would not literally be kept from the site, many feel, as in the case of Ft. Robinson, that at least their versions of the stories of the site essentially are exiled. Healing is difficult if the injured party has no primacy at the site.

Although the dominant society speaks words of healing and reconciliation, the Wounded Knee Landowners ask, why has the government never apologized for the massacre? Many American Indians consider an apology a good place to start if new relationships to the tribes are to be forged.[7] In 2004, such a bill surfaced in the US Senate (2004), but aside from hearings, the bill has languished. The text "acknowledges years of official depredations, ill-conceived policies, and the breaking of covenants by the United States Government regarding Indian tribes." It also "apologizes on behalf of the people of the United States to all Native Peoples for the many instances of violence, maltreatment, and neglect inflicted on Native Peoples by citizens of the United States." Andrew Mollison (2004) quotes Tex Hall, then President of the National Congress of American Indians, who says, "It's only one small step, but without an apology you can't do the healing, and without the healing, we can't come together as one country."

---

[7] An irony is that never having apologized to Indians, in 2004 the US Senate was willing by a vote of 92–0 to apologize regarding Iraq in a resolution saying it "joins with the president in expressing apology for the humiliation suffered by the prisoners in Iraq and their families."

A crosscultural example may put Plains Indian responses to the matter of sites of conscience into perspective. The terrorist destruction of the World Trade Center on September 11, 2001, took innocent lives of people who were no more guilty of "criminal" behavior toward Islamic peoples than the Native American people who were killed at any of the sites mentioned in this chapter. The survivors of the "incident" (the same word used to describe the Wounded Knee Massacre), the families of victims, the people of New York City, and the people of the United States have agonized over the trauma. They have lived in fear that similar horrors will happen again. Their lives have been changed because of it. They also have struggled about how best to memorialize the event and the victims. The "gloating" of the perpetrators about their victory has been difficult to bear, yet can be expected to continue while the conflict goes on. After time has passed and conflict hopefully diminished, would an apology from the perpetrators serve any real purpose? How might the people of the United States respond if Al-Qaeda said they were truly sorry for the attack? What if they said that they would pay to help build the memorial and would like to have their story told along with those of the survivors so that healing and reconciliation could begin? Would it matter who told the story, they or us? Many Americans certainly would have strong opinions about it and reject such a commemoration out of hand, no matter the sincerity of the apologists. That Plains Indian tribes are suspicious or reject the development of sites of conscience, at least on an emotional level, should be easily understood.

Acknowledgments Many people have influenced my thinking regarding commemoration, contested history, and sites of conscience. They include Paul Greenough (University of Iowa), Pat Rowland (Wounded Knee), Doug McDonald (University of North Dakota), Randy McGuire (Binghamton University), and Brian Molyneaux and Larry Bradley (University of South Dakota). Jan Hammil, Maria Pearson, Bill Tall Bull, and Ted Rising Sun helped me a great deal in understanding Native perspectives on some of these issues. They have now passed on, but I hold them dear in my heart.

References

Anderson, Duane C., Maria Pearson, Alton Fisher, and Deborah Zieglowsky, 1980, *Planning Seminar on Ancient Burial Grounds*. Office of the State Archaeologist of Iowa, Iowa City.

Callahan, Kevin, 2001, *The Jeffers Petroglyphs: Native American Rock Art on the Midwestern Plains*. Prairie Smoke, Champlin, Minnesota.

CBS Television, 1998, Kennewick Man. *60 Minutes*. Airdate October 25.

Colwell-Chanthaphonh, Chip, and T. J., Ferguson, 2006, Rethinking Abandonment in Archaeological Contexts. *The SAA Archaeological Record* 6(1): 37–41.

Hill, Richard W., 1999, *Wounded Knee, A Wound That Won't Heal*. http://www.dickshovel.com/hill.html (Viewed 7 March 2006).

Hoig, Stan, 1961, *The Sand Creek Massacre*. University of Oklahoma Press, Norman.

van der Leeuw, Gerardus, 1986, *Religion in Essence and Manifestation*. Princeton University Press, Princeton.

Linenthal, Edward T., 1993, *Sacred Ground: Americans and Their Battlefields*. University of Illinois Press, Urbana.

Mason, Ronald J., 1997, Letter to the Editor. *Society for American Archaeology Bulletin* 15(1): 3.

McDonald, J. D., Larry J. Zimmerman, W. Tall Bull, and T. Rising Sun, 1991, The Cheyenne Outbreak of 1879: Using Archaeology to Document Northern Cheyenne Oral History. In *The Archaeology of Inequality*, edited by Robert Paynter and Randall McGuire, pp. 64–78. Basil Blackwell, Oxford.

Meighan, Clement W., 1986, *Archaeology and Anthropological Ethics*. Wormwood, Calabasas, CA.

Mollison, Andrew, 2004, US Apology to Indians Considered: Bill 'Acknowledges Years of Official Depredations.' *Seattle Post-Intelligencer*, 25 May 2004. http://seattlepi.nwsource.com/national/174821_indian25.html (Viewed 6 December 2006).

Mooney, James, 1991, *The Ghost-Dance Religion and the Sioux Outbreak of 1890*. University of Nebraska Press, Lincoln.

National Museum of Natural History, 1992, Executive Summary: *Naevahoo'ohtseme* (We are going back home) Cheyenne Repatriation: The Human Remains. http://www.nmnh.si.edu/anthro/repatriation/reports/regional/plains/cheyenne_remains.htm (Viewed 7 October 2006).

National Park Service, 1993, *Draft Study of Alternatives, Environmental Assessment, Wounded Knee, South Dakota*. National Park Service, Washington, DC.

—, 2000, *Sand Creek Massacre Project, Volume 2, Special Resource Study*. National Park Service, Intermountain Region, Denver. http://home.nps.gov/applications/ parks/sand/ppdocuments/ ACF33.pdf (Viewed 8 November 2006).

Ševčenko, Liz, 2004, *The Power of Place: How Historic Sites Can Engage Citizens in Human Rights Issues*. Center for Victims of Torture, Minneapolis. http://www.newtactics.org/files/1044/ Ševčenko_Power_en.pdf (Viewed 3 March 2006).

Thomas, David Hurst, 2000, *Skull Wars: Kennewick Man, Archaeology, and the Battle for Native American Identity*. Basic Books, New York.

US Senate, 1995, Wounded Knee National Tribal Park Establishment Act of 1995, S382 1st Session, 104th Congress. http://www.thepeoplespaths.net/political/ s382is.htm (Viewed 7 October 2006).

—, 2004, S.J.RES.37 Title: A Joint Resolution to Acknowledge a Long History of Official Depredations and Ill-Conceived Policies by the United States Government Regarding Indian Tribes and Offer an Apology to all Native Peoples on Behalf of the United States. http://thomas.loc.gov/cgi-bin/bdquery/z?d108:SJRes00037 (Viewed 7 December 2006).

Wanbli Sapa, 1996, Who Should We Believe? Tribal Councils, Traditionals, Survivors Associations, Newspapers, or Others? http://www.dickshovel.com/WKb.html (Viewed 20 August 2006).

Wounded Knee Landowners Association, 1995a, Wounded Knee Landowners Reply to Wasichu's Proposal Part 1. Letter dated 20 March 1995. http://www.dickshovel.com/WKLAltr.a.html (Viewed 7 October 2006).

—, 1995b, Wounded Knee Landowners Reply to Wasichu's Proposal Part 2. Letter dated 20 March 1995. http://www.dickshovel.com/WKLAltr.b.html (Viewed 7 October 2006).

Zimmerman, Larry J., 2005, Public Heritage, a Desire for a "White" History for America, and Some Impacts of the Kennewick Man/Ancient One Decision. *International Journal of Cultural Property* 12(2): 265–274.

Chapter 9
Empty Gestures? Heritage and the Politics of Recognition

Laurajane Smith

Introduction

The politics of identity cannot simply be dismissed as empty or abstract gesturing. The conflicts that occur around the rights to control the expression of cultural identity have important material consequences for struggles over economic resources and struggles for equity and human rights. This chapter examines the role that archaeologists, often unwittingly, play in the arbitration of identity politics and the consequences this has for both the discipline and, more specifically, Australian Indigenous communities. Drawing on a critical reading of Foucault's later work on governmentality (Foucault 1979), this chapter provides a theoretical framework for understanding the conflicts that arise when archaeological knowledge and expertise about the material past intersects with the use of that past as indigenous heritage. This analysis is used to inform a discussion of the ways in which the Waanyi community of far northwest Queensland has asserted an oppositional understanding of the nature and meaning of heritage. In these conflicts, heritage becomes a political resource around which archaeologists, indigenous peoples and other interests negotiate and play out struggles for political recognition and legitimacy. Challenges to received notions of heritage are actively used by the Waanyi to help underpin their demands to access and control of land. In this challenge, the role and authority of archaeological expertise is redefined and renegotiated in more politically useful ways. In short, this chapter argues that heritage is both a resource in, and a process of, negotiation in the cultural politics of identity. Archaeologists and other heritage "experts" are therefore required to make conscious and informed choices in the ways in which they define and engage with heritage, and those communities who have a stake in heritage management.

The Politics of Recognition

Indigenous struggles for equity, sovereignty and land are political conflicts undertaken in the context of the history of colonial disenfranchisement and continuing institutionalized inequity. Conflicts over rights of access to, and control over, heritage

159

H. Silverman and D. F. Ruggles (eds.), *Cultural Heritage and Human Rights*.
© Springer 2007

objects or places are often denounced as simply identity politics of little real material relevance for overcoming inequity. For instance, Appleton (2003) from the British independent political organization "Spiked" has criticized demands by Australian Indigenous communities for the repatriation of human remains held in British museums. She states that archaeologists and museums who supported repatriation requests were indulging in empty "feel good" gestures of little material consequence beyond depriving scholars of important data and knowledge. She also points out that the gestures underlying repatriation do little for indigenous disenfranchisement and struggles for equity and rights, and notes that the return of human remains cannot help provide equitable housing, education, healthcare or welfare to Aboriginal communities. Of course heritage issues have no direct consequence on these issues, yet political struggles over cultural recognition do have important consequences in wider struggles for equity, that will feed back to specific struggles over resources. Certainly, when the archaeological community and other heritage practitioners divorce their attempts at recognizing indigenous issues and cultural concerns over the management of culture heritage from the material and institutional realities of indigenous inequity and discrimination, such recognition can be an empty gesture. However, recognition tied to an explicit awareness of wider political conflict can be significant. Nancy Fraser (2000), for instance, argues that identity politics can represent important emancipatory responses to injustice, and that culture and identity are often significant terrains of struggle in their own right. The issue here is that identity politics should not be seen as replacing struggles for resources. Rather, the redistribution of resources and the struggle for political and economic equity are interlinked with struggles for recognition. Properly conceived, the politics of recognition will work to validate and facilitate wider negotiations for the redistribution of power and resources.

It is important to note that governments and their bureaucracies – the state – do attempt to deal with social problems and conflicts through legitimizing or de-legitimizing particular conflicts and the various parties or interests engaged in that conflict. The state tends to listen only to those interests and interest groups that they believe have enough political legitimacy to warrant their attention. However, interest groups gain political legitimacy through their access to, or control over, various political resources, including, ironically, the ear of the state. The political resources that are drawn on in the negotiation of political legitimacy are many and varied, the most obvious being access or control over financial resources, and the ability to claim democratic representation on a particular issue or concern. However – and this is where the politics of recognition become critically important – political legitimacy may also be gained through the explicit recognition of identity and cultural claims. Subsequently, conflicts over the control of heritage objects and places may be understood to occur in an arena where the symbolic recognition of the legitimacy of indigenous identity claims diffuses out to inform and validate other claims to equity based on claims to cultural identity, cultural knowledge and experiences. Heritage objects or places, and human remains, are often held to be representatives of community identity, and as such, become important symbolic resources in underpinning claims to cultural identity, which in turn have a consequence in wider negotiations for political legitimacy.

In dealing with social conflicts and problems, governments call on various forms of expertise to help them make sense of competing claims and of the various interests and interest groups making claims and demands. Archaeological knowledge is one of the many forms of expertise that the state may call upon to help make sense of particular social problems and conflicts. Consequently, it is important to recognize that archaeological knowledge and expertise do not represent just another interest group in debates over the disposition and management of cultural resources. Rather, archaeologists hold a special position in the disposition of heritage items, due to the way governments and bureaucracies use archaeological knowledge to help make sense of, and regulate, those social problems that intersect with or are based on particular interpretations of the past and its material culture.

Governing Heritage

I have argued elsewhere that conflicts over the control of cultural heritage must be understood as existing within the wider parameters of political negotiations between the state and a range of interests over the political and cultural legitimacy of claims to identity (Smith 2004). Drawing on Foucault's thesis of "governmentality", archaeological knowledge must be understood as a "technology of government", that is, a body of knowledge that the state deploys to help policy makers and legislators understand, make sense of, regulate and govern demands and claims based on appeals to the past. The governmentality thesis recognizes that the governance or regulation of certain social problems and populations can rest on the development of *mentalities* of rule – where populations and the problems they pose are rendered subject to regulation and governance through the way they are defined and represented. Certain "truths" about the representations of populations can more easily be entered into political calculations than other forms of knowledge. In short, the intellectual authority and power of so-called objective, neutral and rational knowledge finds synergy with liberal forms of governance. The mobilization of this knowledge to regulate, translate and render populations and social problems "thinkable" – subject to calculation and the disciplined analysis of rational thought – means that intellectual knowledge becomes directly implicated in the governance of certain populations and social problems (Rose and Miller 1992: 182). Thus, intellectual fields become part of the mechanics or technologies of government (Rose and Miller 1992; Miller and Rose 1993; Dean 1999).

Archaeology's adherence to claims of scientific neutrality and objectivity are central in enabling its deployment as a technology of government. The processual discourse, together with claims to professional pastoral care over the past through the discourse of "stewardship", has been important in both defining and authorizing the discipline's role as a technology of government. This role has also been facilitated by the development of Cultural Resource Management (CRM) policy, legislation and processes.[1] It was no coincidence that CRM, and the pivotal role that archaeology plays within this, was established in many Western countries at the same time as processual theory was gaining ground and giving the archaeological discipline "scientific" gravitas (Smith 2004). The rhetoric of archaeological science and the so-called professionalization of the discipline that dominated much of the theoretical literature of the late 1960s and 1970s were central in demonstrating, through the mechanism of archaeological lobbying for cultural resource legislation and policy, the utility of archaeology as a technology of government. The "common sense" view of science that became embedded in the discipline at this time found synergy with bureaucratic understandings and cultural expectations about the legitimate nature of "knowledge". As Fischer (2003: 4–5) observes, public policy development in this period was dominated by the "rational" model of decision making.

Through the process of CRM, and the various associated policy documents and pieces of legislation, archaeological knowledge and expertise is actively institutionalized as a technology of government. CRM regulates the use, value and meaning given to a range of cultural objects and places, and provides clear procedures and processes through which archaeological knowledge and expertise may be called upon and deployed. In this context, cultural and social conflicts that rest on, or intersect with, understandings of the past become "merely" technical issues of site management or preservation rather than fraught socio-cultural conflicts. In short they are de-politicized.

Nonetheless, conflicts over the disposition of objects and the management of sites and places are part of a wider process in which governments and their agencies confer, withhold or otherwise regulate claims to political and cultural legitimacy. Archaeology benefits in this process by having its authority as a discipline continually underlined and reinforced through its role as a technology of government, and because the discipline's privileged position over the management of material culture assures access to the database. However, to maintain this access, archaeologists must continually invoke the discourse of processual or scientific rationality or risk undermining their authority as intellectuals and the usefulness of their discipline as a technology of government. In effect, archaeological discourse and knowledge become themselves regulated and governed by this process – although often to the advantage of the discipline itself.

It is important to stress that the mobilization of archaeology as a technology of government does not produce a static set of relationships. Nor does the mobilization of archaeology as a technology of government *always* mean that archaeological wishes are upheld. Indeed, archaeological expertise and authority will itself often be marginalized against more powerful economic interests in CRM. Furthermore,

---

[1] Cultural Resource Management (CRM) is the term used in North America for the legal and technical processes of preserving, protecting and managing "cultural resources" or tangible heritage items. In other regions of the world, this process is referred to as Cultural Heritage Management or Archaeological Heritage Management.

from time to time and in certain political contexts, indigenous knowledge may also be granted greater legitimacy than archaeological pronouncements. Nonetheless, the deployment of archaeological knowledge in helping policy makers understand and regulate certain problems or conflicts ensures an overall primacy of place in knowledge claims over the past. Nor is the use of archaeological knowledge to regulate indigenous conflicts over the past necessarily or inherently negative. For instance, during the 1970s the then Australian Labor Government explicitly called on the new archaeological discoveries at Lake Mungo (which suggested that human occupation of Australia was at least 40,000 years old) to help legitimize its attempts to bring in radical land rights legislation (Smith 2004: 154). That this legislation eventuated only in very limited form in 1975 rests more on the fact that this government was overthrown by the nefarious activities of the Australian Governor General and the Conservative opposition party that ousted the Labor Government from power, than the fact that public sympathy had not been sufficiently mobilized to support the legislation. However, the point here is that the authority of archaeological knowledge is used to help legitimize (or refute) indigenous cultural claims. Whether this has positive or negative outcomes is somewhat beside the point, since for the politics of recognition it is vital that recognition flows from an organic expression of identity – that is, that those proclaiming their identity are in control of its expression and thus have a greater chance of influencing how that identity is recognized, while decreasing the possibilities of its misrecognition. Moreover, the archaeological governance of heritage, and the claims to identity associated with that heritage, disallows any acceptance of the legitimacy of *difference* – rather all things must be understood through the lens of archaeological science. Yet, the acceptance of the legitimacy of difference is vital if indigenous knowledge, identity and experiences are to be recognized. This is not to say that indigenous knowledge must always be uncritically accepted or that it must always take precedence over archaeological knowledge, but rather that we accept as a base line that it is legitimate for different knowledge systems to coexist, and moreover to acknowledge and understand the extended political and cultural consequences that will occur when one knowledge system is given greater authority and legitimacy over another.

This theorization of heritage as a resource of power leads us to recognize that archaeology is not simply another interest group in conflict over the interpretation of the past and the management of heritage, but that archaeologists have a vested interest in maintaining their privileged access over "their" database. It also reveals the extent to which certain forms of knowledge have become institutionalized, not only in terms of their incorporation in public policy, heritage legislation and management and preservation practices, but also as self-evident knowledge. They seem natural. Embedded in the heritage management process are certain dominant or authorized discourses that both draw on and underpin the position of technologies of government. The naturalization of these discourses also facilitates the regulation of competing knowledge about the past and conceptualizations about the meaning and nature of heritage places and objects.

In the West, the authorized heritage discourse stresses the material, or tangible, nature of heritage, along with monumentality, grand scale, time depth and aesthetics

(Smith 2006: 29f). While it identifies the symbolic importance of heritage for representing social and cultural identity, it pays scant recognition to the dynamics of how identity is actively constructed or created in association with heritage. This is because the dominant discourse of heritage naturalizes the assumption that heritage is inextricably linked to identity to such an extent that how and why these links occur are hardly ever considered – the heritage/identity dyad just "is". The authorized heritage discourse, informed by archaeological concerns with materiality and assumptions about the representational relationships between material culture and identity, obscures or marginalizes or misrecognizes those identities created using conceptualizations of heritage that sit outside of the authorized heritage discourse.

However, the existence and nature of the authorized heritage discourse does more than render certain identities or populations as subjects of regulation and governance. The authorized heritage discourse not only defines what is or is not "heritage", but also stresses and authorizes a particular ethic. In this ethic, current generations are put under a moral obligation to care for, protect and revere heritage items and places so that they may be passed to future generations for their "education" with the assurance that a sense of common identity based on the past is being maintained. The idea of inheritance, which is embedded in authorized definitions of "heritage", is very important here. "Heritage", synonymous as it is with concepts of "legacy", "tradition" or "birthright", is a discourse that inevitably invokes a sense that the present has a duty to pass on unchanged its inheritance from the past, to protect that legacy and ensure that it remains unsullied by the present so that the next generation may benefit from the past. Subsequently, current generations simply become caretakers of the past, disengaged from an active use of "the heritage". The appropriate experts, who act as stewards and trustees, ensure that heritage is protected and that the present does not actively rewrite the meaning of the past and thus the present. In short, the continuity of the past is maintained, its influence on the present is maintained and, as "the present" becomes "the past" of future generations, social values and meanings represented by "the past" are perpetuated. The symbolic values of heritage, identified, documented and preserved by the stewardship of heritage experts, such as archaeologists, are thus maintained, and competing interpretations or active utilization of heritage to create and recreate identities of relevance to the needs and aspirations of current generations are made problematic.

Another crucial theme of this discourse is the idea that heritage is innately valuable – heritage is inevitably about "the great", "the good" and "the important" that contributed to or "created" the cultural character of the present. Assumptions about the innate significance and value of heritage are also interlinked to assumptions about its materiality. In Western authorized heritage discourse, heritage *is* material: it is an object, place or landscape.

However, it is useful to consider here that heritage is ultimately *intangible*. The idea of intangible heritage is one that has taken on some urgency within recent heritage debates, particularly following UNESCO's adoption of the *Convention for the Safeguarding of the Intangible Cultural Heritage* in 2003. This convention recognizes that not all heritage is represented by physical objects, but can also include intangible events (Aikawa 2004). However, the idea of the intangibility of heritage is one that is difficult to accept within the Western authorized heritage discourse, as witnessed by the ambivalence many key Western countries have towards the convention (Kurin 2004).

Moreover the idea of intangible heritage that I have developed elsewhere (Smith 2006) and revisit here, rests on the idea that while heritage may be represented by a tangible thing or an intangible event recognizable under the 2003 UNESCO Convention, heritage is also usefully conceived as a point or *moment* of negotiation. This negotiation may occur at places or in association with objects identified as having important cultural or social symbolism, or during the performances of intangible heritage events – but that heritage is a process in which identity and social and cultural meaning, memories and experiences are mediated, evaluated and worked out. This negotiation may occur within groups who share a common and collective sense of identity, or between different collective cultural or social identities. This is not to negate the importance of the physical place or object, but rather to de-privilege it. Sites, landscapes or objects of heritage provide a sense of place, or borrowing from Raphael Samuel (1994) a "theatre", in which to negotiate and work out cultural and social identities and the values that underpin them in response to changing cultural, social, economic and political needs and circumstances. The ability to control the moment of heritage – the cultural processes and negotiations that occur at heritage places – becomes vital in projects concerned with the self-determination of identity construction and expression. However, the process of negotiation and mediation of identity and cultural values and meanings, is inevitably arbitrated not only by the authorized heritage discourse, but also by the technologies of government who validate and deploy that discourse.

Challenges to the Authorized Heritage Discourse

The cultural and political "work" done by the authorized heritage discourse is inevitably contested by community groups as they assert their own sense of heritage and identity in negotiations over resources. We see this exemplified in the work the Waanyi community has undertaken in their attempts to assert the legitimacy of their claims to land and resources in far north Queensland, Australia. Waanyi are one of the local community or interest groups who are asserting their rights to have a stake in the management of the Riversleigh World Heritage area and surrounding Boodjamulla (formally Lawn Hill) National Park (Fig. 1).

Riversleigh is part of the Australian Fossil Mammal Sites World Heritage Area, which was listed by UNESCO in 1994 for its outstanding natural heritage values. The Riversleigh fossil fields have been identified as possessing the world's richest Oligo-Miocene deposits of mammalian and reptile fossils (DEST 1993). The well-preserved fossils occur in discrete locations in limestone deposits – although to untrained eyes they are often difficult to recognize. The deposits span a period from 25 million years ago through the Pliocene and into the Pleistocene to possibly about 20,000 years BP (Archer et al. 1989; DEST 1993: 14).

Bootjamulla (Lawn Hill) National Park

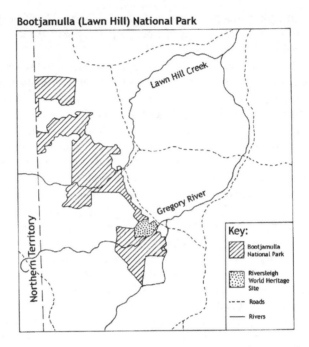

Fig. 1 Location of the Riversleigh World Heritage and adjoining Boodjamulla National Park (drawn by Anna Marshal)

The semi-arid landscape of Riversleigh is characterized by vast limestone plateaus with sparse Eucalypt woodland and spinifex grasslands. This landscape has particular cultural resonance in dominant constructions of Australian national identity: the rugged dry landscape and its eventual taming by early pioneers has come to symbolize a number of national narratives and mythologies about Australian history and cultural identity (Lattas 1992; White 1992; Curthoys 1999). The large Gregory and O'Shannasy Rivers cut through the region, and their narrow bands of riparian forests provide an oasis in the landscape. The strips of forest along the banks of these rivers recall a sense of the rainforests that paleontologists describe as having covered the region at the time when many of the fossilized animals were living (Archer et al. 1996).

This is a highly symbolic landscape because the Riversleigh fossils have captured wider Australian cultural imaginations. Discoveries of exotic animals amongst the fossils – carnivorous kangaroos and marsupial lions, and the whimsically named "weirdodonta" and "thingodonta", the latter possessing large protruding incisors – have drawn significant public attention to the region. Although the Riversleigh landscape has a cultural resonance to mythologies underpinning Australian national identity, the cultural values of the landscape and the fossils are masked by the characterization of the Riversleigh landscape and fossils as "natural" resources (Head 2000; Smith and van der Meer 2001).

Riversleigh is highly significant to Australian paleontologists whose scientific concerns, needs and aspirations drive its management (DEST 1993; Luly and Valentine 1998; Manidis Roberts 1998). In a very real sense, paleontologists are perceived to "own", at least symbolically, the Riversleigh landscape. While some Waanyi people feel marginalized in debates and negotiations over the management of both Riversleigh and the surrounding Boodjamulla National Park, both are areas of cultural significance to Waanyi and within their cultural custodial territories (see Manidis Roberts 1998; Smith et al. 2003a for the extent of these debates). To assert their legitimate right to a voice in management decisions, some Waanyi representatives have started to talk about the repatriation of fossils back to keeping places in the Riversleigh area on the basis that they are part of their cultural heritage (Manidis Roberts 1998). The Waanyi conceive of the Riversleigh fossil fields as part of a landscape defined by personal histories, individual and collective memories, kinship relations and cultural knowledge (Smith and van der Meer 2001: 56). The fossil fields were known to the Waanyi prior to paleontological "discoveries" and investigations, and Waanyi cultural knowledge of the region includes accounts of large kangaroos inhabiting a region in which paleontologists have also uncovered fossils of giant macropods (Smith and van der Meer 2001: 57; Smith 2006: 162f).

Any request for fossils to be held in or "returned" to keeping places at Riversleigh based on "cultural" understandings of the fossils can be incomprehensible to those who privilege "scientific" knowledge as culturally neutral. Animal fossils are not often identifiable as cultural, let alone *cultural heritage* to many scientists and land managers – a conceptual issue that is made all the more difficult by the listing of Riversleigh as a site of *natural heritage* on the World Heritage list. Waanyi requests for fossil repatriation to keeping places can be understood as symbolic demands for recognition of their cultural custodianship over the landscape in a way that challenges Euro-Australian cultural conceptualizations of both the landscape and heritage. Here the Waanyi are asking that land managers not only recognize the validity of their claims to land, but also the validity of the ways in which they conceive and understand that landscape. Their challenges to the authorized heritage discourse demands that policy makers recognize the legitimacy of their cultural difference – and all that subsequently flows from that in terms of economic and political equity. In this, Waanyi are challenging the governance of their identity – by challenging the foundational knowledge and concepts that are drawn on in that governance. As such, this becomes more than an assertion of Waanyi identity. It also becomes a specific challenge to their marginalization in land management practices, through a challenge to the way heritage is defined and meditated by the bodies of expertise that are deployed as a technology of government.

Another challenge to the ways in which heritage is used to govern or regulate Waanyi identity and cultural knowledge was a project initiated by a group of Waanyi women. The Waanyi Women's History Project was concerned with the recording of sites of cultural and historical significance to Waanyi women within Boodjamulla National Park and the Riversleigh World Heritage Area (Smith et al. 2003a,b). Prior to the project, some Waanyi women were concerned that the cultural sites and places within the National Park important to women had not been adequately identified or managed. This situation is exacerbated not only by the colonial history of the region, which has seen many Waanyi people relocated away from their custodial lands, but also because women often have been overlooked in a land management system that has tended to assume that men are the primary spokespersons for cultural issues (O'Keefe et al. 2001; Smith et al. 2003a: 73). Further, much of the information about the sites is knowledge that cannot be imparted to men, and the women were concerned that their sites either were not known by the park managers and thus inadvertently in danger, or that they were being inappropriately managed. At one level, the aims of the project were to identify sites, provide map coordinates for the park managers, and establish protocols for managers to liaise with Waanyi women over their long-term management. On another level, the aims of the project were firstly to allow women to get back in touch with their heritage and to pass on information to younger women and, secondly to assert the legitimacy of the role of women in the management of their cultural sites (O'Keefe et al. 2001; Smith et al. 2003a,b).

The project was carried out by senior Waanyi women in association with three female archaeologists. The archaeologists, of whom I was one, had worked previously in the Riversleigh region, and participated in the project through the invitation of the senior Waanyi women. Our role was to record and map sites identified by the Waanyi women, record oral histories and information about the sites and the region, then discuss and write up management and liaison protocols for use by Park managers. It was agreed that information about the sites and the oral histories would not to be published or used by the archaeologists. The material results of this project were that Park managers became aware of the existence of important sites to women and the need to consult with senior women about site management. The Waanyi women involved in the project have stated that the project had reaffirmed their connections with their heritage and given them some control over its management, and the Waanyi women who initiated the project have been asked to talk about their experiences by other communities in northern Queensland (O'Keefe et al. 2001). The results of the project appear very straightforward; however, what needs to be stressed is the degree to which the women consider that they have increased their authority in negotiations over the management of Boodjamulla and Riversleigh (O'Keefe et al. 2001).

The point to be made here about this project is that the archaeologists involved did not control it; they simply facilitated the collection of data. However, our presence as archaeologists did give the project some intellectual or "scientific" "legitimacy" both in the eyes of the bodies that funded it and the Boodjamulla land managers. However, our role as archaeological "experts" was modified so that the project's primary non-archaeological and community values were met. The archaeologists were not in control of the knowledge produced, nor how it was or was not used. To some extent, the role of archaeological expertise was modified so that we as the archaeologists involved did not regulate or legitimize the content of the knowledge produced – having no control over it or any ability to comment upon it. What we did legitimate by our presence on the project, however, was the legitimacy of the existence of the women's knowledge. The role of archaeology as a technology of government was modified by the Waanyi in such a way that the Waanyi were able to subtly use the archaeological presence to get their message across to the non-indigenous audiences they needed to influence, but yet ensured that they did not surrender control of the knowledge itself. In controlling the project the Waanyi women were able to use our identity as archaeological "experts" to facilitate their aspirations for recognition, and subvert or reorientate the authority and role of archaeological governance to meet their own needs.

As archaeological heritage managers, our role in facilitating the management of women's heritage was entirely redundant in this project. The ways in which women "managed" their heritage centred on the passing on of cultural knowledge to younger women, and in taking opportunities simply "to be" in the landscape and to remember collective and individual memories and experiences (see Smith et al. 2003a for further discussion of this point). None of these things required archaeological knowledge or our recording skills. We simply became a political resource that women used, with our consent, to gain recognition and acceptance of women's cultural knowledge and ways of managing and caring for their cultural heritage.

Conclusion

At the crux of the issues raised by this volume is the definition of "heritage". Certainly, heritage plays a symbolic role in the creation and recreation of a range of cultural and social identities. The argument advanced above is that these identities are important in helping certain populations, in this case an Indigenous Australian community, assert the cultural and political legitimacy of their claims to land and its management. Heritage is utilized as a focal point by governments and their bureaucracies to help them make sense of certain cultural claims. Bodies of expertise, such as archaeology, that have a claim over heritage sites, are called upon to help regulate, interpret and ultimately govern these claims. It thus becomes important in the politics of recognition for subaltern communities to challenge the nature of the knowledge that is deployed in their governance. The Waanyi, in a number of ways, have done so through their attempts to redefine authorized ideas of heritage and its management. The idea of heritage is often a focal point in these conflicts, either as a point through which governance is attempted or though which it is challenged. But what *is* heritage?

One of the things that emerged in considering the cultural and political conflicts that revolve around heritage is the dissonant and negotiated aspect of it. To begin to engage with subaltern ideas of heritage it is useful and necessary to question the dominant or authorized accounts of heritage. To do this it is essential to de-privilege the idea of heritage as a place or thing – as an inanimate object whose meanings and values are immutable. It is perhaps more useful to consider the real *moment* of heritage: this is what is both done at, and with, heritage sites, objects and places. If we take account of this, then heritage is not something in trust for future generations, but rather something we use to address the cultural and political needs of the present. If we conceive of heritage as the intangible process of negotiating cultural identity, value, and meaning in and for the present, then we open the way for challenging the governance not only of subaltern groups, but also our own governance as archaeological and heritage "experts".

Acknowledgments I thank the participants and organizers of the Waanyi Women's History Project for allowing me to participate in that project. Gary Campbell and Emma Waterton read and commented on drafts of this chapter.

References

Aikawa, Noriko, 2004, An Historical Overview of the Preparation of the UNESCO International Convention for the Safeguarding of the Intangible Heritage. *Museum International* 56(1–2): 137–149.

Appleton, Josie, 2003, No Bones About It. *Tech Central Station – Where Free Markets Meet Technology.* http://www.techcentralstation.com (16 January 2004).

Archer, Michael, Henk Godthelp, Suzanne J. Hand, and D. Megirian, 1989, Fossil Mammals of Riversleigh, Northwestern Queensland: Preliminary Overview of Biostratigraphy, Correlation and Environmental Change. *Australian Zoologist* 25(2): 29–65.

Archer, Michael, Suzanne J. Hand, and Henk Godthelp, 1996, *Riversleigh: The Story of Animals in Ancient Rainforests of Inland Australia.* Reed, Melbourne.

Curthoys, Ann, 1999, Expulsion, Exodus and Exile in White Australian Historical Mythology. In *Imaginary Homelands*, edited by Richard Nile, pp. 1–18. University of Queensland Press, St Lucia.

Dean, Mitchell, 1999, *Governmentality: Power and Rule in Modern Society.* Sage, London.

DEST (Department of the Environment, Sport and Territories), 1993, *Nomination of Australian Fossil Sites.* Unpublished report, Department of the Environment, Sport and Territories, Canberra.

Fischer, Frank, 2003, *Reframing Public Policy: Discursive Politics and Deliberative Practices.* Oxford University Press, Oxford.

Foucault, Michel, 1979, On Governmentality. *Ideology and Consciousness* 6: 5–26.

Fraser, Nancy, 2000, Rethinking Recognition. *New Left Review.* http://www.newleftreview.net/ NLR23707.shtml (12 November 2003).

Head, Lesley, 2000, *Cultural Landscapes and Environmental Change.* Arnold, London.

Kurin, Richard, 2004, Safeguarding Intangible Cultural Heritage in the 2003 UNESCO Convention: A Critical Appraisal. *Museum International* 56(1–2): 66–76.

Lattas, Andrew, 1992, Primitivism, Nationalism and Individualism in Australian Popular Culture. In *Power, Knowledge and Aborigines*, edited by Bain Attwood and John Arnold, pp. 45–58. La Trobe University Press, Victoria.

Luly, Jon, and Peter S. Valentine, 1998, *On the Outstanding Universal Value of the Australian Fossil Mammal Site (Riversleigh/Naracoorte) World Heritage Area.* School of Tropical Environment Studies and Geography, James Cook University, Townsville.

Manidis Roberts (consultants), 1998, *Riversleigh Management Strategy, Exhibition Draft, Brisbane.* Unpublished Report to the Queensland Department of Environment, Brisbane.

Miller, Peter, and Nikolas Rose, 1993, Governing Economic Life. In *Foucault's New Domains*, edited by Mike Game and Terry Johnson, pp. 75–106. Routledge, London.

O'Keefe, Eunice, Del Burgan, Anna Morgan, Laurajane Smith, and Anita van der Meer, 2001, *Waanyi Women's History Project and Re-engendering the Riversleigh and Lawn Hill Landscapes.* Unpublished Paper, Sixth Women in Archaeology Conference, Queensland, Australia.

Rose, Nikolas, and Peter Miller, 1992, Political Power Beyond the State: Problematics of Government. *British Journal of Sociology* 43: 173–205.

Samuel, Raphael, 1994, *Theatres of Memory. Volume 1: Past and Present in Contemporary Culture*. Verso, London.

Smith, Laurajane, 2004, *Archaeological Theory and the Politics of Cultural Heritage*. Routledge, London.

—, 2006, *Uses of Heritage*. Routledge, London.

Smith, Laurajane, and Anita van der Meer, 2001, Landscape and the Negotiation of Identity: A Case Study from Riversleigh, Northwest Queensland. In *Heritage Landscapes: Understanding Place and Communities*, edited by Maria Cotter, Bill Boyd, and Jane Gardiner, pp. 51–63. Southern Cross University Press, Lismore.

Smith, Laurajane, Anna Morgan, and Anita van der Meer, 2003a, Community-driven Research in Cultural Heritage Management: The Waanyi Women's History Project. *International Journal of Heritage Studies* 9(1): 65–80.

—, 2003b, The Waanyi Women's History Project: A Community Partnership Project, Queensland, Australia. In *Archaeologists and Local Communities: Partners in Exploring the Past*, edited by Linda Derry and Maureen Malloy. Society for American Archaeology, Washington, DC.

White, Richard, 1992, Inventing Australia. In *Images of Australia*, edited by Gillian Whitlock and David Carter, pp. 23–57. University of Queensland Press, St Lucia.

Chapter 10
Archeology as Activism

K. Anne Pyburn

Heritage and Violence

Archeological sites have become an important defining feature of a nation state; no nationalist agenda is complete without a World Heritage site. Rapidly globalizing postcolonial countries appear on the map symbolized by flags, national anthems, state flowers, and ancient monuments (Barkan and Bush 2003; Kohl 1998). But when heritage and national identity become synonymous with prominent cultural resources, politically motivated destructive impulses are given an effective target (Abu el-Haj 1998; Kohl and Fawcett 1995; Meskell 1998). The most famous recent example of this was the destruction of the Buddhas of Bamiyan in 2002 by the Taliban in an effort to seize control of the global identity of Afghanistan. Other examples are less widely televised or have their significance blurred, as when US and Polish troops' use of the ancient city of Babylon in Iraq as a military depot causing irreparable damage is reported as "a good and decent impulse, to protect the ancient site of Babylon" (McCarthy and Kennedy 2005) that somehow went innocently awry. Often when there is conflict over heritage, sites suffer destruction simply through the inattention of government officials who disregard looting, vandalism, and the recycling of archeological materials. In Babylon, "Vast amounts of sand and earth, visibly mixed with archeological fragments, were gouged from the site to fill thousands of sandbags and metal mesh baskets" (Deblauwe 2005).

Also common are situations in which preservation itself is a means of oppression, as when descendant groups have their cultural identity enforced and economic disadvantages naturalized by constant official and public rhetoric about cultural continuity, authentic heritage, and characterization of the poor as "traditional" and "living in the past." Poverty and the lack of material wealth are cast as the result of choices made by the poor, who in reality have no choice at all (Layton 1989). In a documentary about the identity significance of the perpetuation of traditional medicine, it is impossible to tell whether the people practice magic because they have chosen it over inoculation or because their economic disadvantages have left them with no choices that are intelligible to them (Dreyer 2004). In such cases, identity with romanticized ancient practice and material culture is an imposition of the

H. Silverman and D. F. Ruggles (eds.), *Cultural Heritage and Human Rights*.

modern world system. There is no documentation on how frequently people imprisoned by involuntary identity with the past resort to site destruction.

But a significant amount of looting and intentional site destruction can be better understood as the result of conflicts over the role of heritage in the construction of identity and the real economic and political consequences of that identity on the global stage (Fowler 1987; Mbunwe-Samba 2001). Monuments and material culture all too often become weapons in this type of contest, and documented examples of this are commonplace (Gathercole and Lowenthal 1990). At a site where I was excavating, the owner of a nearby quarry once told me that he had bulldozed the sites around his quarry immediately after my predecessor stopped digging to ensure that the government would not interfere with his business. When archeologist Peter Matthews and his colleagues tried to remove an ancient Maya altar from Chiapas and relocate it for its protection, they were robbed and terrorized. At issue was an ongoing conflict between indigenous people and the Mexican government over land rights; the altar served as their evidence of the indigenous ownership of the land (Hoopes 1997). The Ayodhya riots provide another case in point: Hindus and Muslims worshipping in a shared space flew into a murderous destructive rage over the potential of an archeological report to attribute the origin of their mutually cherished temple to one religion or the other (Bernbeck and Pollock 1996; Bidwai 2003).

Clearly, the politics of identity are not all at the institutional level, nor are such emotions always aroused from the "top-down." Identity may be tied to the material record of the past at a very personal level, as when treasure hunter Mel Fisher promotes his underwater looting as an authentic lifestyle. He presents himself as a crusader for individual rights and democratic opportunity for the ordinary person.

Mel Fisher suffered many personal losses to keep his dream alive during his 16-year search and endured over 100 court battles, which ended in victory in the US Supreme Court. The riches Mel Fisher, his team, and investors had worked so hard for all those years are finally theirs (http://www.melfisher.com/).

Fisher's mantra is that he is fighting against the power of the privileged who would deprive him of his right to be as wealthy as they. The issue at stake here is class, and it should not surprise anyone that victims of exploitation often feel no compunction about practicing exploitation themselves, or that looters like Fisher find a sympathetic audience among the economically disadvantaged. Fisher has tied his practices to the well-advertised popular fantasies about luck and romantic adventure that also sell lottery tickets and movie passes. Ironically, educated art connoisseurs at one end of the social scale and admirers of Fisher at the other make a similar argument about entitlement due to them personally.

Global heritage organizations attempt to discourage such personal possessiveness with rhetoric and legal sanctions (Cleere 2000). But the problem for preservationists is that the emphasis their ethic places on the value of the material past as an important source of identity for both living people and nation states is exactly the factor that renders protecting it impossible (Brodie et al. 2001; Folorunso 2000). The text as written carries the seeds of its own destruction; there must be a way to divert the violent and destructive effects of personal and political identity from the material record of the past. There must be a way in which the record of human history can be used to undermine attitudes of entitlement and hegemony rather than to reinforce them.

Wagging the Dog

The space between the construction of identities through heritage and the repercussions of identity in social context is where archeologists promoting collaborative strategies are needed to change negative correlations and pre-empt violence and site destruction. Where possible, information exchange and collaboration should begin before the community in question has its heritage preserved by foreign intervention, displayed on the world stage, and auctioned in the global marketplace.

When power relations flow backward, when something that is usually a result becomes the cause, we say that "the tail is wagging the dog." Since archeology – in its research, practice, and interpretation – so easily becomes the target of destruction and a tool of violent political action, it might be possible to "wag the dog" – that is, to get local people and various potential competitors who are involved in the globalization of ethnic, social, and national identities to think about heritage in constructive ways before serious conflicts get started. If people have information about the repercussions of the decisions they make about how to handle their material past before they make those decisions, they can better prepare for the consequences. The goal of course is to encourage various groups of stakeholders to think about the past in ways that pre-empt violence and divisive politics. But for this to work, archeologists have to learn to aid and abet grass roots political action by providing useful information.

A number of archeologists have argued for a collaborative approach among stakeholders but only anecdotal evidence of the success of such measures is available (Derry and Malloy 2003; Pyburn and Wilk 1995). Most global heritage preservation organizations (ICOMOS, UNESCO, UPO, WHC, CLT/CH, SC/ECO) assume that economic inequalities are the immediate cause of problems in cultural resource management (CRM) and base their programs of training and support on this assumption. But I believe the relationship is more indirect, because resource access is almost invariably filtered, for better or worse, through identity politics. One reason for the difficulties of global heritage organizations is that few of them are guided by ethnographic research on the local conditions that would identify these political issues in their local manifestations. Instead, research funds are spent on assessments of the condition and vulnerability of cultural resources and estimates of how much money will be required for consolidation, and what legal sanctions deter looting (Prott and O'Keefe 1984). Furthermore, such programs unreflexively use the definitions of heritage and preservation invented in and for wealthy nations as though such ideas reflect a global reality. Nonprofessional stakeholders are stereotyped as protective or disinterested or rapacious, with little real data on the context and origins of these attitudes. What is needed is a combination of research with a deeper level of collaboration at the same time that specific locally designed interventions are tested.

To some extent, there is no time for research whose goal is simply to define the problem. This is because the pace of site destruction is rapid in most areas, and also because the mere presence of preservation specialists can increase looting by drawing attention to an untapped resource. It is imperative that archeologists and other preservationists pursue their research with an applied component, and many international aid institutions have begun to regard preservation as a subfield of economic development. But while some recent global heritage management programs combine archeological expertise with political savvy and economic development theory, they seldom foreground the ethnographic context and the ethnohistoric relations that would make a true collaboration with local and nonacademic stakeholders possible. No other generalization about economic development efforts has achieved more empirical support than the acknowledgment that top-down strategies do not work; at best they last until the funds run out and the visiting experts go home (Cernea 1995). If CRM, including the protection of archeological sites, has a politically positive future in lesser developed countries, it lies in locally engineered sustainable creations that are culturally intelligible and show benefits that people can see.

On the other hand, efforts to improve CRM by involving a wider range of stakeholders, but without ethnographic expertise and training in applied anthropology, have resulted in attempts to foster collaboration among stakeholders that assume local knowledge and academic scholarship are simply two sides of the same coin. But traditional knowledge and acculturation into local values do not prepare a culture bearer to communicate effectively with development specialists, cultural resource managers, scientists, and other interested visitors. Science and scientific archeology as well as the preservation ethics of global organizations are specific forms of knowledge with a set of tenets that – while familiar to many and understandable by anyone – are not immediately grasped by people with no training or experience in these fields. Placing stakeholders with traditional backgrounds in a context with a group of trained academics, CRM specialists, and research scientists places them at a tremendous disadvantage, as is equally the case when archeologists expect to promote economic development in a traditional culture which they understand poorly. The result of this failure to communicate is that little genuine collaboration occurs, while unequal power relations are exacerbated under the surface; a situation that often leads stakeholders to link the archeological record of the past – even their own past – with agendas of the wealthy and oppressive politics (Pwiti and Ndoro 1999). In Brazil, for example, preservation of archeological sites is challenged by the complete sense of alienation that government intervention creates among the public (Funari 2001; Bezerra de Almeida 2003), despite the state's attempts to promote cultural resources as the property of all citizens. The fact that a site has government protection is actually a stimulus to vandalism as an expression of antigovernment sentiment.

The recent spate of community-based collaborations by ethnographically naïve archeologists has achieved mixed results, though little evidence has shown up in the literature, which mostly claims positive results by describing good intentions. However, careful investigation can turn up irate local editorials, instances of violence targeting either the archeological sites or the archeologists digging them, and evidence of utter confusion divulged in newspaper interviews. In candid conversations, archeologists frequently admit cynicism if not fatalism in regard to the potential for success of their plan to "do the right thing."

My own approach has been to pull back and think more carefully about who may best be able to guide me in my desire to advocate for local people and promote respect for a nonviolent human heritage. While it would be a mistake to exclude the voices of any stakeholders from the conversations that must underlie community collaborations, I think the first choice of cultural advisors must be the local professional archeologists who can already speak the language of the academy and who are familiar with tenets of Western science. There are locally rooted or experienced specialists working in or very near any culture area who know how to broaden the perceptions of traditional scholars and government officials without setting up a false and obstructive dichotomy between science and religion or other traditional values. In other words, the beginning conversations should be between archeologists and the local people most prepared to deal with a Western scholarly perspective, and proceed gradually into communication with less accessible groups of stakeholders.

This position may seem high-handed, but an example will clarify the rationale. I was hired by USAID in 1984 to go to Yemen to see why the American agricultural extension college intended to improve the production of food in domestic kitchen gardens was not working. American experts were being introduced to teach gardening techniques, but the young Yemeni men who came to the school were not returning to their villages to help their neighbors grow vegetables but instead were taking their certificates of graduation to urban centers and applying for white collar jobs. A small amount of research showed why this was the case: only women grow kitchen gardens and women from small traditional villages who depend on kitchen gardens cannot travel much less be taught by foreign males. But the lesson I learned from talking to Yemeni women about this situation is one that applies to any cross-cultural collaboration: no group of people is made up of identical units.

Within the group of people who could be identified as "Yemeni women" were women of a variety of faiths and a variety of degrees of conservatism. There also were women of different social status and different age grades. A few of these – for example, women of low status who were past child bearing – *could* talk to male extension agents. Others of extremely high status, having been educated outside Yemen at universities in Europe and Egypt, would be able to take extension training and communicate their knowledge to key women in local female domestic networks. So the way to help Yemeni housewives and the way to reach vulnerable stakeholders in the game of heritage management is to understand and use existing social and cultural networks, rather than to bring them to an alien "table" that is already set with foreign implements and strange table manners for serving unpalatable ideas.

Archeological knowledge and the framework of heritage development have potential benefit for people who find such information and its bearers suspect and potentially dangerous. But in truth, archeology and global heritage *are* potentially dangerous and archeologists are definitely to be suspected. Nevertheless, it is precisely because of the dangerous repercussions of claims about the past and heritage identity that research and preservation issues must be brought to the attention of stakeholders so that they know what their stakes are. Archeologists must explain themselves in a way that allows them both to teach and learn, but that also makes it possible for ordinary people who are vulnerable to global forces to understand what is at stake for them and their future when the archeologists and the tourist developers and the preservationists come to town. We have information that stakeholders need, and they have information that we must have before we can behave responsibly. So, I am arguing that the first stage of collaboration and communication be aimed at a middle ground of people with both local knowledge and experience with outsiders rather than at the extremes of experience and perspective that make conversation impossible.

Participatory Action Research

The conundrum for all outreach efforts to support CRM is that attempts to place stakeholders in lesser developed countries on a more equal footing internationally still must depend on the greater economic resources of developed nations. Collaborative research and training is argued to be a way to equalize power relationships among participants, but the role of the staff developer must change from the top-down provider of information to that of facilitator who establishes an atmosphere that is conducive to conversation in which all participants share their expertise (Richardson 1994).

The real shortcoming of most collaborative attempts is the archeologist's lack of knowledge about how to collaborate. Vague admonitions to "do local ethnography" barely help, because what is really needed is an approach that does not require archeologists to become professional ethnographers but to do the following:

1. Gather enough information about the local context to identify stakeholders and determine what archeological knowledge and heritage management have to offer them.
2. Learn how to share their knowledge so that its usefulness is apparent in the local context.
3. Develop sufficient rapport with stakeholders to design collaborative heritage projects that alert people to the danger of identity politics.

Participatory action research (PAR) is what archeologists are looking for (Kemmis and McTaggart 2001; Robinson 1996). PAR has a long history in lesser developed countries, especially Latin America. Recent work on collaborative ethnography and anthropological research for grassroots knowledge utilization provide crucial models and principles for conducting such participatory research. PAR literature argues that an action research strategy can take emerging solutions into account without sacrificing verifiable results.

PAR is founded on the assumption that the first goal is intersubjectivity; that the first order of business is cross-cultural and interpersonal understanding (McTaggart

1997; Sankaran 2001; Schensul and Schensul 1992). The heritage researcher and promoter must attempt to make sure that local people comprehend the research design and the project goals. Putting what scholars think of as important questions into intelligible language in a local context can only have a salutary effect on science, since an accurate exegesis of research on the origin of civilization to Iraqi villagers or the collapse of civilization to Guatemalan refugees must make local people appropriately aware of the ideas driving the visitor's interest. This is information they must have in order to choose their level of participation. Equally important is that such communication will force the visiting archeologist or preservationist to take the political context of their efforts into account. Gone are the days when the expatriate researcher could ignore local impacts because "*they* will never know."

The most appropriate examples of this strategy for archeologists come from applied anthropology where many versions of PAR are used. One particularly apt example is Bentley's work on crop pests with a group of subsistence farmers in Honduras (1992, 2000). Bentley gathered interested participants at the Zamorano extension college for long enough to explain scientific information about the life cycles of the insects that were affecting the yield. A year later, the farmers returned to Zamorano and taught Bentley how they had used their new information to reduce predation on their food supply. The object of heritage education is to similarly provide information on strategies and consequences of CRM that can be used by participants to solve their local problem themselves in sustainable ways.

This means that at the planning stage it is not possible to say exactly how this will be done. Various areas of teaching, study, and collaborative analysis (about preservation, tourism, museums, stakeholders, grant writing, looting or subsistence digging, methods, and technology) are well documented as relevant to establishing politically effective and economically successful CRM programs. Literature on implementation of programs addressing these topics needs to be summarized for local stakeholders. However, PAR research argues that top-down training – in which experts deliver predetermined solutions and data sets – does not have a lasting or a generative effect. Archeologists are more appropriately conceived as advisors. We must acknowledge that we are also stakeholders who have an interest in preservation, but that our interest is not the only one nor is our perspective necessarily the correct one in a particular local situation. We have the right to make our case, but we must also accept that there will be times when we lose the argument and will have to step aside.

For example, several archeologists promoting community museums have documented their positive interactions with local communities, but some of the resulting institutions have the aura of a successful sales pitch rather than a truly collaborative enterprise. In several instances, community museums have already disappeared along with their alien promoters. Stakeholders in these targeted communities need to be introduced to experts in museum studies, who present technical information in intelligible and locally relevant terms. But after the information has been imparted to them, these stakeholders must be asked to consider how museums ought to play a role in CRM in their own communities and how museums might be used to improve communication among stakeholders and diffuse or avoid politically volatile interpretations of heritage. This involves discussion of the types of museum that are possible in lesser developed countries, turning the conversation back to the expert for more information on extant programs. The importance of including local academics in this process is clear because negotiating the complexities of local government, indigenes, tourism, academia, and other groups of stakeholders is never going to be as familiar to a foreign scholar as to a local one.

Global organizations such as UNESCO and USAID, backed by huge capital and hundreds of experts, are struggling to achieve global standards of heritage management. However, the same wealth that these organizations invest also serves to undermine the development of sustainable and independent solutions in places where local people have little chance of replacing the start-up funds. Furthermore, it is the authority and power entailed by the control of resources that makes the strategies followed and advocated by such institutions seem disconnected, and even suspect, to people at the local level. Most efforts to improve the practice of CRM focus on the needs of the archeological record, rather than on the needs of people whose lives and identity intertwine with the material past on a daily basis.

We desperately need a better understanding of strategies that work and do not work in the development of sustainable CRM programs, and we need to know whether it is possible to design such programs to mitigate political hostilities in the face of globalization. Our goal must be to begin grassroots movements that will reorient CRM from a source of locally irrelevant or politically dangerous knowledge, ethnic circumscription, and economic capital to assume a more positive political authority in the future we create from the past. This does not mean that archeologists are, or should be, neutral. Moral philosophers like Moody-Adams (1997) have made it clear that respecting another culture does not mean refusing to engage with its members in critical discussions about ethics and moral decisions. And radical empiricist/phenomenologist Michael Jackson (1998) has argued that a democratic process of exchange and collaboration is the implicit goal of all social science through the development of intersubjectivity and cross-cultural understanding. Archeologists have an agenda worth promoting; the problem is making sure our voices speak to the political present and ensuring that the informed voices of other constituencies are also heard and understood.

The most difficult aspect of community-based archeology is the factor of time. Despite the effort to speed up the process of information exchange by employing PAR, establishing the trust that must precede information sharing in a wholly new area will be achieved slowly. Furthermore, the trust required will almost always become the foundation of a permanent relationship among the various stakeholders. Gone are the days when archeologists could dig it up, write it up, and go home.

Development Begins at Home

I have recently begun a project in Central Asia to test these ideas. My interest in the area began with the observation that CRM is almost nonexistent in the region, while an interest in the promotion of tourism is developing rapidly (Fig. 1).

Fig. 1 Ready for tourists. (Photo: Anne Pyburn)

Fig. 2 Tourist rugs with "traditional" designs. (Photo: Anne Pyburn)

Markets for artifacts are few but they have the potential to explode along with tourism. Interest in heritage has begun to rise, beginning with the renewed emphasis on local artists, especially those using "traditional" designs and styles, and on practices associated with ethnicity (Fig. 2).

The most dramatic of the latter is the unfortunate resurgence of bride kidnapping, forbidden under Soviet rule, which has the advantage of being a globally stigmatized practice, making it a powerful identity marker on the world stage.

In this social context, I predicted that archeological sites would rapidly begin to appear as national symbols. Kyrgyzstan (where my own research is focused), along with neighboring republics, occupies the territory traversed by the Silk Road, which supported a magnificent variety of cultures with major architectural monuments and material signatures. Today villages are nestled in valleys strewn with ancient burial mounds and dotted with Buddhist, Muslim, and Christian sites as well as remains of various other cosmologies. A small but impressive group of Soviet-trained local archeologists are attempting to document this vast resource without contemporary technological aids. Local communities are aware of the archeologists' work and are interested, but they do not loot to any significant extent because there is no local access to the antiquities market.

Kyrgyzstan and Uzbekistan have recently begun to experience political tension resulting in part from the arbitrary Soviet political boundaries laid down to create the Central Asian republics. These nations encompass people with the same and closely related heritages, but the sense of commonality that once existed is eroding. Recent political events in Uzbekistan drove a number of Uzbek citizens into Kyrgyzstan where many have relatives. The refugees, whose departure infuriated Uzbek officials, were put in an internment camp in Kyrgyzstan where they were characterized by the Uzbek media (which reaches across the border) as dangerous dissidents and terrorists. Local Kyrgyz residents complained bitterly about their unwanted guests until a group of leaders was taken to see the camp. Their visit provoked immediate recognition of common experiences and interests, led to family-to-family interaction, and resulted in the voluntary contribution of food to the refugees. The incident suggests that the window of opportunity to reestablish cordiality is closing but not quite shut.

To address an emergent political conflict likely to heighten interest in heritage identity, I devised a plan to encourage a small village in Kyrgyzstan and another small village in Uzbekistan to create community presentations that consist of their own photos and maps of local resources. This is a strategy that has had some success elsewhere (Chapin and Threlkeld 2001). The villages invited to participate were selected by Kyrgyz and Uzbek archeologists and the curators of the respective national museums, who also will be involved in guiding the collaboration. The village displays will be created using a hand-held GPS and a camera that villagers will use to document what they know – and think – about their material past. The job of the consulting archeologists will be to learn about local interests and knowledge at the same time that they explain what they know about CRM, national interests in archeology, and global politics. When these exhibits are completed, villages will trade their "museums" across national borders. At the end of the project, villagers and the curators of the two national museums of Uzbekistan and Kyrgyzstan will be invited to the US to meet with Native American elders about their approach to heritage in the global arena. This is to ensure that the decisions made by people in the program about how to ultimately handle their material heritage are independent of my ideas as much as possible.

This project already has shown the predicted results. That is, after three months of effort by myself and two assistants, attempts to go beyond basic linguistic competence and establish local trust have failed. I expected this, without knowing how the roadblocks would manifest. In this case, the Soviet legacy of "collectives," which oriented people to a façade of community cooperation thinly covering a totalitarian hierarchy, creates certain expectations of community-based programs. Thus far, people have not responded well to being asked about their preferences and interests in national identity and heritage. Clearly this project will take many years.

On the other hand, as anticipated, archeological sites are beginning to appear as national icons. At the first celebration of the Tulip Revolution that took place this year, a huge banner touting the beautiful resources of the many regions of Kyrgyzstan was displayed in front of the nation's capital. Three of the six regions were represented by archeological sites.

References

Abu el-Haj, N., 1998, Translating Truths: Nationalism, the Practice of Archaeology, and the Remaking of Past and Present in Contemporary Jerusalem. *American Ethnologist* 25(2): 166–188.

Barkan, Elazar, and Ronald Bush, eds., 2003, *Claiming the Stones, Naming the Bones: Cultural Property and the Negotiation of National and Ethnic Identity*. Getty Research Institute, Los Angeles, California.

Bentley, J. W., 1992, Alternatives to Pesticides in Central America. Applied Studies of Local Knowledge. *Culture and Agriculture* 44: 10–13.

—, 2000, The Mothers, Fathers and Midwives of Invention: Zamorano's Natural Pest Control Course. In *Natural Crop Protection in the Tropics: Bringing Information to Life*, edited by G. Stoll. Tropical Agroecology Series, Weikersheim, Margraf, Verlag.

Bernbeck, Reinhard, and Susan Pollock, 1996, Ayodhya, Archaeology and Identity. *Current Anthropology* 37(1): 138–142.

Bezerra de Almeida, Marcia, 2003, O público e o patrimônio arqueológico: reflexões para a arqueologia pública no Brasil. *Revista Habitus* 1(2): 275–296.

Bidwai, Praful, 2003, *Asia Times*, 3/13. http://www.atimes.com/atimes/South_Asia/ EC13Df01.html

Brodie, Neil, Jennifer Doole, and Colin Renfrew, eds., 2001, *Trade in Illicit Antiquities: The Destruction of the World's Archaeological Heritage*. McDonald Institute for Archaeological Research, University of Cambridge.

Cernea, Michael M., 1995, *Putting People First: Sociological Variables in Rural Development*. Reprint. World Bank.

Chapin, M., and B. Threlkeld, 2001, *Indigenous Landscapes: A Study in Ethnocartography*. Center for the Support of Native Lands, Arlington.

Cleere, Henry, 2000, The World Heritage Convention in the Third World. In *Cultural Resource Management in Contemporary Society: Perspectives on Managing and Presenting the Past*, edited by Francis P. McManamon and Alf Hatton, pp. 99–106. One World Archaeology 41. Routledge, London.

Deblauwe, Francis, 2005, Babylon Wrecked by War. *The Guardian*, January 15.

Derry, Linda, and Maureen Malloy, eds., 2003, *Archaeologists and Local Communities: Partners in Exploring the Past*. Society for American Archaeology, Washington, DC.

Dreyer, Nazma, 2004, Minister Urges of Traditional Medicines, *Star & Independent Online* (Pty) Ltd. http://www.thestar.co.za/index.php?fArticleId=349897.

Fisher, Mel, 2006, http://www.melfisher.com

Folorunso, C. A., 2000, Third World Development and the Threat to Resource Conservation: The Case of Africa. In *Cultural Resource Management in Contemporary Society: Perspectives on*

Managing and Presenting the Past, edited by Francis P. McManamon and Alf Hatton, pp. 30–39. One World Archaeology 41. Routledge, London.

Fowler, Don D., 1987, Uses of the Past: Archaeology in the Service of the State. *American Antiquity* 52(2): 229–248.

Funari, Pedro Paulo A., 2001, Destruction and Conservation of Cultural Property in Brazil: Academic and Practical Challenges. In *Destruction and Conservation of Cultural Property*, edited by Robert L. Layton, Peter G. Stone, and Julian Thomas, pp. 93–101. One World Archaeology 41. Routledge, London.

Gathercole, Peter, and David Lowenthal, eds., 1990, *The Politics of the Past*. One World Archaeology 12. Unwin Hyman, London.

Hoopes, John, 1997, Ordeal in Chiapas. *SAA Bulletin* 15(4). Society for American Archaeology. http://www.saa.org/Publications/saabulletin/15-4/SAA12.html

Jackson, Michael, 1998, *Minima Ethnographica: Intersubjectivity and the Anthropological Project*. University of Chicago Press, Chicago.

Kemmis, Stephen, and Robin McTaggart, 2001, Participatory Action Research. In *Handbook of Qualitative Research*, 2nd edition, edited by Norman K. Denzin and Yvonna S. Lincoln, pp. 567–605. Sage, Thousand Oaks.

Kohl, Philip L., 1998, Nationalism and Archaeology: On the Constructions of Nations and the Reconstructions of the Remote Past. *Annual Review of Anthropology* 27: 223–246.

Kohl, Philip L., and Clare Fawcett, eds., 1995, *Nationalism, Politics, and the Practice of Archaeology*. Cambridge University Press, Cambridge.

Layton, R., ed., 1989, *Conflict in the Archaeology of Living Traditions*. One World Archaeology 8. Unwin Hyman Ltd, London.

Mbunwe-Samba, P., 2001, Should Developing Countries Restore and Conserve? In *Destruction and Conservation of Cultural Property*, edited by Robert L. Layton, Peter G. Stone, and Julian Thomas, pp. 30–41. One World Archaeology 41. Routledge, London.

McCarthy, Rory, and Maev Kennedy, 2005, US-led forces leave a trail of destruction and contamination in architectural site of world importance. *The Guardian*, January 15.

McTaggart, R. M., ed., 1997, *Participatory Action Research: International Contexts and Consequences*. State University of New York Press, Albany.

Meskell, Lynn, ed., 1998, *Archaeology Under Fire*. Routledge, London.

Moody-Adams, Michele M., 1997, *Fieldwork in Familiar Places: Morality, Culture, and Philosophy*. Harvard University Press, Cambridge.

Prott, Lyndel V., and P. J. O'Keefe, 1984, *Law and the Cultural Heritage*. Professional Books, Abingdon, Oxon.

Pwiti, G., and W. Ndoro, 1999, The Legacy of Colonialism: Perceptions of the Cultural Heritage in Southern Africa, with Special Reference to Zimbabwe. *African Archaeological Review* 16: 143–153.

Pyburn, K. Anne, and Richard W. Wilk, 1995, Responsible Archaeology is Applied Anthropology. In *Ethics in American Archaeology: Challenges for the 1990s*, edited by Mark J. Lynott and Alison Wylie, pp. 71–76. Society for American Archaeology, Washington, DC.

Richardson, V., ed., 1994, *Teacher Change and the Staff Development Process: A Case in Reading Instruction*. Teachers College Press, New York.

Robinson, Michael P., 1996, Shampoo Archaeology: Towards a Participatory Action Research Approach in Civil Society. *The Canadian Journal of Native Studies* XVI(1): 125–138.

Sankaran, Shankar, 2001, Paper 6: Methodology for an Organizational Action Research Thesis. *Action Research International*. http://www.scu.edu.au/schools/gcm/ar/ari/p-ssankaran01.html

Schensul, Jean J., and Steven L. Schensul, 1992, Collaborative Research: Methods of Inquiry for Social Change. In *The Handbook of Qualitative Research in Education*, edited by M. D. LeCompte, W. L. Millroy, and J. Preissle, pp. 161–200. Academic, New York.

Chapter 11
Genes and Burkas: Predicaments of Human Rights and Cultural Property

Elazar Barkan

Introduction

The validation of cultural property as a manifestation of group identity expanded through the 1980s and 1990s, but since then has encountered major challenges. If previously the control of images and cultural property was viewed as empowering, this has begun to change since the mid-1990s. This was largely due to the revolution in communication including the expansion of the internet and the development of the web. The same type of control – which was viewed as empowering marginal groups, anticolonial forces, and weaker states – has come to be viewed also as possible censorship and repression over individual members of the groups. A moral shift and the inclusion of multiple perspectives within all sides in the debate is at the core of these changing standards. Instead of a binary division between the haves and the have-nots, we encounter pluralistic perspectives at every fluid stage from the individual to the global. Not only can the center not hold, neither does the periphery.

The intensity of the growing communication also led to a severe sense of the loss of the local. By that I mean that ideas, images, and representations no longer circulate only in a confined and anticipated space and do not belong to a culture, but rather everything that was once local has also become global. This is the fundamental essence of colonialism and imperialism. Thus, at some level, today's interconnectivity is not a new phenomenon.

The imposition of Western cultural norms was neither exclusively positive (e.g., the British outlawing of the Hindu practice of sati) nor exclusively negative (e.g., the looting of cultural property in the name of science, salvation, preservation, and pure greed as central to the imperial experience). Certainly it was exploitative.

The cultural construct that framed the exchange has been viewed primarily within the perspectives of a postcolonial critique. Intellectually, Macaulay (1835) articulated most clearly the imperialist rationale: "The intrinsic superiority of the Western literature is, indeed, fully admitted." While Macaulay's views are patently embarrassing in the way they were formulated and for their content, the dilemma remains very much concerning the principles of human rights and of cultural property: is it a responsibility to adhere to traditions and practices even when these are

H. Silverman and D. F. Ruggles (eds.), *Cultural Heritage and Human Rights*.
© Springer 2007

"inferior" or, in our language, abusive and violent to those subjected to them? Macaulay was concerning with the language to be taught – English or Arabic and Sanskrit. We might be concerned more with equality, freedom, dignity, and health. But the dilemma is analogous: *Who determines the right way and for whom?*

The Disappearance of the Local and Diverse Centers

The contemporary disappearance of the local carries a different flavor than that presented above. It is no longer confined to the globalization of the exoticised orientalized *other*, but instead it is distributed everywhere. Thus, the dispute over images of Islam in Europe has subjected the local European tradition to the global gaze. Attitudes in Europe toward minorities, by European society as well as by the minorities resident there themselves, have reconfigured the sense of a group, community, standards, and rights and placed these into a new context where they circulate among others who may or may not share similar geographical location. Globalized culture is no longer a universality that is the expansion of the center imposing its standards, good or bad, on the rest, but rather a continuous flow between the periphery and the center, or rather between diverse centers.

This form of circulating images and ideas underscores the problem of determining who speaks for the group and of what cultural property consists. The predicament of recognizing the group as the crucial element of the identity of its members has led to a series of questions, the most obvious of which may be: if group identity is primary, who speaks for the group? Generally, the answer to this has been its leaders. More recently, the constituency of the group has become a question as has the relationship of the group to the individual members; the focus is on how constrained ought the individual to be by the tradition of the group as understood by its leaders? How hard is the demarcation of the group, and who decides it? This predicament is shared by indigenous artists, who expose sacred knowledge as part of their creativity, as much as by Muslim women, who may seek more individual freedom and equality. It is shared by poor indigenous looters who sell their recovered treasures in a way outsiders decry as destructive to the archeological sites and that, paradoxically, incarnate their own indigenous tradition. And the predicament is shared by performers of sacred rituals. The tension between group and individual rights has been aggravated the more closely a traditional society has interacted with modernity.

These forms of circulation of identities include both tangible and intangible cultural commodities. In the 1980s and 1990s, restitution of cultural property to indigenous peoples, as well as to colonized peoples – both of whom have long been exploited by the modern state – was one small and significant form of redressing those injustices. Initially, cultural property was limited to material and tangible objects, but the concept has expanded to include intangible culture. In both cases, restitution and control over culture was viewed as empowering (Barkan and Bush 2003). This attitude itself has undergone rapid conceptual change as modern technology has recast our approach to intangible property, from music and images to software, movies, and transnational pharmaceutical companies.

The control of such intangible property in certain contexts has come to be identified with the limitation of freedom, indeed oppression. Although the distinctions between Intangible/Intellectual Property (IP) and Patent Property (PP) in contrast to indigenous knowledge or sacred religions may seem clear, it is far from it. Indeed, the appropriation of indigenous knowledge by First World corporations in the last generation led to the construction of the analogy by indigenous peoples who saw others enrich themselves while exploiting the group tradition, with little or no benefit for the group. As long as the contestation was between the subaltern group and the corporation, the morality was largely shaped by the disparity of power, and supporters of indigenous rights knew who was wrong. This changed once the members of the group began to assert themselves as individuals and sought different usages for their knowledge, including marketing secret and sacred knowledge as art.

The constraining of speech in the name of IP is most widely evident on the worldwide web in the attitude of the rich and strong corporation (by analogy, the group) against the "peer production open source" individual whose freedom is constrained. The distinctions are significant: indigenous groups have been victimized and exploited, while Hollywood copyright holders or the Pharmaceutical patent holders are exploiters who rake in excessive profits. Despite such clear distinctions, both claims to ownership of IP present a group versus individual rights argument. The challenge is over the rules of the limitation of use, ultimately a zero sum game. The rationale of privileging the group/corporation over individual users, members of the group, or the public in general, of limiting the access of outsiders to the intangible cultural property of the group is this: if others have access to it, the owner loses. In this there are certain similarities between a traditional group and multinational corporations. The exploitation stems not from the owner having less of what was had before, but, rather, because if the nonowner enjoys the fruits of that good, the owner is injured. In other words, the wider the knowledge is spread, the more it loses value. Not withstanding whether empirical evidence would substantiate this notion, this is the accepted norm regarding IP. These predicaments, in particular vis-à-vis individual and group rights as well as the type of rights (civil vs. cultural, but also economic and social rights) have placed cultural property in its myriad ways at the top of the international agenda.

How Can Human Rights Contribute to Understanding of These Predicaments?

The international law recognizes barely any group rights aside from sovereignty. Article 1 of the International Covenant on Economic, Social, and Cultural Rights (1966) stipulates regarding group rights that "All peoples have the right of self-determination. By virtue of that right they freely determine their political status and freely pursue their economic, social and cultural development" (International Covenant 1966).

All other instances of "culture" mentioned in the Covenant refer to individual participation and enjoyment of cultural rights. But the Covenant is unclear: Who owns the right for cultural property: the group or the individual? Which groups are included and what are the relations between the group and the individual?

Article 1 recognizes a group right as part of self-determination. This would be read to recognize a nexus between group cultural rights and self-determination. That is, these rights are associated with sovereignty, or at least with a legitimate claim for sovereignty. Would that mean that a minority group within a sovereign nation does not have the right for cultural self-determination? Yet we may think that this is the very arena where a group might need a particular recognition of its independent cultural right – that is, when its claims of sovereignty are denied. The clearest example might be an indigenous group that may not have a claim to sovereignty, but would have a claim to cultural autonomy.

Furthermore, entitlement to cultural self-determination, to cultural patrimony, and particularity might, in principle, collide with universal principles of human rights that are, in practice, the very representation of diversity – for many "universal" rights have meaning mostly as they are applied within local variation. This is not limited to non-Western indigenous particularism. For example, freedom of speech is understood locally in numerous divergent ways. In several European countries, it does not include the right to deny the Holocaust. Defamation is construed very differently by the legal system in different countries. These are local varieties of an established universal freedom. An increasing number of people appear to find this controversial, though they are far from the majority.

The conflict between self-determination of a society, norms of freedom, individual agency, equality, and nondiscrimination, among other rights, is played in the public sphere continuously. Relative local variations involving more severe practices are subject to widespread critique. The human body – particularly the female body – is one site where local practices collide with global norms. Violence against women, which in the West has been the subject of extensive criticism and activism for 15 and more years, has focused primary attention on the way sexual abuse is inflicted on women. It might be appropriate to inquire why there is such an intense focus by many parties on female sexuality and female-directed violence as a manifestation of lack of freedom and equality, and not on other forms of discrimination – but that is still another question. Here it suffices to note that the conflict has become a focal point between societies and within societies.

Human rights are considered to be natural-born rights of every human being. These universal rights are supposedly not a privilege: they are not "earned" and do not carry obligations. Although the declaration of "human" attached to rights is frequent, we know these rights are almost always limited to particular groups, and are mostly citizen rights. Humans who are not citizens do not enjoy such rights because they cannot claim these from any government. When an individual does not even have the ability to demand rights from a government, even an abusive government, it means one is barely human. This was the topic of Hannah Arendt's famous chapter on "the Decline of the Nation-State and the End of the Rights of Man" in *The Origins of Totalitarianism* (Arendt 1951). Indeed refugees are humans with few rights, and they can hardly claim those from any specific country. So although we know these exceptions of rightless people include many millions, let us focus on the individual citizen who can claim his/her universal rights and "fundamental freedoms" vis-à-vis his/her government.

How Do These Rights Intersect with Cultural Rights?

The position of the United Nations is that with good will and flexibility it is possible to respect and protect cultural diversity and integrity. The international focus is on establishing "minimum standards" of human rights that incorporate cultural rights. That means that at least within a certain construction there can be "maximum room for cultural variation without diluting or compromising the minimum standards of human rights established by law" (Ayton-Shenker 1995). Indeed, converging "cultural values" around universal human rights and emphasizing "core values" (such as the value of life, social order, and protection from arbitrary rule) would be the UN perspective on the symbiosis between diversity and universality. Whether this is indeed diversity, or merely domestication of differences, is another matter.[1] This perspective can be realistic only as long as there is no controversy. It is one thing to consider "national and regional particularities and various historical, cultural and religious backgrounds" (Ayton-Shenker 1995). It is quite another to focus on the conflict between those and universal rights. The conflict arises when one's culture infringes on someone else's

---

[1] "Human rights facilitate respect for and protection of cultural diversity and integrity, through the establishment of cultural rights embodied in instruments of human rights law. These include: the International Bill of Rights; the Convention on the Rights of the Child; the International Convention on the Elimination of All Forms of Racial Discrimination; the Declaration on Race and Racial Prejudice; the Declaration on the Elimination of All Forms of Intolerance and of Discrimination Based on Religion or Belief; the Declaration on the Principles of International Cultural Cooperation; the Declaration on the Rights of Persons Belonging to National or Ethnic, Religious and Linguistic Minorities; the Declaration on the Right to Development; the International Convention on the Protection of the Rights of All Migrant Workers and Members of Their Families; and the ILO Convention No. 169 on the Rights of Indigenous and Tribal Peoples." "Human rights which relate to cultural diversity and integrity encompass a wide range of protections, including: the right to cultural participation; the right to enjoy the arts; conservation, development, and diffusion of culture; protection of cultural heritage; freedom for creative activity; protection of persons belonging to ethnic, religious, or linguistic minorities; freedom of assembly and association; the right to education; freedom of thought, conscience, or religion; freedom of opinion and expression; and the principle of nondiscrimination." Diana Ayton-Shenker, "United Nations, Background Note, The Challenge of Human Rights and Cultural Diversity," http://www.un.org/rights/dpi1627e.htm

human rights. Since supposedly human rights are "indivisible," this conflict should not in principle arise. But obviously this is not the case.

While the international community is averse to rank human rights violations, it is clear that violations of political and civil rights receive priority. Indeed, the very use of the rights language for economic, social, and cultural claims is contested. Therefore, the rhetoric of cultural rights to justify actions that are understood by others as "torture, murder, genocide, discrimination on grounds of sex, race, language or religion," (Ayton-Shenker 1995) or other fundamental freedoms are particularly frowned upon. In the clash between two rights, cultural traditions of abuse and discrimination do not enjoy parity with other political and civil rights. The very construction of coexistence of tolerance and cultural pluralism is already a partisan view of both culture and universality. A different way to look at human rights is to regard rights as divisible, that is to rank rights as more or less important, and possibly to see cultural rights at best as secondary from a global perspective and subject to the minimum fulfillment of other rights such as security and political freedom. The specific negotiation over the tension between conflicting rights has to be done locally but it must be done with the recognition that a universal minimum applies. I will explore the dilemma as it is manifested vis-à-vis the bioprospecting of indigenous genes and the status of many women in Muslim communities in Europe. (One may feel the urge to state the obvious: not all Muslim women are subject to fundamental oppression and there are numerous liberal voices among male and female Muslims, etc. Or one may feel that such over-explanation may actually raise the specter of the implicit homogenizing gaze at Muslim communities as exclusively fundamentalist. I take the latter view.)

Bioprospecting

The opposition among indigenous peoples to bioprospecting is well known. Several Indian nations have passed antibioprospecting laws. For example, the Confederated Salish and Kootenai tribes adopted a resolution in 1998 that severely restricted genetic research on their Montana reservation. That resolution declared "Scientific research and genetic exploitation of indigenous peoples represents the greatest threat to American Indians since the European colonization of the Americas." This is a very strong statement. One could hardly imagine a more critical situation. Indeed, since the colonization is at times characterized as genocide, one might anticipate that opposition stems from a fear that bioprospecting may lead to destruction of indigenous life and possibly actual killing. This clearly raises the bar. But what does it exactly mean?

Over the last 15 years, the collection of genetic data globally, by public and private institutions, has increased. The research raised many concerns, not least because it was understood against the background of the eugenic movement and racism. There are many complicated and good reasons to suspect these efforts, especially historical precedents. But given the justified suspicion, how does the current research measure up?

One principled objection concerns the ethics of conducting human research and the matter of informed consent. A second concerns who benefits and profits from the research. The latter is most glaring and is possibly a matter of material interests, not morality. Those who secure patents over genetic data seek profits from all types of derivative work done with these data – pharmaceutical as well as research. In contrast, the "true owners," those whose genetic material provides the data, most often receive no or only minimal compensation. This is true of indigenous and nonindigenous subjects alike.

Indigenous peoples are particularly valuable for this research. The vast majority of the world's remaining biodiversity can be found in "indigenous territories" and indigenous peoples are believed to be distinct populations that can facilitate better genetic study. Therefore, the scientific demand is high. A vast number of patents for human DNA have been issued in the last generation and hundreds of corporations are taking part. A large part of the activity occurs in the US and by multinationals. There is little surprise that indigenous people see the demand for their territories and genes as a new gold rush and activists see it primarily as a scientific curiosity and fear appropriation of both land and human genetic material.

Throughout the world, there is a fundamental distrust between the public and companies that harvest knowledge for profit. This is further aggravated in the case of indigenous peoples by the long history of racism and exploitation. There is a lack of clear standards and a history of bioprospecting without prior approval or a full understanding of what is at work, and even changing the purpose in midstream. Gene hunters are viewed as the new colonialists. Given the lamentable history of exploitation of native peoples, any other attitude toward them would be naïve.

A related issue that is creeping into the open is that the next mega-prospecting could yield billions of dollars that in some sense are perceived to "belong" to indigenous peoples who will not see any of the profits. Private companies harvest botanical and human material on reservations without disclosing their true and full goals; they enrich themselves without sharing the bounty with the poor indigenous owners. A long history of colonization has created particular, justified sensitivity among indigenous peoples to issues of honesty, respect, and consent, and these feelings intensify when research subjects are duped with or without consent. Indian communities rarely benefit from genetic studies.

When for example, the Havasupai Tribe consented to collaborate in research in the early 1990s, they believed they had agreed to a specific line of research. Thirteen years later, they filed a lawsuit in 2004 against Arizona State University for taking and misusing their genetic samples. The details of the case are crucial, and I do not believe it has reached legal resolution, but the indigenous perspective was that they were cheated and their samples were used for research to which they did not consent. The research included inquiry into schizophrenia, inbreeding, and migration theories. This is the conventional wisdom among activists about the relation between indigenous peoples and the scientific establishment.

The Genographic Project

In 2005, the National Geographic Society with IBM began a five-year Genographic Project, aimed to collect and analyze DNA blood samples from over 100,000 indigenous people. There are various ways of examining the project, but let me focus on the self-presentation of the project. While it highlights that it is "the world's largest study of its kind in the field of anthropological genetics" much of the language aims at deflecting criticism. It emphasizes its focus on ethics and privacy and states:

> There is no medical research of any kind in the Genographic Project. Also, we will not patent any genetic data resulting from the project. All the information belongs to the global community and will be released into the public domain . . . the Genographic Project research centers will release the resulting genetic data (on an anonymous and aggregate basis) into the public domain to promote further research. The genetic data will be treated as discoveries, rather than inventions, and will not be patented. (The Genographic Project)

This declaration constructs or at least implies that medical research is suspect, an enterprise that aims at pure profit; thus, the project distances itself from it, emphasizing that no medical or any bioprospecting will take place. Yet, in other contexts, these are two activities that are highly valued.

"Openness," "lack of patents," "global community," and "public domain" are all catch phrases that are used in the statement to reassure the audience. The dichotomy between universalism and particular interests is clearly presented, and universalism is the validated approach.

> Ours is a true collaboration between indigenous populations and scientists. Helping communicate their stories and promoting preservation of their languages and cultures is integral. Before any field work begins, we have been and will continue to seek advice and counsel from leaders and members of indigenous communities about their voluntary participation in the project. (The Genographic Project)

Localism is used as a double-edged sword: as a category, "indigenous" places thousands of native peoples with their own traditions into one group that adheres to a minimalist common denominator, the essence of each being localism. Thus, nobody can speak for the indigenous peoples, and ergo, the project can get the support of those who participate, but no activists can object to it in the name of all indigenous peoples. This interpretation of the relation of the "local" to the "global" is not necessarily universally accepted. Indeed, the project attempts to address these conflicts head on, including a presentation of alternative world views and the mutual benefits to be gained by following the guidelines of one of the most prominent Aborigine activists, Professor Mick Dodson. He cannot provide a general authority, since all authority is local, but Dodson clearly has as strong a claim as any indigenous voice (Dodson and Williamson 1999; The Ethical Framework).

The trope of the sinister scientist is meant to be dispelled by these assurances, though there is little inherent correlation between a genetic database aimed at a DNA map of global migrations and one designed to reveal cultures and traditions. These promises attempt to convey respect to the communities, but many indigenous people see that these are untrustworthy words, more manipulative than transparent.

The Genographic Project statement addresses the question of benefits:
Who will benefit from the GLF?
Funded by net proceeds from the sale of the Genographic Project Public Participation Kits,
it is our hope that the Genographic Legacy Fund will establish a positive and ongoing legacy for the Genographic Project that will benefit indigenous and traditional peoples – those
participating in the project as well as others. The GLF will not only recognize the importance of these communities, but aims to empower them as well. (The Legacy Fund)

The sum of the "net proceeds" is not clear. Furthermore, there are no resources explicitly invested in indigenous peoples. Instead, there is a promise to "raise aware-ness of the pressures indigenous groups face and to try to empower these groups." These catch phrases are particularly suspect in light of the fact that the Advisory Board consists of "respected leaders in various scientific and other fields" and more recently added an indigenous representative. There have been so many misrepresen-tations in the past that to attribute an altruistic purpose to the project is impossible, or at least naïve. But let us suspend incredulity and assume that this is the case and that the project successfully addresses all the conventional ethical concerns that are being raised: informed consent, privacy, and even nonprofit status with proceeds reinvested in indigenous communities. What then would be the ethical status of the project?

This brings us to the principle opposition between cultural properties: open knowledge and research versus an indigenous desire to safeguard the sacred. These indigenous claims in the name of tradition cannot be overcome within tradition's own rationale.

Indigenous Responses

It is difficult to gauge indigenous response. On the one side are the representatives of indigenous people, either in international forums or in cyberspace, who advocate traditional and oppositional views to the "Western" view. Many operate within the Western tradition, and are at once both indigenous and Western citizens, but they present the traditional perspective as they see it. One representative group in cyber space is the Indigenous Peoples Council on Biocolonialism (IPCB). The IPCB is an Indigenous organization that addresses issues of biopiracy and formed itself in 1993 in opposition to the Human Genome Diversity Project (HGDP). IPCB advocates noncollaboration with the Genographic Project, although it claims not to "tell" indigenous peoples what to do.

On the other hand are the anonymous individuals and groups who presumably participate in the project and collaborate with various other bioprospecting, whose opinions we do not readily know. The diversity among indigenous peoples suggests that there cannot be a party line. This brings us to the question of who represents the "indigenous," as well as the tension in the representation between the group and the individual.

One dilemma between the collective versus the individual is whether the choice has to be made at the group level, as the indigenous tradition instructs, or by individuals, according to their own private inclination. How is "respect for collective review and decision making" integrated with "upholding the traditional model of individual rights" (Harry 2001)?

The indigenous opposition contrasts "mainstream ethical protocols," which focus on "individual consent" with the reality that "in many indigenous societies, people may not be free to sell their knowledge because either the knowledge cannot be sold according to the group's ethical principles or permission of a larger group is required first" (Indigenous People 2000).

Sacredness

How does one incorporate or reconcile a traditional perspective and indigenous world view with Western science? Consider the following statement by the IPCB (IPCB):

> Many indigenous peoples regard their bodies, hair, and blood as sacred elements, and con-
> sider scientific research on these materials a violation of their cultural and ethical man-
> dates. Immortalization, cloning, or the introduction of genetic materials taken from a
> human being into another living being is also counter to many indigenous peoples' cultural
> and ethical principles.

The objection to having one's family human remains displayed or stored in a museum as material for biological anthropological research, when first articulated by indigenous activists, was largely dismissed by the scientific community because such treatment was deemed essential for the progress of science. Indigenous bodies were viewed as scientific material while white bodies were treated as sacred. We view this today as racism, but in its day it was a convention hardly worth noticing. In the last two decades, the indigenous demands for equality in the treatment of their bodies and remains has been more clearly understood by the wider society, and indeed the process initiated by the Native American Graves Protection and Repatriation Act (NAGPRA) of 1990 has attempted to attend to many of the indigenous concerns. Exceptional cases clearly remain, such as the dispute over the Kennewick skeleton. Yet the older practices have vanished from many museums, and human remains are treated with much more respect to traditional and religious beliefs, Western and indigenous. However, there is the legacy of a history of the conflict between the scientific establishment – including the legacy of racist dehu-manization of indigenous peoples – and the traditional that frames, for certain activists, all science concerning indigenous life. These activists oppose such science as a violation of the natural world:

> Genetics, as a discipline, has little regard for the life forms it manipulates. Their interven-
> tions – inserting foreign genetic material into an organism, adding or deleting genes – can
> permanently alter life forms that have evolved naturally over thousands of years.
>
>   This contrasts sharply with an indigenous worldview. For us, all life is sacred-it is a gift
> from the Creator. As indigenous peoples, we carry the responsibility of insuring a healthy
> future for our children and unborn generations yet to come. (IPCB)

The fast pace of scientific innovations concerning manipulations of the human body and health destabilizes many belief and ethical systems. The debates over stem cells or contraception/abortion divide American society in a way that is played out in unexpected ways globally. At the heart of these debates is the question of sacredness, but the essence of sacredness is articulated in various ways. The issues of prolonging versus terminating life, life worth living, how death is determined, and who determines death are the basic questions that modern life imposes on older belief systems, and indigenous peoples are not spared. Despite enormous variability, a basic tenet among indigenous peoples is that all life is sacred. Those who oppose genetic research argue that any intervention with the body, presumably to remove part of it, even a blood sample, can restrict one's ability to pass into the next stage of life. This clearly calls on complex interpretation of "removal" among other issues. Bleeding as such would not entail "removing," so while the blood or other DNA samples are tangible, its collection does not hinder life in a tangible or conventional way. The meaning of the "removal" becomes an interpretive matter that somehow is related to the essence of life or is made into an essential part of life by the use made of it in the scientific realm. The significance is gained by incorporating the knowledge from one system of culture – science – in its negation. The potential conflict is principled and practical, and certainly not insignificant.

One result of the Genographic Project will be the mapping of human migration. This is very likely to conflict with the creation narrative of various indigenous groups. How would such knowledge impact indigenous groups? This would likely be one more manifestation of the polarization of world views and historical narratives between tradition and science, but it is clearly entirely new. After all, creation and evolution give sufficient ground for disagreements. However, the specific act of attributing to a specific group an origin, which contradicts its own narratives, is hardly trivial for those indigenous peoples who object to it. For example, the question of migration goes to the heart of native American beliefs in their local origin. In the lawsuit mentioned earlier by the Havasupai Indians, one concern is that their blood samples were used in migration research. This was particularly offensive because their religion and culture attribute their origins to Red Butte in the Grand Canyon. Contrary scientific conclusions would most likely confront these beliefs. The case is too complex to pursue in detail here. The issue at stake is the control of cultural narrative, particularly when that narrative is at the heart of a religious belief system. One can respect the Native American tribe's wish to preserve its belief system. But how then does one deal with the similar demand from fundamentalist Christian groups to teach their children their nonscientific version of creation and Intelligent Design?

This goes to the heart of the Genographic Project. A map of the migratory history of humankind through DNA is in direct opposition to indigenous creation stories and languages that describe genealogy and ancestors. Therefore, it is not surprising that this research is viewed as desecration. The dispute about the Ancient One found at Kennewick, Washington, was multilayer, and the opposition was over the violation of sacredness, and the taking of DNA samples. The court decided in favor of allowing research, which violated the principle of the indigenous position.

Lack of clarity also means that different tropes compete. Indigenous culture is envisioned in a spectrum from strong to weak. There is the "vanishing cultures" trope that sees the salvaging of the genetic data as a means to preserve the diversity of humanity. The vanishing trope has been traditionally associated with racist notions of inferiority, linked to scientific racism and eugenics but not exclusively so. Indeed, some of the indigenous narratives often integrate significant parts from anthropological research. Furthermore, the fact that the vanishing trope was part of a notion of progress that dismissed "primitive" cultures does not negate the fact that indigenous cultures do disappear at a fast pace and that the number of languages is diminishing rapidly. Conversely, one aspect of the opposition to the Genographic Project is a self-validating objection among certain indigenous activists who view surviving in the face of colonialism a testament to their superiority. This, the argument goes, means that there are "some strong genes" in the indigenous pool, which is "something that scientists in industry are interested in." Survival becomes evidence of valuable cultural property that is embedded in the genes, and should not be appropriated by others.

In addition to concerns regarding the sacred, the new scientific research might be used to challenge aboriginal rights to territory, resources, and self-determination. Because of this, intangible cultural property has potential for tangible consequences. Whether this fear is real or not, the rationale of justifying indigenous claims – whether on the basis of first occupation or penultimate occupation – is up for discussion.

The Dilemma of Multiculturalism and Islamic Women in Europe

In a recent essay, the Dutch scholar Ian Buruma (2006) describes how leaders, often self-appointed, of ethnic and religious communities appropriate the right to speak in the name of the group and to control what is said about the group by others. Buruma sees the censorship and intimidation that comes with limiting speech as a crime. Indeed, he says, "leaders of minorities are a bit like bosses of criminal gangs" and ventures that second-generation minorities would rather be part of the nation than be represented by the ethnic leaders. "We should treat individual Muslims, Christians, Jews, Sikhs, and the rest with courtesy and respect, but what they think or believe must not be exempt from criticism, or even from ridicule." He says this is why the British proposal to criminalize criticism of religion as a hate crime is well intentioned but wrongheaded. He prefers the melting pot model, the official French approach that earlier characterized American culture. But, he concludes that "this has begun to unravel as the worship of ethnicity and the politics of 'identity' emphasize and celebrate differences rather than a universal American civic identity" (Buruma 2006).

This, alas, provides an easy culprit and a wrong solution. As the violent Muslim demonstrations in France in the Fall of 2005 showed, and what Americans have known for a long time, ethnic pride is not merely a self-affirming celebration, nor a manipulation by some self-appointed community leaders; it can also be a response to discrimination. The validity of claims in the name of the community stems from the experience of many in the community who suffer from the melting pot, a social model that maintains the power structure and allows foreigners and immigrants to trickle only very slowly into acceptance.

The idea that multiculturalist community leaders are merely self-promoters is one-sided at best. Yet, the construction of a binary choice – between delegitimizing identity politics and imposing extensive censorship – is false. The dilemma is how to avoid legitimizing racism (anti-Muslim, anti-Semitic, anti-Sikh, etc.) yet not fall prey to the many whom Buruma rightly describes as community-leader thugs; in other words, how to protect the weak without subjecting them and the surrounding community to another form of intimidation.

At the heart of the global cultural existence is the question of the right to offend: when a subjective perspective of one's own culture becomes offensive to surrounding cultures. The permeated border does not have to be physically close, and certainly not overlapping as does the minority space in the larger nation. This dilemma of a group's ownership of its tradition as an uncontested space faces challenges everywhere. For instance, Japan's colonial aggression against Asian countries has become an annual topic of protest in South Korea, China, and domestically in Japan itself, as Japanese Prime Minister Junichiro Koizumi each year insisted on visiting the Yasukuni Shrine where Japanese war criminals are buried among Japan's other war dead. This example shows how one country's culture impinges on the memory and the culture of another's by merely domestically commemorating a subjective perspective of history. This is not a political statement; it is not ostensibly directed in any way at the other countries, but memory is a contested space, and validation of one country's memory can be regarded as an infringement on that of another. The latest contention between Germany and Poland revolves around the memory of the German expellees at the end of World War II. Should Germany, and German expellee organizations, be at liberty to equate their own suffering with that of the Holocaust, or the Polish victims? Does such a comparison violate the memory of the victims of Germany? An exhibit in Berlin in Summer 2006, called "Forced Paths," organized by the League of German Expellees, has bold historical revisionist aims. The controversy results from a growing attention to German suffering during World War II relative to their victims. The exhibition does that by focusing on various expulsions of ethnic Germans from Poland and the Czech Republic in the immediate post-World War II years. The organization represents a one-sided account of wartime suffering (Der Spiegel 2006).

Who Speaks for Muslim Tradition?

An analogous type of conflict was at the root of the Danish cartoons published in September 2005 that caricatured Muhammad. They were taken as an offense by some Danish Muslims. A few months later, the dispute spilled into the Middle

East and other Muslim societies, leading to demonstrations, boycotts, violence, and an international crisis over respect, blasphemy, freedom, as well as the correct interpretation of the offense within the Muslim world. Was it the freedom of speech or the Muslim tradition that was being violated? Was the violent response warranted? As the antagonism toward the West within Muslim societies has increased over the last decade (especially but not exclusively toward the US) and fear of Muslim terrorism has become a news staple, discussions of cultural practices within Islamic societies have become even more controversial and subject to political manipulations. Huntington's (1996) theory of the "clash of civilizations" has provoked an explicit political and intellectual controversy, exploited in different directions. These controversies should not, however, silence the discussion of cultural practices within Islamic societies, but rather make these more central. Azar Nafisi (2003), in *Reading Lolita in Tehran: A Memoir in Books*, presents a strong liberal Muslim perspective on the internal struggle in Iran. It is clear that this is most important an internal matter for Islamic societies, though here I discuss briefly Islamic communities as minorities within the west. Indeed, in the middle of World War II, on the eve of the birth of the modern human rights movement, President Franklin D. Roosevelt responded to Harry Hopkins's skepticism about the willingness of the American public to embrace freedom for all in the world, saying "the world is getting so small that even the people in Java are getting to be our neighbors now" (quoted in Borgwardt 2005: 21). In the global society, maintaining borders between cultural norms becomes less and less feasible.

Recognizing the diminishing space of the local community, in particular, to engage in a behavior deemed offensive to others – whether the actors belong to the same group or are outsiders – is a major question in global discussion today. It involves, for instance, the place of women in Islam. How can this topic be responsibly discussed? Given the political stakes, it is more likely than not to offend some. Therefore, whatever the reader may think of the following discussion, I hope the recognition that such a conversation has to take place, can be recognized.

The topic can be approached from several perspectives. The Islamic world suffers from repeated violence, external and internal. Beyond and related to the political violence, there is an internal contest within Islam over the soul of its culture, of the struggle among fundamentalist Islamists, religious moderates, and secular yet self-identified Muslims for cultural tradition and freedom. In some African nations (Sudan and Nigeria, to give but two examples), there are individuals and communities who fall victim to the clash between Islam and Christianity. Numerous fatwas are issued by religious authorities, and although relatively few come to the attention of the West, the number of fatwas listed on the web gives an indication of it as a growing issue. The fatwa as a cultural practice is an attempt by a decentralized religion to determine the behavior of its believers, wherever they may be (dispersed as they are among numerous nations on all five continents). It also tries to determine the behavior of non-Muslims. The ease with which fatwas are issued and the obscurity of most is a real example of the infinite expansion and the double edge of claiming tradition as a group right to control behavior and ideas.

Among the numerous ways to illustrate the political dilemmas in the West in
discussing these issues, we could refer to the fortune of Ayaan Hirsi Ali, the
Somali-born refugee who became a Dutch politician and achieved international
fame as a symbol of the contentious struggle over modernization among Muslims
in Europe. Hirsi Ali challenges notions of cultural authenticity and of the legitimacy of traditional Islamism, as well as the understanding of political right and left
and ethical right and wrong.

Hirsi Ali experienced the oppression of Muslim women firsthand in Somalia.
When her father attempted to force her into an arranged marriage, she fled to
Holland in 1992 where she later renounced Islam. In 2006, she was stripped of
her Dutch citizenship for about a month after her admission that she had provided false information on her refugee application because, as she explained,
she was fleeing violence and had to hide her identity. As a filmmaker she part-
nered with Theo van Gogh in the 2004 film *Submission* and was forced to go
into hiding in November of that year after his murder by an offended Islamic
fundamentalist in Amsterdam. The attacker left a death threat against Hirsi Ali
stuck to his corpse with a knife. Because of this and other threats against her by
radical Islamists, she has been frequently under protection by the Dutch
government.

Several quotes from Hirsi Ali will suffice to demonstrate her political position
regarding Islam:

> Not a day passes, in Europe and elsewhere, when radical imams aren't preaching hatred in
> their mosques. They call Jews and Christians inferior, and we say they're just exercising
> their freedom of speech. When will the Europeans realize that the Islamists don't allow
> their critics the same right? . . . the same thing happening that has happened in the
> Netherlands, where writers, journalists and artists have felt intimidated ever since the van
> Gogh murder. Everyone is afraid to criticize Islam. Significantly, *Submission* still isn't
> being shown in theaters. (Hirsi Ali)

Her criticism is aimed at the Dutch left, which makes the political alignment so
unsettling.

> Muslim women at home are kept locked up, are raped and are married off against their
> will – and that in a country in which our far too passive intellectuals are so proud of their
> freedom! (Hirsi Ali)

One of Ali's criticisms is that The Netherlands directs money to Islamic organizations that violate human rights and oppress women. Instead she wants social services and economic assistance to be directed toward women and organizations
that care for the welfare of the weaker members of this minority – children and
women – not to the traditional Muslim powers who advocate and practice oppression
of women.

As a victim of forced marriage and a refugee, Hirsi Ali has the legitimacy
acquired by identity and cultural experience that is celebrated by human rights
defenders. Yet, she is not alone as a member of a group (any group) speaking
against what is conventionally considered the group's tradition. In exploring the
relation between cultural property – the question of who owns the culture – and

human rights, Hirsi Ali provides a striking example of the impossibility of privileging the group over the individual in today's society.

It could be argued that positioning Hirsi Ali on one side and Islam on the other oversimplifies the issue. This is certainly true, but it allows the central issue to emerge more sharply. The question of the place of women in Islamic society, both in Islamic countries and in the West where Islam is a minority religion, raises a host of issues that includes gender, nationalism, globalism, localism, and universalism. Many of these exist in opposite relation, yet none of the dichotomies are clean cut. Despite this, politics often demands a choice between two diametrical positions. Subtleties hardly find room in heated debates. Is politics of this type not part of the cultural property debate? I think it is. The French dispute over wearing the veil in schools, for instance, is very different from the Turkish debate about the veil, and in both societies there are feminists who support wearing the veil as a statement of opposition to the State that forbids it, as a visible resistance to state hegemony, and as a form of cultural independence.

My argument is not that there is a correct way to interpret the actions for all those involved, or that I have a general solution. Far from it. In fact, my argument is that with the disaggregation of traditional societies and with the disappearance of the local, the notion of an intangible or even tangible cultural property comes up against multiple forces, internal and global, that challenge the group's right to make pronouncements about that cultural property. On the other hand, to shift the legitimacy to the individuals at the expense of the group altogether would not only entail a loss, it would also presumably fail. We are all part of groups, and our identity might be as members of several groups; we would be very poor humans if we lost these affiliations.

Conclusion

We all live within "society," itself composed of multiple and imbricated groups within which our identities are formed and reside. In Germany, Japan, historically Islamic nations, and indigenous and minority communities, people everywhere hold to cultural and political beliefs that they see essential to their own identity and culture, yet that are at the same time offensive, at time violently so, to others, both members of the groups themselves, and outsiders. These beliefs are subject to controversies, and in places to political violence. The trespassing – internally or globally – cannot presumably be avoided. Human rights scholars are yet to formulate a theory of "group rights" in between the individual and the sovereign. Minorities' rights have been a cause for conflict for a very long time. If ever we thought that we can at least privilege group cultural rights as an autonomous space, clearly, we no longer have that privilege.

References

Arendt, Hannah, 1951, *The Origins of Totalitarianism*. Harcourt, New York.

Ayton-Shenker, Diana, 1995, *The Challenge of Human Rights and Cultural Diversity*, United Nations Department of Public Information DPI/1627/HR – March 1995. http://www.un.org/rights/dpi1627e.htm

Barkan, Elazar, and Ronald Bush, eds., 2003, *Claiming the Stones/Naming the Bones: Cultural Property and the Negotiation of National and Ethnic Identity*. Getty Research Institute, Los Angeles.

Borgwardt, Elizabeth, 2005, *A New Deal for the World: America's Vision for Human Rights*. Harvard University Press, Cambridge.

Buruma, Ian, 2006, How Communities Control Language. The Freedom to Offend. *The New Republic*, September 4.

Confederated Salish and Kootenai Tribes, *Resolution to Oppose the Human Genome Diversity Project and Condemning Unethical Genetic Research on Indigenous Peoples*. http://www.ipcb.org/resolutions/htmls/res_salishkoot.html (adopted 1998).

Der Spiegel, 2006, *New Setback in German-Polish Ties*, September 4. http://service.spiegel.de/cache/international/0,1518,435066,00.html

Dodson, Mick, and R. Williamson, 1999, Indigenous Peoples and the Human Genome Diversity Project. *Journal of Medical Ethics* 25: 204–208.

Harry, Debra, 2001, *Biopiracy and Globalization: Indigenous Peoples Face a New Wave of Colonialism* (comments for the International Forum on Globalization Teach-in held in New York City), February. http://www.ipcb.org/publications/other_art/globalization.html

Hirsi, Ali, 2006, *Spiegel Online*, Spiegel Interview with Ayaan Hirsi Ali: Everyone Is Afraid to Criticize Islam, February 6. http://www.spiegel.de/international/spiegel/0,1518,399263,00.html (accessed 9 January 2007).

Huntington, Samuel, 1996, *The Clash of Civilizations and Remaking of World Order*. Simon and Shuster, New York.

Indigenous People, Genes and Genetics, 2000, *What Indigenous People Should Know About Biocolonialism: A Primer and Resource Guide*, June. http://www.ipcb.org/publications/primers/htmls/ipgg.html

International Covenant on Economic, Social and Cultural Rights (1966; ratified 1976) http://www.unhchr.ch/html/menu3/b/a_cescr.htm

IPCB (Indigenous Peoples Council on Biocolonialism) http://www.ipcb.org

Macaulay, Thomas B., 1835, *Minute on Indian Education*. http://www.english.ucsb.edu/faculty/rraley/research/english/macaulay.html

Nafisi, Azar, 2003, *Reading Lolita in Tehran: A Memoir in Books*. Random House, New York.

The Ethical Framework, *National Geographic*. https://www3.nationalgeographic.com/genographic/pdf/Genographic-Project-Ethics-Overview.pdf (accessed 6 January 2007).

The Genographic Project, *National Geographic*. https://www3.nationalgeographic.com/genographic/faqs_about.html (website accessed 6 January 2007).

The Legacy Fund, *National Geographic*. https://www3.nationalgeographic.com/genographic/faqs_legacy_fund.html (accessed 6 January 2007).

Index

9 780387 765792

Cultural H